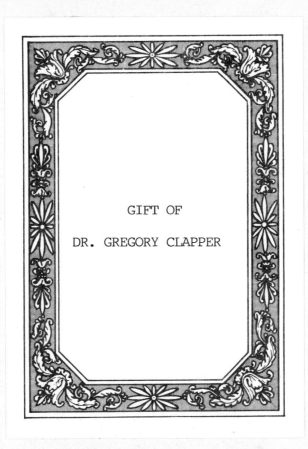

A SHORT HISTORY
OF POLITICAL
PHILOSOPHY

Gaetano Mosca

A SHORT HISTORY
OF POLITICAL
PHILOSOPHY

TRANSLATED BY SONDRA Z. KOFF

State University of New York at Binghamton

Thomas Y. Crowell Company · *New York* · *Established 1834*

L. C. Card 77–179774

ISBN 0–690–73378–X

First American edition of *La Storia delle Dottrine Politiche* published in 1972 by arrangement with Gius. Laterza & Figli, Bari, Italy.

Manufactured in the United States of America

Preface to the English Translation

Few writers who have made a major contribution to the development of political thought have also written specifically for students. Gaetano Mosca was such a writer. A professor by vocation, but also with extensive and varied experience in government, Mosca was always concerned with the clarity and directness of the political ideas he was writing about. This book, *A Short History of Political Philosophy*, is evidence of his efforts in this direction. Based on a series of lectures he gave at the University of Rome, the work is clearly related to the teaching of political philosophy. Mosca's prime concern for politics and his endeavor to be rigorous are very apparent in *A Short History of Politcial Philosophy*. Mosca stresses the close interdependence of political ideas and applied politics; he examines political institutions and practices throughout recorded history and interprets them within their cultural and temporal contexts.

Although dealing primarily with the history of western political thought, Mosca does not limit himself exclusively to this area.

In this concise history, which also points out the relationship between political thought and political institutions, Mosca discusses the great and near-great political philosophers and places them in clear historical contexts. One gets a lucid picture of each political thinker and his relationship to the major characteristics and governmental institutions of his period.

Starting with a brief treatment of primitive societies, with an acknowledgment to Aristotle that man is a social animal, Mosca discusses the ancient oriental empires and their political theories. The subsequent discussions of the organization and exercise of power in the ancient Greek and Roman periods and the Middle Ages provide keen insights into the political cultures of those times.

With Mosca's knowledge of and interest in Italian history, the material such as that on the Florentine historian Guicciardini, the Piedmontese writer Botero on leadership and power, and above all Machiavelli and his time is most illuminating. Mosca's treatment of the development of the British parliamentary system of government is particularly noteworthy. Although he discusses most of the major English political writers and thinkers, especially before the 19th century, the emphasis of the book in some respects is continental. The author mentions certain continental thinkers, particularly Italians, seldom treated in other political theory texts available in English.

The discussion of Saint-Simon and Sansimonism is particularly interesting because of Mosca's readily acknowledged debt to this French writer. Saint-Simon was one of the first writers to divide societies into two classes, one giving moral and intellectual direction and one fulfilling national needs. Mosca built on this idea in developing his theory of the ruling class. The inclusion of a discussion of Henry George reflects the fact that Single Tax arguments were popular in the 1920s and especially in the Depression, the time when Mosca was writing. Also of great interest to Mosca was George Sorel, not only because of his syndicalist thought so pertinent to Italy, but also because of his ideas relating to the organization of power and the use of a myth, the general strike.

In the chapter on racist theories and the doctrine of the superman, Mosca relates Nietzsche and others to historical arguments in this area.

In the last chapter Mosca sets forth his foremost idea, the notion of the "ruling class." This theory of the ruling class is discussed at length in the section at the end of the book entitled "Gaetano Mosca: The Man and His Times." However, one point should be mentioned here: Mosca's call for a mixed state with something of a balance of power as the best possible political system. While he rejected Aristotle's classification of governments by number, he saw some value in the great Greek philosopher's concept of a balance of power. His notion of an equilibrium among the members of the ruling elite combines a power analysis with the historical notion of constitutionalism, or limited government.

In spite of the vast arc of time Mosca deals with, he gives the reader a fundamental understanding of major thinkers. The ideas of these figures are treated primarily in a descriptive fashion. However, in dealing with historical evidence throughout all of his writings, Mosca elsewhere supported or disputed these theorists to substantiate other points. The Aristotelian classification of governments, which for so long was generally accepted, came under Mosca's realistic political criticism in several works, including the last chapter of this book. However, in the early chapter on Aristotle, Mosca set forth these ideas thoroughly and objectively. Similarly, Montesquieu and his classification of political systems and Rousseau's general will, both rejected by Mosca but of great interest to him, are given fair treatment.

The author's dedication to the teaching of history and the historical method marked all his intellectual endeavors. In this book he carefully relates historical experience to political ideas. Furthermore, the work is useful as a teaching instrument because of its brevity and conciseness. It presents the student with a comparatively brief survey of the history of political thought and thus this overview may be supplemented by selections from the original works. In this manner the student not only will be familiar with the classics themselves but also will have the benefit of an interpretation by a disciplined critic and thinker from another culture.

Sondra Z. Koff
Stephen P. Koff

Great Barrington, Massachusetts
July 1971

Translator's Note

The original edition of this work was published in 1933 in Rome under the title *Lezioni di storia delle istituzioni e delle dottrine politiche*. Mosca later revised the work and it was published in 1937 under its present title. This translation is from the 1965 edition, which is fundamentally the same as the 1937 edition.

The translator wishes to acknowledge the assistance of several people in the preparation of this manuscript. First and foremost, Mr. Vittorio Sicherle was always willing to bring to bear his love and knowledge of languages when called upon. Professor and Mrs. Dino Moggi spent time and effort in responding to questions put by the translator. Professor Frank J. Munger of the University of North Carolina labored long and hard on the manuscript after the translation was completed. Also Dr. Kenneth Culver and Mrs. Susan Bass of Thomas Y. Crowell Company deserve credit for seeing the work into its final form, and Stephen P. Koff constantly brought a critical reading of the manuscript at all stages of the translation. In spite of such assistance the translator bears sole responsibility for the final result.

S. Z. K.

Author's Preface

The volume now appearing is an accurate and rather ambitious summary of lectures on *The History of Political Institutions and Theories*, which for eight years with some variations from year to year I gave at the University of Rome. I began by noting the oldest accounts of political thought and then, slowly proceeding across the different historical eras, arrived at the most recent doctrines that have interested and interest men born toward the end of the nineteenth century and at the beginning of the twentieth century.

Naturally, given the vastness of the material, it was not possible in all parts to present an adequate and, above all, precise notion of all the thinkers who in such a long period have dedicated themselves to the study of political problems. Therefore, I tried to draw the students' attention particularly to those authors, such as Plato, Aristotle, Saint Thomas, Machiavelli, Rousseau, and Marx, who better represent the historical eras in which they thought and lived and who exerted influence on both their contemporaries and posterity.

Today, monographs are not rare that are concerned with the political writers of a given age or with a writer distinguished by his originality or by the singularity of his doctrines. Certainly the utility of that type of work is not contestable; but, having to teach young people who almost always lack detailed preparation in the subject, I find it didactically preferable to give them a basic idea, be it even summary, of all the phases through which philosophy and, parallel to philosophy, political institutions have passed.

I would fail in fulfilling my duty if, before closing this brief preface, I did not mention the work of my assistant, Doctor Leonardo Donato, who with much intelligence and competence has so excellently assembled my lectures and has seen to their printing with great diligence.

G. M.

Rome, June 1933

Contents

A SHORT HISTORY
OF POLITICAL
PHILOSOPHY

1
The Relationship between Political Theory and Political Institutions

In every human society that has reached a certain cultural level two types of forces ensuring cohesion can be distinguished: one is of an intellectual and moral nature, the other material in character. Those in the first category consist of identities or similarities of fundamental ideas and beliefs shared by the individuals who are part of the same political society. They would include, for example, a common religion, a consciousness of belonging to a society different from all others, or a traditional fealty to a dynasty. Meanwhile the material forces act through those hierarchies of functionaries who, being in a position to use the necessary means of coercion, are able to guide the action of the masses toward ends that are sometimes desired by the masses themselves, but in each case conform to the views of the ruling class.

Now, particularly when a people have reached a higher intellectual level, the material forces ordinarily try to justify their actions in terms of at least some of the intellectual and moral forces, while the intellectual and moral forces in turn seek to secure power to achieve in practice the political organization they desire.

Thus the combined hierarchies guiding a society materially and morally form what today is coming to be generally defined, at least in Italy, as *the ruling class*. The doctrines and beliefs that provide a moral base for the power of the rulers correspond to what many people now call *the political formula*.

By necessity the political formula has to be suited to the level of intellectual maturity and to the sentiments and beliefs prevailing in the given age and society. At the same time, it has to be in harmony with the fashion in which the ruling class is formed and organized. Thus, a ruling class that justifies its power as derived from divine will must necessarily be formed and organized differently from a ruling class that bases its power on the presumed or real consensus of popular will. Accordingly, change in the formation and organization of the ruling class must alter the political formula, and also change in the latter will alter the former.

This reciprocal influence of ideas on political actions and of actions on philosophy explains why it is impossible to study the history of political theory without studying at the same time the history of political institutions. We cannot know a given doctrine well unless we consider the type of political organization to which it refers, whether it defends or opposes the organization. In other words, without a precise notion of the political organization of a given age and society it is impossible to acquire a clear idea of the theories formulated in that era and by those people.

We can become acquainted with the ideas as well as the institutions of more or less remote eras by studying the past of all those peoples who have had what is commonly referred to as a *civilization* and who thus have acquired a place in the history of humanity. The belief is still prevalent that history can only furnish us with doubtful data and uncertain teachings. In truth, so long as history is limited to telling us of the deeds of the individuals who have politically and militarily directed nations, it cannot be denied that this belief has some foundation. It is rather difficult, even among contemporaries, to evaluate with precision the actions of the men representative of an era, the motives that moved them, and the kinds of obstacles they overcame. It is also true that, given the infinite variety and complexity of human events, it is usually impossible to find two perfectly identical situations such that what happened before can shed light on what occurred subsequently. But there is a part of history that furnishes more precise data and it is this part that is the more interesting in the study of political science.

With the help of the documents left to us—books, ancient manuscripts, records, and the monuments of past civilizations—we can in fact succeed in reconstructing with sufficient exactness the thought of men who lived two or three millennia before us and of the functioning of the institutions that governed them. And, with a knowledge of the thinking, laws, and customs of the societies whose civilizations developed before ours, we can discover reasons why nations and flourishing political institutions declined, were transformed, and sometimes died.

2
The Beginnings of Political Thought

The First Human Communities

Man appeared on earth at least one hundred thousand years ago, yet the most ancient documents and monuments hardly go back five or six thousand years. It is from this era, therefore, that the historical period begins, and from this date the study of philosophy and political institutions can be commenced.

In order to reach a certain level and to create what is now commonly called a civilization, it was undoubtedly necessary first to establish basic rules of social morality, to collect and hand down to succeeding generations a quantity of experiences and knowledge, and to accumulate the first capital in the form of domesticated animals, agricultural supplies and instruments. All this could be accomplished only after many human groups had been fused into a single political society and then through the conscious and unconscious collaboration of the individuals who composed it.

But long before even the most ancient civilizations arose, man was unable to live in complete isolation. Each individual maintained stable relations with others. Society, no matter how embryonic in form, is indispensable for human life; this has been clearly affirmed ever since Aristotle defined man as a political or social animal. Besides, sociability is a phenomenon common to many animal species; we have examples of it among insects such as bees and ants, and even among mammals where monkeys, beavers, and a large part of the herbivora live in the wild state in groups of greater or fewer members.

In the most remote parts of Oceania, Africa, and America some human groups still survive that can provide us with an idea of what primitive societies were like. For example, the natives in Australia, where they have not been destroyed, still form hordes of several hundred individuals who live by hunting, fishing, and gathering the vegetables furnished naturally by the soil.

Toward the end of the last century a school of writers led by Spencer thought that, by studying the functioning of primitive political organizations, they could discover the laws regulating the action of the more developed ones. But we no longer believe such a method can produce truly scientific results; otherwise, it would seem to be as necessary to study the anatomy and physiology of a superior animal, such as man or any mammal, first in an inferior animal, such as a polyp, whose organs are not distinctly different.

In fact, it is difficult to find in *hordes* the beginning of any true political organization. In each of these is a leader, who is the strongest man or the best hunter, and some old men or women who are consulted in difficult times; but in either case it is entirely a matter of personal influence, which lasts only as long as the individual continues to display the necessary qualities.

Where the wild fauna offered species of animals susceptible to domestication, where man found plants he could cultivate, and perhaps even where the race had greater potential for progress, the horde could become more numerous and be slowly transformed into a *tribe*, that is, into a human community of several thousand individuals. In the tribe we can begin to identify the first elements of hierarchy and political organization.

In fact, every tribe generally has a supreme leader who is chief in war and who in peacetime metes out justice according to customary law. However, in cases of importance he must consult the council of elders, that is, the heads of the most numerous and influential families; and in even graver cases he convenes an assembly of the freemen of the tribe which, when it is not yet converted to some world religion such as Christianity or Islam, generally recognizes a special god as its particular protector. Furthermore, the true or supposed community of blood, that is, the common descent of all individuals from the same ancestor, is still today in many places the moral chain uniting all members of the same tribe.

The *primitive city* appeared in those parts of the world where, because of propitious natural conditions, the tribe could abandon nomadic life and acquire fixed residences, where sheep-rearing was partially replaced by permanent and regular cultivation of the fields, and where the population grew more dense. This primitive city is the type of human community that has left us the most ancient documents and monuments recording intellectual and material activity. In both the tribe and the primitive city, we always find slaves in addition to freemen and almost always a third class of persons who are not slaves yet are not considered members of the political community either because they are descended from freed slaves or from resident foreigners who abandoned the tribe or city they originally belonged to. The members of this last class might at times be admitted to the tribe by means of more or less complicated ceremonies. Among the most common means was, and sometimes remains, a symbolic blood transfusion with a member of the tribe.

The Great Eastern Empires

Just prior to the beginning of the third millennium before the Christian era the first large political organizations were formed that united vast areas and numerous populations under a single ruler and that reached and surpassed a million people. This occurred when a city was able to enslave so many others as to assume the importance of an empire.

Some modern writers, such as the Frenchman De Gobineau and more recently the German Oswald Spengler, have attempted to list the different cultural centers that have arisen in the world contemporary to the emergence of these great political organizations. But the calculation can never be exact; there are many reasons for this, one being that it is often impossible to determine if a given civilization is completely original or if it has received cultural elements and instruments from a previous one. At any rate, it would seem that the oldest great human societies are those formed in lower Mesopotamia, irrigated by the Euphrates and the Tigris, and in Egypt, irrigated by the Nile. However, very recent discoveries suggest that the ancient civilization of Mesopotamia was preceded by a still more ancient one that had its origin in Elam, a mountainous region to the northeast of lower Mesopotamia.[1]

In any case, it is clear that in Egypt and in lower Mesopotamia (or in the country inhabited by the two peoples of different tongues who were called Sumerians and Akkadians) there existed natural conditions more suitable to the formation of large states. Both countries are flat so that the different parts are not divided by large natural obstacles; both countries had irrigation systems which, in order to function smoothly, required the irrigated area be subject to a single power. Before Xenophon, Herodotus had already observed that unity was necessary to distribute water with the maximum possible common advantage.

It seems certain that Egypt was first unified under a king called Menes about thirty centuries before the Christian era; but even earlier the valley of the lower Nile possessed a degree of culture, had begun controlling the waters of the river to which it owed its fertility, and had invented—if not perfected—hieroglyphics. In Mesopotamia, Lugalzaggisi, King of Uruk about two thousand eight hundred years before the Christian era, subjected all other cities of the lower Euphrates and the lower Tigris. Almost a century later Sargon the Elder, King of Akkad, having subdued all lower Mesopotamia, pushed on to Syria and created an empire that lasted less than a century and extended from the Persian Gulf to the Mediterranean.

Other large states arose in southwestern Asia after those of lower Mesopotamia and Egypt. North of Babylonia beyond Assyria, during the second millennium B.C., the empires of the Mittanni and the Hittites arose, the first extending even into upper Mesopotamia and the second into northern Syria. Still in the second millennium B.C. the Aryans invaded India, found an earlier civilization, and formed some fairly extensive states. Probably about the same time other important groups, creating a civilization partially original, organized themselves politically in central and northwestern China

---

[1] Recent discoveries have shown that prior to the invasion of the Aryans a very old civilization had been born in the valleys of the Indus and its tributaries. These valleys, like Mesopotamia and Egypt, are suitable for irrigation.

where, until Confucius' epoch, i.e., the seventh century B.C., the peoples of this Chinese civilization were divided into several local principalities.

These eastern empires had some characteristics in common and others that varied from empire to empire and in different eras of the same empire; however, their unchanging nature was more apparent than real. An almost general characteristic was the subdivision of governmental tasks on a geographical rather than functional basis. Thus the local official was at the same time military leader, supreme judge, and tax collector. This concentration of power in the same person often allowed the chief official in distant provinces to become independent of the central power, even to the point of making his position hereditary. The Egyptian monuments preserve in their inscriptions evidence of this continuous struggle between the central power and the local leaders. Other indications are found in the struggles between Assyria and Babylonia. After conquering Babylonia, the king of Assyria left it to be governed by a younger brother. The latter, urged on by Babylonian separatists who wanted to recover their independence, was placed at the head of the new rebels.

To impede the rebellions of the distant peoples they enslaved, the Babylonians and especially the Assyrians often used effective but cruel means. Thus, after partially exterminating the conquered, they would transport the rest in mass to regions far from their native country. In this way at the end of the eighth century B.C. the ten northern tribes of Israel were transported by the Assyrians beyond the Euphrates, and about a century later the two remaining tribes of Judah and Benjamin were transported by the Babylonians to Babylonia.

Within the great eastern empires the ancient political institutions of the tribe and the city could not be observed. Because the state was too vast the assembly of all the citizens could not function and not even the council of elders consulted by the king could survive; this did not, however, exclude the exercise of influence by those in high office, by courtiers, and by some important families. Nominally, therefore, and for really intelligent and energetic individuals actually, the power of the sovereign was, as would be said today, absolute. His authority had a religious basis because he interpreted the will of the national god under whose special protection the people whom he governed were placed. The national deities included Ammon in Egypt, Marduk or Shamash in Babylonia, and Asshur in Nineveh, the capital of Assyria. Palace and harem intrigues often caused the rapid degeneration of royal families and ruling classes who lost their original strength. Assassinations of sovereigns were not uncommon and sometimes at the moment of succession the numerous brothers of the heir to the throne were eliminated.

Given the magnitude of the eastern empires, the political differentiation between classes was accentuated, and ruling classes were formed that ordinarily included the chiefs of the warriors and the priests of the national god. Also, they often included judges, bankers, and those who possessed knowledge forming the scientific heritage of the period. As we have noted, whoever believes that the political organization and social conditions of the eastern peoples were unchanging is in error. We find the most important offices, although frequently, were not invariably hereditary. In both Egypt and Babylonia, funeral records describing careers of the deceased give us examples of persons born into the most humble classes who rose to the most elevated ranks. Such cases naturally could occur more readily in uneasy times of internal revolution or long wars against foreigners. They represented exceptions to the rule. In this respect, the Greek Xenophon passes on to us a characteristic response by Ariaeus, the commander of the Persian contingent who campaigned with the ten thousand Greeks. When Cyrus the Younger was dead, the heads of the Greek auxiliaries offered to Ariaeus their support for his candidacy to the Persian throne. He replied that he was not noble enough and, therefore, the great personages of Persia would never accept him as king. Moreover, Herodotus relates that, having killed the false Smerdis who had usurped the throne by pretending to be the son of Cyrus the Great, only seven important Persian noblemen decided among themselves which of them should be king.

The Persian empire—about which much information has been left by the Greeks of the classical era, having many contacts with it in both war and peace—was the first state to unify all the countries of more or less ancient civilization and notable antiquity. It extended from the Aegean Sea to the borders of India, even including Egypt. The Persian empire was thus the result of the forced fusion of the ancient Babylonian, Lydian, Egyptian, and Median empires under Medo-Persian hegemony.

The work started and carried to an advanced stage by Cyrus the Great, whose reign began in 559 B.C., was completed by Darius, the son of Hystaspes, who died in 485 B.C. Assyria had earlier tried to enslave the other states of southwest Asia and Egypt but, weakened by an invasion of northern barbarians, had to yield to the coalition of the forces of Media and Babylonia.

Within the Persian empire many provinces of diverse language and civilization were governed by satraps chosen from the Persian nobility and given considerable liberty of action; in others, such as Armenia and Cilicia, the indigenous dynasties were maintained but were required to pay tribute. At the same time in the midst of the empire some tribes of mountaineers, including the Kurds of whom Xenophon speaks, escaped almost completely from the authority of the great king. On the whole, it can be affirmed that Persian hegemony was preferable to the bloody contests between the peoples of southwest Asia to which it put an end. Thus, it inaugurated a period of relative peace which lasted for almost two centuries.

In the seventh century of the Christian era an Arab-Moslem empire was established on the model of the ancient eastern empires. It imitated in part the organization and institutions of the Byzantine empire but even more those of the neo-Persian empire of the Sassanids which the Arabs had destroyed. The Moslem religion did not, of course, have the character of the older national religions because Allah was and is a universal God. Yet in the Moslem state the members of the political community were those who believed that Mohammed was a revelation of Allah who had given Mohammed inspiration for the Koran—the holy book constituting at one and the same time a religious, political, and civil code. Followers of other religions were tolerated but were subjected to a special tax and excluded from military service and public office. Thus the organization of the state had a religious base but without a church separate from the state and without a theocracy, for there was not and is not in Moslem society a clergy distinct from the laity. The chief of state, that is, the caliph, vicar of the Prophet, is the prince of the faithful (*amir al-mum'inin*) and should govern according to the norms prescribed by the Koran. The first four caliphs were elected by the most authoritative Moslems. Subsequently the office became hereditary within the members of the same family. Theoretically, a single caliph should have governed all the Moslems, but schisms soon developed among the faithful and different caliphates appeared. After that change the Moslem state, modeled more or less on the ancient eastern states, was organized or disorganized in such a way that any governor of a distant province had the potential to become independent. Soon many local sovereigns were independent, paying, at most, formal homage to the caliph, leaving his name on the currency, and remembering him in the Friday public prayer. Later, even this formal homage ended in many countries and the local sovereign acted as caliph.

Political Theories of the Eastern Peoples

In the ancient eastern civilizations no true political theories existed. The great Asiatic empires and Egypt did not consider possible any form of government other than absolute sovereignty exercised in the name of God, the protector of the nation. The concept of political liberty, as we Europeans understand it and as it was passed on to us by the Greco-Roman civilization, was unknown to the eastern peoples, who considered themselves to be free when they were not dominated by another people of a different race and, above all, of a different religion. For example, in the Old Testament we find that the Jews deemed themselves fallen into servitude when they were enslaved by the Midianites and the Philistines.

But if the eastern civilizations furnish us with only sparse fragments of true political doctrines, they did more or less succeed in creating a political art. They attempted to codify determinate rules to serve as a guide in obtaining power and keeping it.

Thus from ancient Egypt we have the teachings on the art of ruling that King Merikara left to his son about 2500 B.C. and also the book that King Amenemhet, founder of the Twelfth Dynasty, wrote for his son around 2200 B.C. The former is more optimistic in tone and the latter less so.[1] To date nothing similar has been found

[1] It appears that the two cited works are actually by later authors, who, in order to enhance the authority of their writings, attributed them to Merikara and to Amenemhet.

among the numerous documents that the Babylonian civilization left us.

In India we find Manu's books, written about ten centuries before the beginning of the Christian era. These provide a justification of the division of the Indian people into hereditary castes, affirming the *Brahmans* or priests came from the head of Brahma, the *Kshatriyas* or warriors from the arms, the *Vaisyas* or merchants from the legs, and the *Sudras*, the artisans and cultivators, from the feet of the god.

It is noteworthy that the religious reform, begun in the seventh century B.C. by Sakyamuni and named Buddhism, maintained that the members of inferior castes by leading an ascetic life could rise closer to the perfection of those in the superior castes; in a way personal merit replaced birth. But Buddhism, which had triumphed in several Indian states at the time of King Asoka, the third century B.C., was later eradicated from its native country as a result of the reaction of the Brahmans. Expelled from its native country, it nevertheless spread to the island of Ceylon, to Indochina, China, Tibet, and Japan.

In about the sixth century A.D., a treatise of political art was prepared in India by a man called Kamandaki. This work somewhat resembles Machiavelli's *Prince,* particularly in the emphasis given to the military sections where Kamandaki highly recommends the employment of a national militia. But for the rest Kamandaki's advice is less specific than Machiavelli's, so that the theoretical wisdom of the Indian statesman's counsel does not eliminate the difficulty of executing it. For example, Kamandaki teaches that the art of ruling is summed up in knowing how to know oneself and others. While largely true it would also be necessary to teach how one comes to know oneself and others—a very difficult undertaking when the pupil lacks natural inclinations, and a superfluous one when he has them.

In China Confucius (K'ung Fu-tse), who lived in the seventh century B.C., insisted on the moral duties of sovereigns. Mencius (Meng-tse), who lived about two centuries after Confucius, taught that it was a prince's duty to punish prevaricating ministers who, in turn, had the task of deposing a vicious and intemperate prince if he did not listen to their admonitions. In practice presumably the placement of blame could only be determined by the success of one or the other. But it is also necessary to recognize that the Chinese men of letters of Confucius' school, sometimes risking their lives, had the courage to criticize the administration of the state when, interpreting popular dissatisfaction, they believed it defective.

In the rich Hebrew literature collectively making up the Old Testament some genuine political doctrines were unintentionally expressed in allusions and brief digressions which throw light upon the political thought of the epoch in which they were written. Thus, for example, in the Book of Judges, having told the story of the near destruction of the tribe of Benjamin by the other tribes of Israel because the concubine of a Levite had been treated with violence and died in a city inhabited by the descendants of Benjamin, the narrator sets forth the perils of anarchy. He concludes with these words: "In those days there was no king in Israel: every man did that which was right in his own eyes."

An apologue found in the same Book of Judges is used to suggest that the popular choice selects the worst people for supreme power because the best do not like to enter into competitions. In illustration, the author relates how Gideon, one of the judges or dictators of Israel, died and Abimelech, his illegitimate son, supported by the people of Shechem, had his seventy legitimate brothers exterminated and was proclaimed dictator. But Jotham, the only legitimate son to escape the slaughter, told the inhabitants of Shechem how once the trees, wanting to select a king, had offered the crown to the olive, the vines, and the fig, how all three rejected the offer because they were busy producing fruits very useful and gratifying to man, and how the bramble then came forward and obtained the supreme power by threatening to set fire to the other plants if they did not obey him.

And evidently the inconveniences of absolute monarchy, the form of political organization common to almost all the east, were not unknown to the ancient Israelites. In the Book of Samuel it is told that when the elders of Israel went to Samuel to ask him to choose a king from the people, he explained that they would then have to pay to the king tithes on the products of the land and the sheepfolds, that the king would take their sons for soldiers and their daughters for cooks and bakers, that he would dispossess them of their best fields to give them to his officers, and that he would requisition their servants and domestic animals to make them work for him. In spite of this the elders insisted on their demand because all the other societies had kings who in peacetime judged their complaints and during war led them.

An institution peculiar to the Israelites was that of prophecy. The prophets were men who considered themselves inspired by God and their word carried great influence with the people, so that even the king had to take them into account. They taunted the sovereigns, great men, and sometimes the whole people for their sins, their luxurious life, and the adoration of gods other than the national one. Largely through these efforts the national god assumed the character of a universal god. In addition, the prophets harshly censured the injustices of the powerful, unrighteous judgments; and lastly, at times they sought to guide what now would be called foreign policy. This last was a very arduous task in an era when both the kings of Israel and those of Judah were continuously battling with the nearby small nations. They also had to maneuver between two great empires—Assyria, which in 609 B.C. was replaced by Babylonia, and Egypt—who were contending for supremacy in Palestine.

Thus, we read that Nathan harshly reprimanded King David for abducting the wife of Uriah the Hittite and causing Uriah's death by ordering his general to put Uriah in the most dangerous place of battle.[2] The prophet Elisha reproached King Ahab and his wife Jezebel for unjustly condemning Naboth to death because he had not wanted to sell the king a vineyard inherited from his forefathers.[3] We see also Amos frowning upon the great men who with usuries and iniquitous judgments dispossessed the poor. Finally there is Jeremiah, who prophesied defeat, the destruction of Jerusalem, and the captivity of its people to the kings of Judah, Joachim, and Zedekiah, and the great men of the reign who believed that the support of the king of Egypt would give them the power to escape the servitude of the Babylonian king.

In the extensive Arab literature of the tenth century A.D. and up to the fifteenth century, works dealing with the art of politics do exist in which glimmers and sometimes visions of political science can be found. Worthy of mention is the *Sulwan al-muta'* or the *Conforti politici* [4] by Ibn Zafer, a twelfth-century Sicilian Arab. Among

---

[2] See the second Book of Samuel.   [3] See the Book of Kings.
[4] Michele Armari translated this work in 1851 with this title.

the rules contained in this work two should be cited: one of an un-Machiavellian nature and the other of a more refined Machiavellism than that of the Florentine secretary. The first asserts that a mountain of astuteness is necessary to counterbalance a small grain of force; the second compares lies to those poisons that, taken by themselves, are fatal but mixed with other substances and wisely consumed, can become beneficial drugs.

The now famous prolegomena to the history of the Berbers by the Tunisian Arab Ibn Khaldun, who lived in the second half of the fourteenth century of the Christian era and apparently died in 1406, are of greater importance. Above all, it is noteworthy that Ibn Khaldun points out the importance of the *asabiyyah*, a term that could be translated as clique, ruling class, or political class. According to him, the rise of an Arabo-Berber state in northern Africa had always been the work of some organized minority, a tribe of highlanders or of desert people, which superimposed itself on the richer but more enfeebled populations of the city and the shore. Once the new ruling class had conquered an empire, it gradually became enfeebled and lost its moral cohesion as the tribal spirit—the sentiment of the original community to which this cohesion was owed—weakened; then another *asabiyyah* replaced the old one.

Accordingly the author studies in detail the causes producing the rapid rise and decay of the Arabo-Berber empires of northern Africa such as those of the Almoravides, the Almohades, and so on. He is less successful, however, when he tries to apply the law of the *asabiyyah* to other Moslem countries outside of northern Africa.

In conclusion, it can be affirmed that our inheritance in the political thought of the ancient eastern empires was very poor chiefly because, as we have already pointed out, the concept of political liberty, as the Greeks and Romans understood it and as we understand it, was lacking in the ancient Asiatic east and in Egypt. But, in spite of this deficiency, we must not forget that in other fields the cultural inheritance transmitted to the European peoples by the ancient empires born on the banks of the Tigris, the Euphrates, the Nile, and in Asia Minor was great.

In fact, considering the material aspect, it is enough to remember the domestication of animals useful to man and the cultivation of edible plants. Included among the former were the ox, the ass, the horse, and the sheep, which furnished man, in addition to food and clothing, the first agricultural machines and the first means of transportation. And among the latter were wheat, barley, and rice, without which it would have been impossible for millions of men to live and collaborate within relatively limited spaces.

As far as intellectual progress is concerned it should not be forgotten that Egypt and Mesopotamia were the birthplaces of mathematics and astronomy, that there the first glimmers of scientific thought were found. Moreover, in these countries the first ideographic alphabets were devised and in Syria about thirteen centuries before the Christian era they were transformed into the phonetic alphabet that afterwards was spread all along the Mediterranean by the Phoenicians.

And perhaps still more notable is the contribution of the ancient eastern civilizations to the moral progress of humanity. In the ancient *Code of Hammurabi,* drawn up in Babylonia about 2,200 years before the Christian era, we find decreed the most indispensable norms of social morality, the nonobservance of which would render impossible any human society. The ancient Egyptian *Book of the Dead,* whose most recent part is traced to the eighteenth century B.C., prescribes that one should not lie, not give false evidence, should give food to the starving and drink to the thirsty, not cheat the worker of his wages, and observe other norms of private and social morality. And lastly, it was in the east that the great world religions were born, first Buddhism and then Christianity and Islam, the last two detached from the old root of Judaism.

And finally it was in the ancient eastern empires that the difficult art of public administration faced its first tests. Chiefly this art consists of doing things in such a way that in a great society, with the least possible restraint, the activity that each individual undertakes spontaneously for his own advantage also benefits the total community. In addition, it tries to restrict all forms of individual activity contrary to the general interest.

3
Greek Political Thought

The Political Institutions of Ancient Greece

Greek civilization reached its greatest spendor in the period
from the sixth to the fourth century B.C. The unexpected revelation
of the Greek genius and the seemingly sudden maturity of the Hellenic culture have caused many contemporary scholars to speak of
the Greek miracle. The very great contribution of classical Greece
to world civilization must be recognized; however, of some use perhaps in explaining the miracle is the now verified fact that the culture of this historical period was preceded by two other civilizations,
both interrupted by foreign invasions. The excavations and the discoveries of the last forty years have indeed shown us that in a pre-
historic time dating back to about the thirtieth century B.C. a
prosperous civilization existed in the Aegean with its center at Crete.
This civilization, in frequent contact with Egypt and Mesopotamia,
extended into the Peloponnesus where it was represented at Mycenae
and Argos. Toward the eighteenth century B.C., following an invasion by northern peoples called Ionians and Achaeans, the first
Greek middle ages took place. In the twelfth century B.C. the Dorians,
a race similar to the Achaeans and the Ionians but less civilized, who
had remained until that time in their original place of residence,
pushed forward into the Peloponnesus and to Crete. They forced
some of the Ionians and the Achaeans to migrate to Asia Minor where
they then formed a center of Greek culture. After the Dorian invasion a second middle ages took place at the end of which the historical epoch began and classical culture was born.

But all these extensive movements of peoples could not entirely destroy the material achievements of the civilization during its two periods of prosperity. The most beautiful buildings and the best works of art were ruined and the cattle could be stolen from their original owners, but wheat, barley, wine, and oil were spared and the land continued to produce them in both good and bad quality. The victorious population merged with the conquered and they lived together in stable settlements. Nor was the intellectual and moral inheritance less important than the material as the blood of the vanquished was mixed with that of the victors. As a result even in temporary barbarity the Hellenic offspring preserved attitudes that are indispensable for the achievement of a higher level of culture. Reciprocally, however, these attitudes are themselves the inevitable consequence of the high level of culture.

At the dawn of the historical period, the end of the ninth century B.C., the age when Homer probably lived, the political institutions of Greece were not particularly original. They can be defined with the term *patriarchal monarchy*. Every city had its king and its council of elders; in serious questions the assembly of all the citizens was convened. In addition to the citizens a class of freemen were considered guests of the city and did not share political rights; finally, there were the slaves. The king commanded the armed forces in war, acted as a judge in peacetime with the assistance of the council of elders, and offered sacrifices to the gods in the name of the city.

However, this type of political organization experienced an evolution profoundly different from that of the eastern empires. The Greek city never became an empire: it was hindered, in part, by the topography of Greece where every valley is cut off from the others by mountains and other natural barriers and, in part, by what is called the genius of the race, to use a rather vague expression. With each city isolated, the patriarchal monarchy remained weak and, beginning in the eighth century, the aristocratic families that formed the council of elders were no longer willing to recognize the superiority of the royal family; the monarchy was abolished completely or retained only those religious functions traditionally exercised by the monarch. Other traces of the monarchy remained only in conservative Sparta and in areas on the border between the Hellenic and barbarian worlds, such as Epirus.

The seventh century B.C. was an era of profound changes in Greek society. In the commerce of the eastern Mediterranean and, to some extent, in the western, the Greeks replaced the Phoenicians, and Hellenic colonization extended on the east to the southern coast of the Black Sea and on the west to the coasts of Sicily and Magna Graecia (southern Italy) and even farther. Growing trade and an increase in population required an expansion in agriculture and, as happens when new goods are produced, the distribution of wealth was altered. Some families who belonged to the old citizenry became poor while others, descended from the resident foreigners, became rich; but among the latter the greater number were reduced to extreme poverty because of the increased rent of the lands and usuries. Whether they were rich or poor, it was natural that those who were excluded from political rights aspired to citizenship in order to be able to participate in the formation and application of laws.

For these reasons there were violent civil conflicts in most Hellenic cities toward the end of the seventh century B.C. continuing to the last decades of the sixth with supremacy alternating between an aristocratic conservative party and a democratic party. A member of one of the old aristocratic families was often placed at the head of the latter, and he, with the support of the people, exiled the rival families, confiscated their goods, and distributed them among his followers. This was the form of dictatorship that the Greeks called "tyranny," a word that came to acquire the meaning of arbitrary and cruel government, although the conduct of the tyrants was not always deserving of blame. On this subject it is enough to recall Pittacus and Pisistratus.

Finally, however, toward the end of the sixth century B.C. and largely with the help of Sparta, the preponderant state in European Greece, tyranny was almost everywhere abolished and the old and the new citizenry arrived at agreements creating the classic constitution of the Hellenic "polis." A result of one of these compromises was the constitution that Solon gave to the Athenians and that we know a good deal about.

The truly sovereign organ of government was no longer the council of elders, which almost everywhere became elective, but the assembly of all citizens to which was entrusted the approval of the laws, the nomination of almost all public officials, and the power to declare war and conclude treaties with other Hellenic cities or even with barbarian kings. All those whose families had been domiciled for some time within the territory of the city were generally admitted to citizenship and if some distinctions were maintained among the various classes of citizens, income was the basis, not birth. However, those who subsequent to the constitutional reform established residence in a city where they had not been born did not enjoy this advantage, nor did their descendants; therefore, especially in the commercial cities the class of *metics*, or resident foreigners, was reinstated. Furthermore, we know that only by a special law could Pericles give citizenship to a child that he had by a woman not Athenian.

All the magistracies were temporary as the incumbents held their positions at most a year and often it was preferred that different people hold the same office for short periods of time. Similarly the army was commanded by up to ten *polemarchs* who in practice either commanded in rotation or yielded command to those among themselves best known for their skill. All those holding public office, if they could not be called to account for their work during the time they were in office, could be summoned before the assembly of the people after the expiration of their term to answer for their behavior.

The liberty enjoyed by the Greek cities, the fact that law was not unchanging and sacred but emanated from the will of the citizens to which it applied, and that the magistrates who applied it were chosen by the citizens themselves, undoubtedly contributed to the intellectual and moral elevation of the Hellenic people. The contests that took place in the assembly sharpened minds and inspired a rivalry among the citizens based on the services they could render to the country. Oratory of high quality often was one of the most necessary requisites for those who aspired to a brilliant political career.

But with the advantages came inconveniences. Very important among these was the need for the frequent presence of the citizens in the assembly, which impeded both the granting and exercise of citizenship to those living outside the city and its territory. So much was this the case that the Greeks, in spite of the richness

of their language, had only one word for the state and the city—
"polis." And it is necessary to bear in mind that the many Greek
colonies, unlike the Roman, became politically independent from
the mother country with which they maintained only religious and
moral ties. The only important exception to this rule came during
the Peloponnesian War when the *cleruchs,* Athenian colonists assigned lands in Euboea and in other islands of the archipelago, kept
their citizenship; but Euboea was very near to Athens and those
who had been granted lands in places farther away very often remained in Athens and rented their lands, generally to the original
residents.

Some effort was made to compensate for the Greek state's
low capacity for expansion with the practice of *hegemony,* that is,
with the formation of confederations in which a city of major importance forced a number of minor cities to ally with it. But a
serious defeat of the hegemonic city was generally enough to dissolve the confederation, because the confederated cities would then
take advantage of the defeat to recover their independence. So it
happened to Athens after the unhappy result of the Peloponnesian
War and to Sparta after the battle of Leuctra. Only in the third
century B.C. were the Achaean and Aetolian leagues founded in which
many cities joined a confederation with all members equal. These
were formed when Greece was already seriously impoverished of
men, riches, and power and when states of such large size, possessing
an element of the Greek population, had been established in the
vicinity that the political mission of Hellas in the world could be
termed exhausted.

And it is also necessary to bear in mind the Hellenic city-
state lacked two great elements of stability found in the modern
state: bureaucracy and a standing army. In the Greek city, public
offices were filled by citizens in rotation and often by lot. Public
order and upholding the constitution depended on the good will of
the citizens, who were the only persons to possess arms. As a result,
the city was a very delicate organism, the correct functioning of
which required of the individual a strong sense of legality and a
profound devotion to public good. For these sentiments to prevail
it was necessary that there should not be too much disparity of
wealth among those who were part of the state; there should be, as

one would now say, a numerous middle class; and the majority of citizens should not hope to better themselves by violent change, by civil war. When the middle class was very small, and wealth, consisting principally of property, very centralized, the rich frequently formed secret mutual aid associations called *hetairies* and bought the votes of the poor with gifts and favors, thereby excluding them from public office. Or else the poor, by prevailing in numbers and by winning power, systematically expelled from public office the members of the ruling class, provided for compensation to those who filled these positions and to those who participated in the assembly, and met the expenditures through taxes on the wealthy so heavy at times as to border on confiscation. Furthermore, where citizens were relatively few and slaves numerous the citizens had to fear slave revolts, as happened in Sparta where the insurrections of the Helots were frequent.

It is necessary to bear in mind these special characteristics of the Hellenic city-state in order to understand the problems that troubled the minds of the Hellenic political writers of the classical period, particularly Plato and Aristotle.

The First Political Doctrines of Ancient Greece

It is widely known that in ancient Greece poets preceded the prose writers; the most ancient literary texts of classical Greece are the Homeric poems, which in their original form were probably written in the ninth century B.C.

The deeds immortalized in these two poems preceded by about three centuries the era in which the author, or authors, lived. Therefore, it is reasonable to believe that when he described the conditions of the society contemporary to the heroes he praised, he wished to convey a vision of a time remote from his. And probably this was his intention, although it must be remembered that what could be called a sense of history (i.e., reconstruction of the philosophy, institutions, and customs from centuries past) requires a maturity of judgment. It can only be found in times of great and long-established culture and among men versed in the study of documents and monuments of a bygone time.

At any rate, in the times described in the Homeric poems patriarchal monarchy and the upper classes maintain their prestige in entirety; thus the poet tells us that government by many is insane and, for him, kings are the leaders of people. They are almost invariably gallant in war, wise in the council of elders, and eloquent in the assembly of the people. The episode of Thersites makes evident that even in those days malcontents and critics of the powerful were not lacking, but the poet makes Thersites appear ridiculous. However, it is necessary to remember that in the Homeric age it was the gifts of kings and great men that gave poets the means to live by.

In the epoch described by Homer, military preponderance lay with the upper class, whose members wore heavy and expensive armor and fought mounted on war chariots. But with the end of the seventh century B.C., the strength of the Greek armies came to be provided by the hoplites, heavily armed infantry soldiers who fought in close order and came from the middle class. This change in the military order contributed a great deal to the evolution of the political establishment.

The patriarchal monarchy had already lost part of its prestige in the epoch of Hesiod, who probably wrote his poem *Works and Days* toward the middle of the eighth century B.C. In fact, the poet exhorts his brother Perseus to stay far away from kings and noblemen, who are devourers of gifts and who sell justice.

The seventh century B.C. is a brilliant period in Greek poetry. One can find many hints of political life in the poetry of the seventh and early sixth centuries B.C.

Archilochus, one of the greatest poets of this period, who lived a little after the middle of the seventh century B.C., was rarely concerned with political subjects, but in his verses the word "tyranny," which it seems is not of Greek origin, is mentioned for the first time. He speaks of it incidentally when he says that he does not aspire to the possession of the treasures of Gyges, king of Lydia, nor to tyranny.

Alcaeus, as it is easy to see from his verses, is of aristocratic sympathies. A little later than Archilochus, he fought against several tyrants in his native city of Mytilene. He also fought against Pittacus, the last of the tyrants of Mytilene, who exiled the poet but after many years permitted him to return and even gave him back his property.

An avid follower of the aristocratic faction was Theognis of Megara, also a poet of the first order, who lived in the sixth century B.C. when the conflicts among the ancient aristocratic families and the *nouveaux riches* were still burning in many Greek cities. For the poet those of his faction are always the good and the others, naturally, the wicked. Believing a mixture of blood to be fatal, he deeply laments that often a young lady of an impoverished noble family marries an enriched provincial, and an economically ruined nobleman marries the daughter of a wealthy plebeian. He clearly expresses his unsatiated desire for revenge against the enemies who compelled him to go into exile.

On the other hand, another poet of that epoch, Phocylides, can be regarded as inclined toward democracy, since in his verses he affirms that it is better to be a good orator and of wise counsel than to be descended from a noble family.

Tyrtaeus and Callinus, members of the same poetic circle, exalt patriotism and praise those who are willing to fight and die for their city, but abstain from participating in the civil wars.

Political hints are found also in the maxims of the Seven Sages of Greece, who lived around the sixth century B.C. Although we know that the ancient authors were not in agreement about who should be included among the Sages, one of the sages provided a rather exact definition of political liberty, affirming that it exists when the law is stronger than those who intend to violate it.[1] But another sage compared laws to webs because flies are caught in them while swallows break them. A third, who must have been Pittacus, speaking from his own experience, commented that tyranny was a beautiful country, but that once one had entered it, it was not easy to find the way out.

Heraclitus, a philosopher who lived in the sixth century B.C. and a native of Ephesus, left us some fragments that are famous for their obscurity and have drawn much attention from some modern scholars. In respect to politics, it appears that he was inclined toward aristocracy, since in his own country he was a member of the aristo-

[1] The same concept is found in one of the *Pensieri* by Guicciardini.

cratic party. In one of the fragments he affirms that the multitude does not know how to obey the best, nor to tolerate superiority.

Herodotus seems to have been born in Halicarnassus, a Greek city in Asia Minor, in 479 B.C., but he became Athenian by adoption. In his *History* there are passages that have a connection with politics. Among these it is important to point out a discussion, which he attributes to three Persian nobles, on the merits and defects of monarchy, aristocracy, and democracy. This discussion demonstrates that among the Greeks of that time the distinction among the three forms of government, enunciated about a century later by Aristotle, was already popular. It was Greek thought naturally that Herodotus had the three Persians express. According to the Persian mentality, the only possible conclusion to the dispute had to be favorable to monarchy.

Most probably the true Persian philosophy on the political regime of the Hellenic cities was that which Herodotus attributed to Cyrus the Great responding to the Spartan ambassadors who warned him not to attack the Greek cities in Asia. Cyrus replied that he did not fear people who had in their cities a square where they were in the habit of assembling to deceive one another.

Toward the end of the fifth century B.C., the Sophists appeared in Greece. The majority came from Magna Graecia and were teachers who sought to teach the young every kind of discipline and eloquence of expression. Of their doctrines we know only what their adversaries have referred to us. It is known that their research at first was concerned with the study of natural phenomena and that, according to them, in every question both the pro and the con could be upheld. This view was a cause for scandal to many Greeks and later to the Romans. Subsequently the Sophists also concerned themselves with morality and politics. According to Plato, the Sophist Callicles distinguished two types of justice: one artificial and created by men according to the laws of a particular society, and the other followed from nature. In the first, a legal equality was often created contrary to human nature. In the second, the strong prevailed over the weak. According to Callicles, all weaknesses in political arrangements originated in the insuperable gulf between legal equality and natural inequality.

Aristophanes, because of some of his comedies, can be in-

cluded among the political writers of classical Greece. He lived at
the end of the fifth century and the beginning of the fourth century
B.C. When he began his career as a playwright his characters were
real people, played by themselves. Thus, in a manner, the theater in
Athens substituted for satiric newspapers and modern caricatures. In
the play entitled *The Clouds* the dramatist attacks Socrates, erroneously identified as a Sophist, who teaches how to make the unjust become just and the just unjust. In the *Knights* he attacks Cleon,
a common leather-maker who for some time exerted much influence
on the people of Athens. Two other characters supported by the
knights, that is, by the aristocracy, in order to fight Cleon turn to a
sausage-maker who, even more deceitful and common than his
antagonist, succeeds in taking the favor of the people from Cleon.
Perhaps this is the most cruel satire on democracy ever created.
In another play the idea of holding property in common is ridiculed.
This would imply that at that time in Athens some followers of communist theories could be found. The *Lysistrata*, one of the most
noted plays of Aristophanes, defends the peace between Athens and
Sparta which was obtained only through a sex strike on the part of
the women. This play seems to have been written on the eve of the
peace of Nicias, which suspended for several years the Peloponnesian
War.

Thucydides, a contemporary of Socrates, wrote the history
of the Peloponnesian War. In the first book he describes the conditions of primitive Greece when the Greeks, for the most part, lived
on brigandage and piracy. Later he draws a very effective picture
of the profound demoralization produced in Greece by the long
struggle for primacy between the two leagues, the Athenian and
the Spartan. This conflict had an echo in the internal politics of all
the Greek cities because everywhere the aristocratic party was supported by Sparta and the democratic by Athens. That Thucydides
was an exceedingly impartial writer is indicated by the fact that,
though himself of aristocratic sentiments, he still put in the mouth
of Pericles, chief of the Athenian democratic party, one of the most
beautiful eulogies of democracy ever written. Thucydides' mag-
nanimity is also notable in that, though unjustly condemned to
exile during the Peloponnesian War, he devotes only a few lines to
describing the episode that caused him this unjust condemnation.

Socrates, who exerted so much influence on contemporary thinkers and on those of subsequent generations, left nothing in written form and his thought passed to posterity through the works of Xenophon and Plato. It is debatable whether one or the other has transmitted to us more faithfully the teachings of the master. It is probable that in some of his dialogues Plato at least improved upon and developed Socratic thought. Particularly notable in Xenophon's *Memorabilia* is the exposition of the Socratic method aimed at showing how apparent truth often does not correspond to real truth.

In politics Xenophon's Socrates does not expressly profess either aristocracy or democracy. He maintains that the citizen ought to obey the law even if it is unjust and, like almost all the Greek intellectuals, he censures the system under which the citizen who had to fill a public office was chosen by lot. He observes that one does not choose by lot either the engineer to direct the construction of a house, or the captain to direct the course of a ship. In a dialogue also handed down to us by Xenophon, the philosopher points out to a young man of noble family how unprepared he is for the political life to which he wants to dedicate himself.

Xenophon was definitely a member of the aristocratic faction, although it has now been verified that the work on the constitution of Athens in which democracy is criticized is not his. Exiled from Athens, Xenophon obtained Spartan citizenship and was given some land in the Peloponnesus by the Spartans. It seems that in his old age he was able to re-enter Athens.

Democritus of Abdera, a Greek philosopher born in 460 B.C., undoubtedly possessed some successful insights into the natural sciences. In politics he appears to have been a partisan of a moderate democracy since he wanted the best to govern but, at the same time, declared that he preferred to live free and poor in a democracy rather than rich and dependent in an oligarchy.

The Political Theories of Plato and Aristotle

With the exception of Aristotle, Plato was the most important of the classical Greek political writers, and with Aristotle he has exerted much influence on all thought since their time. Plato was born in 427 B.C. and died at eighty in 347 B.C. Thus his life was encompassed almost entirely within the period when the genius of Hellas reached its zenith; that is, from 450 to 350 B.C.

Perhaps Plato was the first of the ancient thinkers to publicly allude to one god as the single creator of the universe and father of humanity. His is the theory of innate ideas, such as those of the just, the good, and the beautiful, which man cannot derive from the senses but which are transmitted in man's soul by divine creation. The notion of a parallelism between the social organism and the human individual is also attributed to Plato. In both the philosopher found mental direction (νοῦς), willful energy (θῦμός), and sensual appetites (ἐπιθυμία).

Although political subjects are mentioned elsewhere, there are three platonic dialogues that are principally concerned with political topics: the *Statesman*, the *Republic*, and the *Laws*.

In the *Statesman* Plato, among other things, seeks to establish what objective the statesman ought to attempt to achieve. According to Plato, the true aim of rulers ought not be to engrandize the state or make it rich and powerful, but instead to make the citizens morally better and happier. These two ends should be related to one another since happiness ought to be closely linked to morality.

In order to achieve these objectives the statesman should have two means at his disposal. The first should consist of a system to better the race by arranging suitable marriages between strong personalities and kind ones, and the second of an educational system to develop the germs of the elevated sentiments that God has put into the human spirit. According to Plato, one of the most practical ways to develop these sentiments is by music.

More important is the dialogue in the *Republic*, in which the philosopher describes the ideal city and identifies the origins of the decadence causing the ideal city to gradually become a tyranny, which is the worst form of government.

According to Plato, in the human organism there are mental direction, willful energy, and a part devoted to material life. The same elements are found in the social organism and a special class corresponds to each. Thus the mind is represented by the class of wise men, and courage or willful energy by warriors. The task of production, whether agricultural or industrial, falls to a third class deprived of political rights which furnishes material sustenance to the other two classes. These other two classes, for the most part, are formed according to age, and the class of wise men is recruited from among the warriors who have reached forty years of age.

In describing the organization of his ideal city, Plato intends especially to suppress conflict between private interests and those of the state. Thus he does not tolerate private property, which causes inevitable strife between rich and poor. Nor does he acknowledge family ties because often they cause love for children to prevail over devotion to the public good. Thus marriages are to be temporary and prearranged by public authority, and children are to be educated by the state, remaining unknown to their own parents. It follows that education must aim at developing elevated sentiments and, above all, at ridding the citizen of any self-centered beliefs and making him always ready to sacrifice himself for the good of the state. The state is viewed as a large family and the number of citizens is not to surpass a certain limit. Also the city is to be located some distance from the sea in order to avoid frequent contacts with foreigners, which potentially could become dangerous by introducing new customs and destroying the moral unity of the citizens.[1]

In the same dialogue it seems that Plato wishes to reserve to the third class the task of maintaining the wise men and the warriors, and Aristotle, in his critique of Platonic concepts, points out that it is not clear whether private property, forbidden to the first two classes, is allowed or tolerated in the third.

Plato himself recognized that it was impossible for a city organized along the lines he described to exist in his own time. However, he believed that it would have been possible in a remote age when there still existed in the world what he called the golden age.

---

[1] In the dialogue in the *Republic* Plato limits the number of warriors to a thousand and, if as many were wise men, the real citizens could not have surpassed two thousand. In the dialogue in the *Laws* the philosopher asserts that the number of citizens should reach five thousand.

It has already been noted that the Hellenic city-state could not function well if its territory and, consequently, its population surpassed certain limits. Aristotle in the seventh book of the *Politics*, without fixing precisely the number of citizens, points out the inconvenience of cities that are too large and he deems it necessary that the citizens know one another well if they are to be able to choose carefully the proper persons for public offices.

After the golden age that of silver, which he called *timocracy*, would have come about. In this period the warriors would have placed themselves over the wise and then, since love of wealth would develop among the warriors, the age of copper or *oligarchy* would follow. At this point the poor would be counted and, being superior in number to the rich, oligarchy would be transformed into *democracy* and the age of iron would evolve. But inevitably, democracy would deteriorate in turn into *anarchy*, which is the mother of *tyranny*, the worst among all forms of government. Tyranny is the natural enemy of those who excel because of their wealth, intelligence, or virtue.

In the *Laws*, his third political dialogue, Plato, modifying what he had written in the *Republic*, describes a form of government that he, perhaps, believes could be realized. With greater realism he accepts private property on the condition that there is not an extraordinary inequality of wealth among the citizens. To guarantee this he established the principle of the inalienability of each lot of land which must be passed on to only one of the sons. He also recognizes the difficulty of abolishing the family, but wishes the young to follow the advice of the rulers concerning marriage. In this dialogue Plato suggests that all forms of government can be reduced to two: one in which authority is transmitted from the top downwards, which he calls *monarchy*, and one in which authority is transmitted from the bottom upward, which he calls *democracy*. He believes that the best results are obtained by moderating the extremes of the two systems and, on the basis of this concept, proposes a mixed form of government but with the supreme authority—the custody of the laws—residing in the responsibility of a council of wise men.

Even recognizing the great merits of Plato, one has to affirm that the greatest thinker of ancient Greece was Aristotle. He dealt with all branches of knowledge and his works form a virtual encyclopedia in which all the wisdom of the most brilliant age of Hellenic civilization is set forth. The influence of Aristotelian thought was great in classical antiquity and very great in medieval Europe. From the start of the thirteenth century and even before, he was known and esteemed by the Arabs. Without being so preponderant and exclusive as in the Middle Ages, Aristotelian influence continued in Europe in the sixteenth and seventeenth centuries, and even modern political thought draws some of its basic elements from the great philosopher from Stagira.

Born in this city about 384 B.C., Aristotle later moved to Athens, the intellectual center of Greece, and appears to have achieved fame rather quickly, because in about 342 B.C. Philip, the king of Macedon, called upon him to teach his son Alexander. One of his works describing the constitutions of many cities of Greece has been lost, but at the beginning of the 1900's the section of this work concerning the *Constitution of Athens* was found nearly intact in Egypt. Finally, we have almost all of his classical work on the *Politics*. Before beginning a brief explanation of these works, it will be useful to recall that, like Plato, Aristotle bore in mind the Hellenic city of the classical era which during the youth of these two great writers still maintained its splendor; only in the second half of the fourth century B.C. did the signs of decadence become easily recognizable. Neither Plato nor, with some exceptions, Aristotle thought the political organizations of the barbarians worthy of study which, with some reason, they deemed much inferior to those of the Greeks.

It is necessary to add that in the *Politics* Aristotle also concerns himself with subjects related to this discipline in a very broad sense, for example, the justification of private property, the family, and slavery. This occurred because in ancient times the word *politics* had a somewhat broader meaning than the one we generally give it today.

First of all, the philosopher from Stagira starts by affirming that man naturally is a social animal: Ὁ ἀνθρωπός ἐστι ξῷον πολιτιχόν. According to Aristotle, man can reach the level of perfectibility that nature has endowed him with only in society and with the help of society. Isolated man would have to be a god in order to maintain his human faculties, but not being a god he would become a beast.

The first nucleus of human society is the family, but the family is not enough to nourish the development of all the human faculties in man.

After the family the village, formed by several families, offers a still more developed type of human society. But a more complete nucleus exists and it is the state or the "polis," which is the sufficient group because in it man can develop all his potential capacities. Aristotle is not concerned with political communities very much larger than the Hellenic city—that is, with the great Asiatic empires—because, since these are populated by barbarians, he views them as the product of an inferior civilization.

According to Aristotle, as opposed to the principle that existed in primitive Roman law, in the family the authority of the father over the children and the wife is not absolute like that of the master over the slave. Instead it is a moral authority in which kindness is used more often than violence.

Private property is viewed as the most suitable means to make man work and produce, and if it yields profit to individuals it also brings profit to the group as a whole because when all the citizens are abundantly supplied with the basic necessities of life, the city is also rich.

Slavery is justified as a consequence of the inequality found among men because some have so little intelligence that they can only be guided by others. According to Aristotle, the coupling of the material force of the slave with the intelligence of the master is profitable to both. In an explanation of Aristotelian thought it is necessary to bear in mind that at the time slaves in Greece were for the most part barbarians. Also it is worth noting that Aristotle acknowledges that there could be a slave who has the soul of a free man and vice-versa. But it is possible that this phrase was later interpolated by a copyist who probably was a slave.

Aristotle distinguishes two forms of enrichment: οἰκονομία and χρηματική. The οἰκονομία is the form of private enrichment useful to all that comes about when the father in the family through his work and that of the children and the slaves provides for their needs and, if necessary, for those of other citizens. In this way he obtains the maximum income from his work because the family grows rich and thus creates abundance in the city. The χρηματική would be the form of private enrichment obtained by speculation, commerce, or usury. On this subject the philosopher from Stagira cites the example of another philosopher, Thales from Miletus, who, thanks to his meteorological studies, foresaw that in a given year there would be an abundant olive crop and hired beforehand all the oil-pressers in Miletus. Thus he was able to control the prices for oil pressing and made a considerable profit.

Such a form of private enrichment in the *Politics* is judged dangerous or at least not profitable for society because no augmentation in collective wealth corresponds to the enrichment of the individual. Still worse than commerce and speculation is usury, or loans with interest, because, according to the Stagirite, lent money does not multiply. This error in judgment is explained by the fact that lending money in those times was often a speculation on misery or on the vices of the children of the family. In truth, in the age of Aristotle in Athens and in other maritime cities commercial and industrial borrowing that could be advantageous even for the debtor was no longer unknown. But this was a relatively recent practice and it is well known that the importance of contemporary or nearly contemporary facts sometimes escapes the attention even of superior minds. Thus, for example, Machiavelli did not recognize the importance of firearms, and Thiers in the beginning ignored that of railroads.

Having spoken of the two forms of enrichment, Aristotle perceptively examines some types of constitutions conceived by various writers as well as some existing constitutions known to him. We have already pointed out the reasons why he contradicted Plato in respect to the abolition of private property. Now we can add that the Stagirite is also opposed to the abolition of the family because he maintains that those altruistic sentiments from which a man sacrifices for his family would be lost if the family were abolished.

Aristotle also objects to Phaleas of Chalcedon who wanted property divided into equal parts because, he insists, private property does not always lend itself to being divided equally. Even if equal division were possible, property so divided would remain that way only for a while because in a brief time the old inequalities would be renewed.

And afterward he concerns himself with Hippodamus from Miletus, an architect who, having given rules for the construction of cities, also sought to draw up their political constitution. According to him, in every city there should be two classes, that of the warriors and that of the artisans. Property was to be divided into three equal parts, one for the warriors, another for the artisans, and the third for public needs. Aristotle notes that the warriors in short time would become the only masters of the city.

After this the philosopher analyzes some of the principal constitutions in force at the time, such as those of Crete, Sparta, and Carthage. Judging correctly the infantility of the procedure in Crete, he criticizes, among other things, the system for election of magistrates by which the choice was made on the basis of the amount of applause roused by the proposal of each name. He also criticizes the constitution of Sparta as oligarchic and in decline, noting that the perfect citizens required by the constitution were barely a thousand because eligibility for public office required participation in very expensive public banquets, and thus the offices were not accessible to everyone.

After writing of the Spartan constitution, Aristotle makes one exception to Hellenic pride by speaking of Carthage, a Phoenician and thus barbaric city. He argues that the Carthaginian constitution must necessarily have some merits because it had endured. Although this constitution was in fact aristocratic, it made provision for poor citizens by sending them to establish new colonies.

After bringing this quite accurate analysis to a conclusion, Aristotle examines what should be the qualities expected of a perfect citizen, that is, one eligible for all public offices. According to him, not all the free inhabitants of the city should be considered eligible; together with the *metics* or resident foreigners it was necessary also to exclude the artisans and small businessmen because, due to lack of education, they were incompetent to deal with public affairs and, being attached to their own small interests, would not know how to bring to the government of the state the disinterest necessary to govern well.

After making this point Aristotle concerns himself with three fundamental forms of government, *monarchy, aristocracy*, and *democracy:* a classification almost universally accepted today.

Monarchy exists when all the sovereign powers are concentrated in one person, aristocracy when only a small class of citizens possesses sovereignty, and democracy when all power originates from the will of the majority of the citizens. According to Aristotle, perversions of these three forms are *tyranny, oligarchy*, and *extreme democracy* respectively. The proper criterion to distinguish whether a constitution is normal or perverted is essentially ethical; that is, of a moral order. If the ruler or rulers direct their efforts toward protecting the general interest, the constitution is normal. If instead they are concerned with their own personal advantage, it is perverted. Such a criterion is, in practice, unreliable since it is often difficult to separate precisely the interest of the rulers from that of the ruled and, more particularly, because those who govern may in good faith believe that their government is the best possible one even if it does not correspond to the truth.

In the fifth and sixth books Aristotle examines the causes of violent change and identifies the conditions necessary for the political life of a Hellenic city to function normally. Very rightly he believes that the most indispensable condition is the existence of a numerous middle class, because in a city where there are few rich and many poor, either the former oppress the poor or the latter dispossess the rich.

Finally, in the seventh and eighth books the Stagirite speaks of the best location for a city, the preferable size of the citizen population, and, especially, the education to be given young people. He even provides many rules for public and private hygiene and, among other things, affirms that the best age for marriage is thirty-seven for men and eighteen for women.[2]

Points of contact between Aristotle and Plato are not lacking. Both consider the Hellenic city-state to be the only possible form of state for a civilized people, and in both prevails the ethical criterion, according to which power finds its justification and its legalization when it is exercised in the interest of the governed. But Plato believes that the will of the wise man is preferable to a law which is by its nature rigid and adapts poorly to the infinite diversity of particular cases; while Aristotle believes that law, precisely because it does not recognize particular cases, is the product of impartial human reason, while on the contrary the will always submits itself to the influence of human passions. Furthermore, while Plato aims to dictate the norms according to which the perfect city ought to be ruled, Aristotle explains the conditions according to which the Hellenic state of that time, the "polis," could better function.

---

[2] Modern critics are not in agreement on the preferable order of the eight books of the *Politics*. We have endeavored to follow the order most generally adopted.

The Last Political Theories of Ancient Greece

Plato and Aristotle were still alive in the fourth century B.C., an age in which the decay of the Hellenic political organization was still not manifest, although toward the end of the century it had commenced. But after Aristotle and especially in the third century B.C., the symptoms of decadence became more evident. The cities of Greece slowly waned as their best energies were absorbed by the Hellenic-barbaric empires of Syria and Egypt, which had formed after long struggles following the death of Alexander the Great (323 B.C.). These empires carried the germs of Hellenic culture as far as southern Egypt and northwestern India but, at the same time, caused the breakdown of the country from which they took the elements of their civilization.

In addition, the pressure of neighboring and semi-barbaric Macedonia, one of the three successor states into which the inheritance of Alexander the Great was divided, destroyed the independence of the Hellenic cities or at least posed a continued threat. Literary and scientific decadence was naturally linked with political and social decadence. No Greek writer of the third century B.C. can be compared to Plato or Aristotle.

The first Greek philosophic school to emerge after Aristotle's was the Cynic School, of which Diogenes was the protagonist. It denigrated patriotism because the Cynics declared themselves "cosmopolitans," that is, world citizens. All their efforts were directed toward the attainment of happiness, which they thought could be best realized by reducing their needs to a minimum. According to their views, private property was to be abolished.

Another school arising at the beginning of the third century B.C. took its name from Epicurus. Perhaps to this school we owe the conception of a contract as the source of political cohabitation and thus the germ of that doctrine by which limitations on the powers of rulers and guarantees for the governed are derived from an original contract.

The Stoic School also began in Athens in the first years of

the third century B.C. Its doctrines were especially developed and somewhat modified when Stoicism was propagated in the Roman world during the last century of the Republic and the first two centuries of the Empire. Stoic morality taught the individual to bear pain like a man, to master his passions, and to allow himself to be guided only by reason. The philosopher Seneca, a follower of Stoicism, distinguished a natural right based on reason that was different from a civil right based on law. In politics the Stoics, especially those of the Roman period, believed that the ideal state was governed exclusively by reason and embraced all of humanity regardless of nationality.

During the second century B.C. the decay of Greece—poor in people, wealth and, in comparison to previous centuries, talent—was still more accentuated. However, even in this era Greece still produced a great writer, Polybius, born in Megalopolis in Arcadia about two centuries before the Christian era.

In 168 B.C. the conflict between Macedonia and Rome ended with the defeat of the former. It appears that during the struggle there had been some Macedonian partisans within the cities of the Achaean League. At least so their political adversaries claimed and extended the charge to a thousand of their fellow citizens who were compelled to go to Rome to defend themselves. Having arrived in Italy, they were dispersed throughout the various Italian cities where they remained for seventeen years after which they were permitted to return to their own country. Among these was Polybius who, having become a guest of the Scipio family, received special treatment, resided in Rome, and could even travel throughout Italy and go to Cisalpine Gaul. He learned Latin and wrote a well-documented and very accurate history of the Punic and Macedonian wars. He has been reproached for his many digressions but they give us much valuable information on Roman customs and institutions in that era.

Very important is the part left to us of the sixth book of the *Histories,* in which Polybius discusses the Roman constitution and the organization of the Roman army. According to him, the success of Rome was due, in part, to her military order and, above all, to the stability of her government which resulted from the fact that in Rome until that time there had been no civil war. Examining the causes of the stability of the Roman constitution Polybius sets forth a complete system for the philosophic interpretation of history. According to him, in the first stage of their political organization men are governed by a patriarchal monarch, but the monarchy inevitably decays into tyranny against which the aristocracy rebels to form an oligarchic government. From this in turn through the insurrection of the popular classes democracy results and then, because of successive internal changes, tyranny evolves and thus a new cycle begins. According to Polybius, all forms of government inevitably decay and become corrupt by the exaggeration of the principle on which they were founded.

In Rome, however, these changes would not have occurred because monarchy, aristocracy, and democracy were wisely combined in the constitution. In fact, the power of the consuls was comparable to that of the king, the senate was an aristocratic assembly, and the *comitia* provided the democratic element. Thus, by fusing together the three fundamental forms of government, the usual constitutional deterioration affecting other cities was avoided.

We, born more than twenty centuries after Polybius, can easily ascertain that the coexistence of the three elements—monarchic, aristocratic, and democratic—is a fact that can be observed in different combinations in all forms of regimes; wherever a person or a very small number of people is at the head of a political hierarchy, there can be noted also the existence of a ruling class. Finally, it is necessary everywhere to consider the acquiescence or dissatisfaction of the popular masses.

Instead, as we shall see, Roman success was due—in addition to political wisdom and excellent military organization—most particularly to her very great capacity for organization and assimilation which led her with prudent cautiousness to extend the right of citizenship to a major part of the conquered Italic population. She maintained this right also for the settlers sent out to distant places even if it was exceedingly difficult for them to attend personally the *comitia*. Thus Athens in her best moments at the beginning of the Peloponnesian War possessed barely thirty-five to forty thousand citizens, while Rome at the outbreak of the first Punic War had two hundred and ninety thousand and thus, in spite of very heavy losses, could always recruit her own legions and crews for her fleets.

4

Roman Political Thought

Institutions and Political Theories of Ancient Rome

It is quite clear that at the beginning of the historical period the political organization of the Italic cities showed many analogies with that of the Hellenic city-state. These similarities resulted either from a distinct ethnic relationship or from the influence of the nearby Greek colonies of southern Italy which had a great impact from the sixth century B.C.

In fact, in Rome, the most noted of the Italic cities, we find originally a king, a senate composed in the most ancient times of the heads of the numerous patrician clans, and a *comitia* or assembly of the people. As in Greece, a hereditary royalty was later abolished and supplanted by the consulate and other temporary magistracies which were elective and almost always "multiple." Also in Rome there was soon friction between the old patrician citizenry, consisting of those who were part of the ancient *gentes,* and the new plebeian citizenry, composed for the most part of descendants of the resident foreigners and liberated slaves. And for a while it seems that two cities coexisted *in urbe* with magistracies peculiar to each until finally they were almost completely fused by a constitution very similar to that of the Hellenic city-state. However, this constitution was different in some original details. The principal ones perhaps are the greater facility with which citizenship or partial citizenship was gradually granted to the larger part of the conquered people, the maintenance of all the rights of citizenship for the settlers sent to places distant from the capital, and lastly, the distinct aristocratic character that the Roman constitution retained until the last century of the Republic as compared with that of almost all the Greek cities.

In fact, the Roman Senate in the historical period was composed of those who were chosen by the "censor" from among the people who had held high office. Only in a relatively late period were the *comitia centuriata* reformed in such a way as to eliminate the preponderance in them of the highly taxed classes. The *comitia tributa*, in which numbers prevailed over wealth, were admitted to equality with the *comitia centuriata*. However, a law could not be approved unless it was in the precise form in which the magistrates had proposed it and the Roman Senate had possessed powers and authority much greater than those given to analogous bodies found in some Hellenic cities. And as far as elected offices were concerned, custom more than law thwarted their being conferred on true commoners until the last days of the Republic. Indeed, the military tribunate, the first step to be mounted by those aspiring to political office, until the end of the Republic was accessible in practice only to members of the equestrian order who had to possess a rather high income.

But when Rome, having subjugated Italy, had conquered almost all the lands around the Mediterranean, it seemed clear that the constitution of the city-state, even modified in this way, was no longer capable of functioning. The remoteness of the large majority of citizens was in actuality an obstacle to the orderly and prompt gathering of the *comitia* in the Forum which were ultimately attended only by the plebeians who lived *in urbe*. Furthermore, it became impossible to retain the practice of yearly installation in the higher offices when the consuls had to undertake long journeys to faraway provinces.

Besides there was a profound change in the distribution of property, which slowly concentrated in the hands of a small number of landowners. Thus the class of small proprietors that for a long time constituted the strength of the Roman armies was gradually diminished. In order to remedy this situation two laws were promulgated. One, proposed by Caius Gracchus in 123 B.C., provided that the cost of armament no longer was to be borne by the soldier but was to be paid out of the Public Treasury. The other, proposed in 108 B.C. by Caius Marius, the reformer of the Roman military organization, provided that not only proletarians but also the sons of freedmen could be admitted to the legions.

In consequence of these laws and of the long and distant wars, the citizen army was slowly replaced by an army of professional soldiers recruited from the lowest sectors of the population. In practice, the command (*imperium*) given to the commanders of the legions at first only temporarily and with the possibility of revocation came to be unlimited and was prolonged for many years. In this way the soldiers became easy instruments for their leaders who nourished their ambitions with promises that they would participate in the rewards of victory. Given this situation, we find one of the principal causes of the civil wars. They resulted in a remarkable change in private property; during the first and above all during the second proscription, many lands were taken from the rich and from average proprietors and were distributed to the soldiers; that is, the armed proletariat.

Modern historians have debated and some maintain that Augustus wished to create a new form of government and to replace the Republic with the Empire. Others are of the opinion that he saved the republican form of government and revised it where necessary.

To us, the question put in such terms seems poorly posed because people not fully acquainted with the details of Roman institutions could imagine that in ancient Rome the Republic was a form of government nearly comparable to modern republics and that Augustus' Empire was very similar to modern empires. The truth is that Augustus saw that the ancient constitution of the city-state could no longer function after Rome had subjugated the entire Mediterranean coast and Roman citizens numbered in the millions. Thus he added new and more efficient governmental organs to the old, while adapting as much as possible old organs to new needs.

In this way the *comitia*, as legislative organs, started to become obsolete, although Augustus made them approve two important tutelary laws concerning the family institution: the *Julia de adulteriis*

law and the *Papia Poppea de maritandis ordinibus* law.* The last
law known to have been approved by the *comitia* is Nerva's agrarian
law of A.D. 97.

The *comitia's* legislative function passed to the emperor and
the Senate which issued *Senatus consulta* having the force of law.
But the old prerogatives of this political body were remarkably
limited. In fact, financial affairs and foreign policy that had been
within its competence were in large part entrusted to the emperor.[1]

The Empire was divided into *imperial* and *senatorial* provinces.
The former were directly administered by the emperor through
functionaries nominated by him and the latter through functionaries
appointed by the Senate. It should be noted that almost all the imperial provinces were located on the borders of the Empire and the
legions—of which the emperor was commander-in-chief—resided in
them. Consequently, he held the military force in his hands, and in
the imperial provinces where there was military government he
exercised absolute authority.

In Rome and in the senatorial provinces the emperor was a
civilian magistrate but he accumulated in his own person so many
offices that his will became predominant. Almost all the old republican magistrates were retained but next to them were instituted new
and more efficient offices, manned by common knights or by the
emperor's freedmen who were directly dependent on him. Thus
little by little the imperial bureaucracy replaced the old magistrates
who in time became purely honorific.

The only trace or memory of the old political regime remaining was the *lex regia de imperio*, through which the Senate as

---

* The *lex Julia de adulteriis* made adultery a crime and the *Papia Poppea de
maritandis ordinibus* law modified the *lex Julia de maritandis ordinibus*, which
penalized the unmarried and the childless and rewarded parents of large
families.—Trans.

[1] In ancient civilization the clear subdivision of responsibilities among the different sovereign organs that exists today at least in theory in the countries
of European and American civilization was not found. Often the same function, such as the legislative power, was alternately exercised by two different
organs. In fact, in Rome in the first two centuries of the Empire the powers
of the Senate were enlarged and restricted according to the emperors' will.
In general, those emperors who left a good name, such as Trajan, were more
respectful of the Senate's authority, while those who were deemed wicked
by their contemporaries and posterity were much less so.

representative of the Roman people nominally conferred power on the emperor; in reality, however, it was the favor and the disfavor of the praetorians and then of the legions who appointed and brought down the emperors. At any rate, until the third century A.D. the law cited above allowed the constitution of the Roman Empire to be distinguished from that of the ancient eastern empires in which the sovereign derived his power from the national god or from his family's hereditary privilege. This concept concerning the origin of the Roman emperor's authority is still found in Justinian's *Pandects*. At the end of the sixth century A.D. Saint Gregory the Great, writing to the emperor of the east, likewise affirmed that while the foreign sovereigns (*reges gentium*) were lords of slaves, the Roman emperors (*imperatores vero reipublicae*) commanded freemen.

One of the weakest points of the imperial Roman constitution was the uncertainty of the rule of succession, which caused frequent conflicts among the various pretenders to the throne. The first five emperors, ending with Nero in A.D. 68, were members of the Julio-Claudian family by blood or by adoption. After a year of civil war the Flavia family until A.D. 96 provided three emperors: Vespasian, Titus, and Domitian. In that year the custom of adoption through which the living emperor designated his successor was instituted, and thanks to this custom a series of good emperors succeeded until A.D. 180.

At that time natural succession was restored and Marcus Aurelius was succeeded by his unworthy son Commodus. After Commodus was killed in A.D. 192 civil wars between would-be successors, each supported by his own legions, broke out again. With the renewal of these conflicts the first symptoms of the decay of the Empire and of the ancient civilization became evident.

The political theories of the Roman writers are not very original. The Romans, eminently men of action, did not much like to theorize. Furthermore, in the last century of the Republic, an unsettled era of civil wars, theories were of little use and the influence of Greek doctrines was preponderant. Under the Empire there was no practical purpose for theoretical investigations into political problems.

At any rate, among the Roman writers whose thoughts can

be found relating political life Lucretius can be noted first of all. In his poem *De rerum natura*, having acknowledged the existence of the gods who would not concern themselves with things of this world, he searches for the origins of political institutions. He asserts that in the beginning men gathered in the city under leaders chosen from among the strongest and the most outstanding; this is the meaning that must be given to the adjective *pulcher* that Lucretius uses. The leaders became degenerate, abused their power, and collected in their own hands all the wealth, thus causing rebellion against the government and provoking a state of anarchy that necessitated the formulation of laws and the election of magistrates. In these theories is much eclecticism, and the influence of both Plato and Polybius is evident.

Sallust in his work *Bellum jugurthinum* attributes to Caius Marius a violent invective against the Roman aristocracy. Furthermore, in his description of Catiline's plot he illustrates in very effective manner the corruption of Roman political life in the last days of the Republic.

Another writer concerned with politics was Cicero, who in the *De republica, De legibus,* and *De officiis* examined the three traditional forms of government and stated his preference for a mixed government in which the three forms were fused. The influence of Polybius is clearly apparent. Speaking of slavery, Cicero does not tolerate the Aristotelian theory of the inequality of men but justifies slavery with a principle of international law, affirming that in war the vanquished whose lives are spared become slaves. It is worth recalling that Cicero meanwhile treated his slaves very humanely, especially the educated ones from the east and, in fact, the letters he wrote to his freedman and collaborator Tiro are very affectionate.

Seneca, basing his argument on the distinction between natural and civil law, maintained that slavery was not justifiable from the point of view of natural law but rested on the basis of civil law.

Tacitus, in the fourth book of the *Annals*, writes that it is easier to praise than to put into effect mixed governments of monarchy, aristocracy, and democracy, and that, if realized, they do not last. Apparently Tacitus was not a republican in the sense that he desired a return to the old form of government prior to Caesar and Augustus. He was averse only to bad emperors and praised the good ones who had known how to reconcile supremacy with liberty; that is, with respect to the laws and authority of the Senate.

Causes of the Fall of the Roman Empire and the Dissolution of Ancient Civilization

Greece made the greatest contribution to the development of ancient civilization, but Rome's merit rested on extending the achievements of Hellenic culture to a major part of Asia, North Africa, and to Europe south of the Danube and west of the Rhine, even to the southern part of Great Britain. An even greater merit of Rome was to introduce near equality of laws, ideas, and customs wherever it extended its authority, replacing without apparent compulsion the multitude of barbaric languages in the west with Latin and in the east with Greek, and erasing with time every distinction between conquered and conqueror. In fact, with the Edict of Caracalla in A.D. 212 Roman citizenship was extended to almost all the conquered areas; thus political and moral unity was achieved over more of the civilized world than has ever again been realized.

Urbem fecisti quod prius orbis erat. Thus sang the Gallic poet Rutilius Namatianus at the beginning of the fifth century A.D., summing up in a few words the grandiose work that in the course of several centuries Rome had accomplished.

The search for the causes of the fall of the Roman Empire in the west is still one of the most obscure problems among the many that history presents. It is a question of explaining not only the fall of a political organism, but the dissolution, not complete but certainly great, of a civilization. An observation perhaps until now not made concerns China and even to a certain point India. Both are countries whose civilization had few contacts with Hellenic and Roman civilization and in which several barbarian invasions took place. After a couple of generations the conquerors absorbed the civilization of the conquered and this civilization continued its course without a long or very perceptible decline. This did not occur at the fall of the Roman Empire in the west. It can be supposed that the reason for the difference was due principally to internal causes.

It is already known that the first serious symptoms of the crisis were seen in the third century A.D. and that they are visible also in art and literature, which demonstrate a remarkable decline in taste and thought. The lack of a norm regulating succession to the throne also points out a deficiency that gave rise to a series of civil wars during which there were sometimes as many emperors as there were important provinces. About the same time the first barbarian invasions took place spreading devastation in Gaul and the Balkan peninsula and at one moment even reaching northern Italy.

The Illyrian emperors, Claudius II, Aurelian, Probus, Carus, and lastly, Diocletian, succeeded in driving back the barbarians but abandoned to them Dacia and that part of Germany east of the Rhine and extending to the sources of the Danube. In order to reinforce the central power, Diocletian completed the evolution already begun by Septimius Severus and gave the Empire the shape of an absolute monarchy of the eastern type, transforming also in this sense the etiquette of the court. With the coexistence of two *Augustuses* and two *Caesars,** who reappointed themselves by co-option, Diocletian even tried to fix the norms for succession to the throne in such a way as to avoid civil wars. But after the retirement of Diocletian the civil wars were renewed until Constantine re-established the unity of the Empire, which, however, lasted only a little while until, after various vicissitudes, with the death of Theodosius in A.D. 395 it was broken definitively.

During the entire fourth century A.D. and the first part of the fifth the political, economic, and moral dissolution of the Roman Empire in the west continually worsened until it became an incurable evil. As has already been noted, it is difficult to ascertain the primary cause of this decadence. It was probably due to a set of causes primarily of an internal nature. Some of these are well enough known.

First of all, it is necessary to note diminution of population, owed to frequent pestilences and famines, in addition to the barbarian invasions. Neither public hygiene nor the transportation system were at that time sufficiently perfected to forestall the deaths caused

---

* The *Augusti* were the two coequal emperors administering the eastern and the western parts of the Empire. They each selected an assistant and successor, known as a *Caesar.*—Trans.

by these destructive forces. In addition, the birthrate was very low because Christianity was still not so diffused among the rural plebeians to eradicate the use of voluntary abortions and the abandoning of infants. The decrease in population naturally resulted in the abandoning of cultivation of many fields. An attempt was made to remedy this situation with the institution of *serfdom* binding the farmer and his children to the land, but this was an artificial and insufficient remedy.

Another cause was the decline of the middle class due, above all, to the fiscal system. Besides customs duties and a five percent inheritance tax the major income of the imperial treasury was a tax on landed property. This was allocated through a quota system on the basis of which the central government established the share to be assumed by each municipality. The *decurions*, or members of the city council, recruited from among the highest taxpayers, were charged with the collection of taxes. They were required to cover with their private income the difference between the established sum and that actually collected. The large proprietors, residents of Rome or other major cities of the Empire, were easily exempted by the *decurionate*. Thus the burden fell entirely on the shoulders of the average and small proprietors and ruined them.

In addition, the uncertainty of the value of money necessarily aggravated the economic crisis. During the period of military anarchy in the second half of the third century, debased currency began to be coined in the state mints by mixing lead with the silver and sometimes with the gold. Naturally in trade these coins were accepted for their real value with a consequential rise in prices. Diocletian tried to find a remedy with a single schedule that established in all the territory of the Empire the maximum prices for all commodities and for all services. This was absurd, however, because, among other things, it was impossible for a commodity to have the same price in all parts of such a vast empire. Thus in spite of the grave penalties threatened to those who violated it, the schedule was not enforced.

It is also known that in many parts of the Empire brigandage was a permanent plague. This helped to disturb the security of property and to impoverish especially the middle classes because the rich defended themselves with private guards and the poor were defended by their own poverty.

But above all else aggravating the consequences of the errors of the government and rendering fruitless all those remedies that might have been useful was the corruption of the numerous and all-encroaching bureaucracy. After the third century the bureaucracy continually extended its power to the detriment of individual liberties and municipal autonomy. Historians recall some typical cases of this corruption. Toward the end of the fourth century when the Goths, driven by the Huns, asked to settle in the territory of the Empire south of the Danube, the emperors granted this demand and promised them provisions for a year plus seed to cultivate the land on condition that they relinquish their arms. The bureaucrats entrusted with this work robbed them of the supplies and seeds and, allowing themselves to be corrupted by gifts, left them the arms. The barbarians rebelled, devastated the Balkan peninsula, and defeated and killed in battle Emperor Valens.

But all this explains only in part the fall of the Roman Empire in the west and the more serious aspect of this fall; that is, the very great decline (to avoid saying dissolution) of ancient civilization. In fact, in every civilized country and in every generation alongside the dissolving forces there are always conservative and reconstituent forces represented by noble individuals devoted to the public good. Men of this type were not unknown in the Roman society of the fourth and fifth centuries A.D. The church at that time possessed a series of men, such as Saint Ambrose, Saint Jerome, Saint Augustine, Saint Paulinus of Nola, Salvian, Paulus Orosius, and so on, who were without a doubt of superior character.

But these men, superior because of their intelligence and morality, could not postpone the fall of the Roman Empire in the west because they were part of the ecclesiastical hierarchy that, while not lacking in patriotism, put aside the salvation of bodies for that of souls. The pagan ideal (active participation in the life of the state, a feeling of civic and military duty, an immanent conception of life) was replaced in large part and necessarily by the Christian ideal (disinterest in things of this world and thus also of the state; an aspiration to eternal beatitude; a transcendent conception of life, considered to be an exile, a passage, an obstacle to the attainment of Christian perfection). Thus that ensemble of ideas and sentiments, which until then had directed the movement of the civilization, dissolved and the moral force that is the essential coefficient of the collective efforts of every human society was lacking. Such a deficiency necessarily produced, under the thrust of a somewhat serious external impact, the dissolution of the political organism and of the civilization inspired and sustained by that moral force.

Thus the Roman Empire in the west crumbled. Less favorably situated than the Empire in the east, it had in addition the misfortune of being attacked and invaded by the barbarians precisely at the most acute period of the moral crisis caused by the spread of Christianity among its ruling class. Meanwhile the Empire in the east had time to reinstate its own material and moral forces, to overcome the worst moment of the crisis, and to still endure for almost a millennium. There Christianity, becoming the national religion of the Empire in the sixth century A.D., helped to increase its force and maintain its framework in the face of attacks first by the Persians, then by the Arabs, and for a long time by the barbarians from the north.

5

The Medieval Period

*Boundaries of the Period and the Principal
Characteristics of Medieval Thought*

Generally the Middle Ages are said to begin in A.D. 476, the
year in which the Roman Empire in the west disappeared, and to
terminate in 1492, the year in which America was discovered. These
precise divisions always contain something artificial but, to a certain point, they answer a practical necessity. As we have just noted,
the political and intellectual decline of ancient civilization began
more than two centuries before the year 476, and before the middle
of the fifth century A.D. the emperors in the west had already become puppets appointed and dismissed at will by the leaders of the
barbarian mercenaries. However, the formation of the absolute
monarchic state, the immediate ancestor of the representative state,
was only realized on the European continent toward the end of the
seventeenth century. Only at that time was the mentality of the
European ruling classes divested of the last medieval notions, acquiring a decisively modern complexion.

Perhaps it would be more exact, therefore, to say the Middle
Ages began in A.D. 395, the year of the death of Theodosius and the
definitive separation of the eastern Empire from the western, and
ended in 1715, with the death of Louis XIV, or perhaps with the
beginning of his effective reign, which commenced at the death of
Cardinal Mazarin in 1661.

At any rate, whether the commonly accepted dates are
adopted, or if those just now proposed are preferred, the historical

period that is understood as the Middle Ages includes a minimum of almost ten centuries or a maximum of almost thirteen. It does not require a very profound knowledge of historical phenomena to realize that in such a vast period of time political organization and human mentality had to undergo many changes. Between man of the sixth and seventh centuries A.D. and man of the fifteenth and sixteenth centuries there was naturally a very great difference, and if the psychology of the individuals was different, the institutions and prevailing ideas in human society necessarily had to be diverse.

The principal characteristics of the Middle Ages in the narrowest political sphere are the confusion of private law with public law which allowed the proprietor or owner of land to consider that he was invested with sovereign rights over the inhabitants of that land. It also allowed for the creation of an intermediary entity, the *fief* or *commune*, between the representative of the sovereign being (emperor or king) and the individual. Another purely medieval concept was the assimilation of the state's sovereign rights into the private patrimony of a family with all the consequences derived thereof.

So far as exclusively intellectual characteristics are concerned almost all medieval writers show a deficiency of criticism and of historical sense; only occasional and imperfect observation of facts; and an excessive obedience to the principle of authority, with controversial views supported with passages from the Bible or from Aristotle and often applied with forced analogies. But in the Middle Ages can be found also writers who displayed great logical capacity and who knew how to build comprehensive intellectual systems. On this point it is enough to remember Saint Thomas and Dante.

All things considered, there can be no doubt that modern thought, or that of the last two or three centuries, resembles more closely the philosophy of classical antiquity than the medieval. This is so true that the first manifestations of modern thought were generated toward the end of the fifteenth century after the Renaissance when classical studies had their place of honor reinstated. A similar kind of comment can be made about medieval sentimentality which, perhaps due to the effect of Christianity, has a more pronounced likeness to modern sentimentality. On the subject it is enough to consider some episodes from *The Divine Comedy* (Francesca da Rimini,

Count Ugolino, and so on), Abelard's letters to Héloïse, and especially, Héloïse's to Abelard, as well as many Provençal, French, and Italian verses and tales.[1]

Medieval Political Thought Up to the Eleventh Century

It has already been noted how much Christianity contributed to the modification of the human mentality. Now we will examine how much and what its influence has been in the field of political theory.

In early times the Christians were completely uninterested in mundane powers: Jesus Christ had said that his kingdom was not of this world and Saint Paul had added that *non est potestas nisi a Deo,*[*] thus teaching Christians to respect any constituted authority. But this complete lack of interest in earthly things could not last after the great majority of the Empire's inhabitants and the emperors themselves became Christians.

In the Roman Empire the emperor was also the pontiff; consequently, lay power was merged with religious power. But the organization of the Christian church did not permit this fusion: Christianity had the character of a universal religion and it was destined thus to spread beyond the borders of the Empire; its supreme hierarchs, the bishops, were not nominated by the emperor and from its beginning it aspired to complete autonomy from the state.

Under Constantine and his immediate successors, with part of the population still pagan, the church was under the control of the state. This control was felt in the first ecumenical councils and it was maintained in the Empire in the east because of tradition and because the structure of the state retained greater force. But in the

[1] Modern critics have placed in doubt the authenticity of Héloïse's letters, which perhaps were written by an unknown fourteenth-century author. This would explain the more refined sentimentality than that in Abelard's letters. At any rate, even admitting the indicated hypothesis, the author of the letters still would have lived in the Middle Ages.

[*] There is no power but from God.—Trans.

west the state's authority became continually weaker and more divided. The church soon aspired to independence; after achieving independence it sought supremacy because, in guiding souls, it deemed itself superior to those who had responsibility only for the direction of the body.

The first symptom of this split was evidenced when Emperor Theodosius was prohibited by Saint Ambrose from entering the cathedral in Milan to celebrate Easter because, having ordered the slaughter of Thessalonica, he had hands marked with blood. This action openly signified that in exercising his duties the bishop was superior to the emperor.

At the end of the fifth century A.D. the theory of the coexistence and separation of the two powers was publicly enunciated by Pope Gelasius I (492–496). This pontiff wrote that in consideration of human frailty, it was God's will that the spiritual power be separated from the temporal power so that these two authorities, combined in the hands of a single person, would not give rise to deplorable abuses. In ecclesiastical matters the bishop was superior to the emperor, and in lay matters the emperor was superior to the bishop. Still another step had been taken in the direction of supremacy of the ecclesiastical over the lay authority.

One can note also a letter by Saint Gregory the Great (the end of the sixth century) to Emperor Maurice who, in the Empire in the east, had compelled some monks to become soldiers. Although the letter begins with humble phrases it ends by warning the emperor not to impose military service for the benefit of the state of Christ's soldiers.

The seventh century and the first half of the eighth were too turbulent for the doctrine of ecclesiastical supremacy to continue developing. The barbarian reigns of the Franks, the Lombards, and the Visigoths of Spain were disrupted by almost continuous internal conflicts, and the royal authority little by little weakened to the advantage of the local *signori*. Germany was still in large part pagan, and the Mohammedan Arabs at that time detached Northern Africa and the Iberian peninsula from European civilization, threatened the coasts of Italy, and invaded France.

But Charles Martel in A.D. 732 stopped the invasion of the

Saracens at Poitiers and he and his successors pushed them beyond the Pyrenees. His grandson Charlemagne then reunited under his scepter France, almost all of Italy, and Germany up to the Elbe River, and, forcing the Saxons to accept baptism and to settle in fixed centers, put an end to the movement of the Teutonic people toward western and southern Europe. With Charlemagne the first period of the Middle Ages closes and the restoration of the Roman Empire in the west begins. Thus, within the limits of the possible, the unity was reestablished of the people of Christian civilization, which tradition tenaciously maintained and continued to maintain despite the long centuries that had elapsed and were still to elapse from the fall of the Roman Empire in the west.

The period during which Charlemagne reigned (A.D. 768–814) and for several generations was distinguished by an awakening, albeit temporary and partial, of studies and culture. However, the culture remained almost completely a monopoly of the clergy and especially of the monks. It is therefore not to be marvelled at that the doctrine of the superiority of the ecclesiastical hierarchy over the lay hierarchy was in that period developed and reaffirmed.

The first symptom of this awakening came with the famous *False Decretals* attributed to Saint Isidore of Seville, a bishop who at the beginning of the seventh century had acquired much fame for his *Etymologies*, in which he explained the significance of many words used in the classical age but whose meanings had become doubtful in the author's time. It appears that these *Decretals* had been compiled in the convents of France from A.D. 809 to 851 and were then attributed to several pontiffs beginning with Saint Clement, the successor to Saint Peter, and ending with Saint Gregory the Great. The falsifications aimed at maintaining two theses: the superiority of the Roman bishop over all other bishops and the supremacy of the ecclesiastical authority over the lay authority.[1]

Pope Nicholas I (A.D. 858–867), in the second half of the ninth century, was inspired by the same principles in a letter directed to Austentius, Bishop of Metz. In it the Pope supported the supremacy

[1] In the Middle Ages it was not uncommon for an unknown writer to attribute his work to a famous author and in this way confer on his own ideas a greater authority.

of the ecclesiastical power over the lay power and invited the clergy to refuse obedience to those wicked princes for whom the name of tyrant was suitable.[2]

And identical was the thought of Hincmar, Bishop of Rheims, who set forth his views in a treatise *De potestate regia et pontificia*, almost contemporary to the *False Decretals* and the letter of Pope Nicholas I. First Hincmar repeated in his treatise the thought expressed by Pope Gelasius on the prudence of the separation of the two powers, but, in addition, Hincmar added the argument that since the ecclesiastical power governed souls and the lay power governed bodies, and since the soul was superior to the body, it resulted that the ecclesiastical authority was superior to lay authority. Besides, the lay power, being subject to commission of sin, was always subject to the judgment of the ecclesiastical power.

It may provoke some surprise that this theory concerning the supremacy of the ecclesiastical authority, already a mature doctrine by the end of the ninth century, remained ineffective in actual events for nearly two more centuries; but the conditions of European society at that time explain the enigma.

Cultural decline and the dissolution of state authority had been halted under Charlemagne and for the first decades after his death, but this period did not last long. Toward the end of the ninth century and in the first half of the tenth the darkness thickened and the murkiest and most tormented period of the Middle Ages took place. New inroads by the Hungarians, Normans, and Saracens, who were nestled even in the peaks of the Alps, spread misery and terror everywhere, and the central authority of the state, represented by the kings, dissolved and divided into hundreds of large and small ecclesiastic and lay fiefs. These fiefs were in continuous conflict among themselves and with their nominal leader. Frequent plagues and famines added their devastations to those of war. Religious feeling

---

[2] The distinction between kings and tyrants, which was to have so much importance for the medieval political writers, was known to them above all through the above-mentioned *Etymologies* by Saint Isidore of Seville. Indeed in it, in seeking to explain the meaning of the word "tyrant," it is said: *jam postea in usum cecidit tyrannos vocari pessimos atque improbos reges.* On the subject see A. J. Carlyle, *History of Mediaeval Political Theory*, Volume I, Chapter 18, London.

was very strong but it often degenerated into base superstition and did little to hinder the violence of the feudal chiefs; these men placed their relatives in office as bishops and the bishops often held views and interests hardly less mundane than those of the lay *signori*. The papacy itself frequently became a prize over which the *signori* of the neighboring Roman countryside disputed with arms.

But in A.D. 962 the Roman ideal of the unity of all civilized and Christian people under a single scepter was again reaffirmed in the practical sense through the work of Emperor Otto I of Saxony. At the same time the last barbaric invasions were repelled, the bands of Saracen adventurers were expelled or exterminated, and the Normans established themselves firmly in northern France. Hungarians, Poles, Bohemians, and Scandinavians took baptism toward the year 1000 and thus joined the now large family of people who had received the germs of their civilization from Rome and had embraced Christianity. A degree of order was introduced into feudalism by the stabilization of the powerful families and the first signs of the future constitution of the communes manifested themselves.

At the same time the monks of the Abbey of Cluny in Burgundy, of Hirsau in the Black Forest, and of still others adopted more severe rules of conduct, emancipated themselves from lay influences, and through their teaching spread the concept of the superiority of ecclesiastical authority over lay authority.

Given the political and intellectual conditions of European society once the lay power had been stabilized and the unity and independence of the ecclesiastical power re-established, conflict between the two had to explode sooner or later. By this time the independence of the church had been realized and its discipline under the pope made more rigid through the work of a man of faith and genius, Gregory VII. Favored by circumstances, he was able to induce his immediate subordinates to confer upon the Roman clergy the election of the pope, release of the papacy from the influence of the Roman nobility, and prohibition of marriage of priests, which had made it easier for the lay nobility to occupy episcopates and to become ruling powers over their regions.

Once the struggle between the Empire and the papacy burst into the open, the majority of the feudal lords and bishops (who, for the most part, came from the nobility) favored the Empire. In general, allied with the papacy were the lower clergy and especially the monks, as well as the plebeians who almost by instinct joined the side opposing the nobles.

The conflict was fought with sword and pen and the pontiff immediately took part. In his letters to Hermann, Bishop of Metz, one can detect not only the views of a head of the church, but those of the son of a carpenter from Soana expressing the popular sentiments against the oppression of the nobles. The nobles are accused of having arrived at power, either by themselves or through ancestors, through shameless violence and fraud, thanks to the help of Satan.[3] Inspired by the nobility, some bishops replied to the pope; among them was Waltram of Naumburg who, after the death of Gregory VII under the pontificate of Pasquale II, wrote a work entitled *De unitate ecclesiae conservanda*. In this treatise Waltram calls attention to the pride of a pontiff who speaks as if he were God, proclaims himself master of the world, and believes himself infallible, abandoning Christian humility and evangelical modesty.

Waltram, like the other imperialist writers, opposed particularly the claim made by the pope to be empowered to release vassals from observance of their oath of fidelity. It is easy enough to understand the animosity against this claim if one bears in mind that the oath of fidelity was then the base of the entire social hierarchy, the tie that supported the political structure in such a way that, if all were exempted from observance of their oaths, the feudal world of the time would have fallen into total anarchy.

---

[3] The words adopted by Gregory VII in one of the two letters addressed to Hermann, Bishop of Metz, are the following: "Does he not know that princes originally have had their power from men enemies of God, that with pride, robbery, perfidy, homicide, and crime, animated by the devil, prince of the world, they sought with a blind passion and an unbearable presumption to dominate over their equals, that is over men?"

It is important to relate verbatim the words of Gregory VII because in various publications even by competent scholars it is sometimes said that according to Gregory VII, the state had its origin in the devil. The truth is that Gregory VII could not have had any conception of the state as we have it in the twentieth century and that, on the other hand, he had a very clear idea of the oppression that the armed nobility imposed upon the unarmed common people, and it was natural that he attributed to the devil the role of protector and instigator of oppression.

Political Doctrines during the Second Phase of the Conflict between the Papacy and the Empire. The Communes and the Signorie

By the twelfth century progress in culture over the preceding century is already apparent. Accordingly, the conflict between that current of ideas advocating superiority of ecclesiastical authority over lay authority and the current asserting reciprocal independence of the two powers, both seen as direct emanations of divine will, necessarily continued not only in fact but in writing. Perhaps it is not superfluous to recall that the positions of importance assumed by the communes, especially in northern and central Italy, were of much help to the pope in the struggle that he carried on against the imperial house of the Hohenstaufen in that century and in the next.

In the intellectual duel between the two powers, in which each of the two parties tried to take advantage of the renewed interest in juridical studies, the Canonists in general upheld the authority of the pope, and the Romanists that of the emperor. To the former is owed the *Decretum* by Gratian, a collection of partly apocryphal texts, exemplified by Emperor Otto I's oath of fidelity to the pope and a document concerning the donation of half the Empire by Emperor Constantine to Pope Sylvester.

On the other hand, the jurists at the University of Bologna, immersed in the study of Roman law and considering the emperor to be the legitimate successor of the ancient Caesars and thus possessor of complete sovereignty, upheld the imperial authority. Such was the principle they upheld at the Diet of Roncaglia where, summoned by Frederick Barbarossa and accepting the *Pandects*, they pronounced an opinion favorable to unlimited imperial supremacy.

In letters addressed to the Duke of Carinthia and to the French bishops at the end of the twelfth century, Pope Innocent III clearly and decisively formulated the theory of papal supremacy over all temporal powers. To the Duke of Carinthia he actually wrote that if, because of ancient custom, the German nobles elected the emperor, the election had to be examined and confirmed by the pope. In the same letter Innocent III recalled attention to the coronation of Charlemagne by which the pope had transferred the imperial power from the Greeks to the Germans.

Even in England the conflict between the two authorities was lively in the twelfth century. The two most eminent representatives of this struggle were, on the one side, King Henry II, and, on the other, Saint Thomas Becket, Archbishop of Canterbury. The contrast was at first doctrinal until the King either had the archbishop assassinated or else permitted his assassination. Alongside Saint Thomas we find the monk John of Salisbury, who went so far as to uphold the legitimacy of tyrannicide, excepting only the case when the tyrant was a priest and, in any case, never with poison.

In the thirteenth century new cultural elements were introduced into the world of western Europe, in part due to contacts in the east during the crusades with the Byzantines and the Arabs. Another home of Arab culture at that time was found in the southern part of Spain from which ideas could more easily penetrate the rest of Europe.

Toward the end of the twelfth century, therefore, an Arab from Cordova, who was called ibn-Rushd and whom the Europeans named Averroës or Averrhoës, had prepared a commentary on the works of Aristotle from a viewpoint that could be generally defined as pantheistic. The views of the Arab philosopher soon infiltrated Europe, and translations into Latin of the works of Aristotle, whether directly from the Greek or from the previously known Arab translation, began to spread and acquired very great authority. Aristotle was rightly deemed the most authentic representative of ancient culture, and thus the "teacher of those who know." The church was at first not favorable to Aristotelianism, because it was presented under Averroist guise, and in about 1207 the Sorbonne in Paris condemned it. Subsequently, however, it was deemed more opportune to demonstrate that science, as personified in Aristotle, could be reconciled with faith. This was the task undertaken by one of the greatest medieval thinkers, Saint Thomas Aquinas (1225–1274).

Saint Thomas studied at Cologne under Albert the Great and his principal work is undoubtedly the *Summa Theologica*, in which he is concerned also with politics and social themes. In agreement with Aristotle, he is favorable to private property, judging that property ownership furnished the best way of utilizing man's work and provided a means for the rich to help the poor.

Concerning slavery, which in his time still existed in western Europe, although on a very limited scale, Saint Thomas closely approximates the opinion of Aristotle. He believes that, given the limited intelligence of the slave, slavery is of use both to the slave and to the master. However, he does not fail to recommend that the master treat the slave humanely.

On strictly political matters Saint Thomas needed to overcome the major obstacle presented by the words of Saint Paul: *non est potestas nisi a Deo.* Interpreted to the letter, the phrase justified obedience to any government. But in the *Summa* it is explained that though God wills that government exist, its form is left to the free choice of men.

Saint Thomas then distinguishes a tyrant *a titulo*—that is, one who usurps power—from a tyrant *ab exercitio*—that is, the original legitimate sovereign who then abuses his power. He argues that a tyrant *a titulo* can legitimize his power if he governs with justice; that is, in the interest of his subjects. He admits that in extreme cases when tyranny becomes unbearable and inflicts sinful actions on the subjects, rebellion is justified.

A point often debated is the question whether Saint Thomas, in certain cases, even justifies tyrannicide. This controversy arises because in his *Commentary on the Sentences* he quotes a passage from Cicero saying that the people are accustomed to praising and rewarding him who kills the tyrant. In this passage, however, the author of the *Commentary* does not express his own opinion. Following Aristotle, Saint Thomas judges that any form of government can be legitimate if the rulers act according to the interests of the community, but, approaching Cicero, he judges preferable the mixed government in which even the democratic element has its representation. He says *Oportet ut omnes partem aliquam habeant in principatu.*[1]

---

[1] It should not be taken to mean, however, that Saint Thomas alludes to universal suffrage. Such would have been contrary to the mentality of the Middle Ages. He evidently refers to those who at that time were believed the natural leaders of the people and interpreters of the popular will. These would include the barons, ecclesiastics (churchmen, clergy), the representatives of communes and guilds, and sometimes even doctors.

Finally Saint Thomas deals with the difficult question of relations between church and state. He affirms that the guidance of souls belongs to the former and the guidance of bodies to the latter. Thus each of the two institutions would have its own power and neither should invade that of the other. But in the case of conflict the papacy is always able to judge if the sovereign has sinned, because the pope *utriusque potestatis apicem tenet.*

Another political work attributed to Saint Thomas is the *De regimine principum.* In it, among the various forms of government, preference is given to monarchy, provided that it be tempered; to the monarch is assigned the mission of protecting the weak against the oppression of the strong. The authenticity of this work is much debated because while the thought expressed is, in general, that of Saint Thomas, too often the form is rough and elementary, especially in the last part of the book. Most probably the work represents a course taught by Saint Thomas at the University of Naples and not completely revised by him.

A contemporary of Saint Thomas was Egidius Colonna, who taught Philip the Fair, King of France, before Philip was crowned, and the author of a work also called *De regimine principum.* In it he recommends to the prince the practice of the theological virtues and favors the superiority of the ecclesiastical over the lay power. Generally, Egidius Colonna conforms to Aristotle's teachings, but is not lacking in some original conceptions. For example, he notes that the medieval reign constitutes a type of political order more vast than the Hellenic city-state, because it was a confederation of cities and of castles joined together for common defense under a supreme chief. It will shortly be seen that his royal pupil did not actually conform to the precepts of his teacher so far as relations between state and church were concerned.

During the thirteenth century important changes in the political arrangements of western Europe came about. After the death of Frederick II of Swabia and the great interregnum (1254–1273), the imperial power was weakened in Italy and Germany, while the French monarchy became stronger. In Germany, the large and small feudatories profited from this loss of strength, as did the communes. In Italy the communes and later the signorie profited.

The rise of the communes is an extremely important historical phenomenon which, having begun before the twelfth century in northern Italy, spread to central Italy and subsequently to Germany, Flanders, and, in less accentuated form, to France, England, and even the Iberian Peninsula.

At first the communes were leagues of men who were free from feudal ties or had become free, who swore to defend each other and to obey their elected heads, and who, according to the country, took such names as consuls, scabini, and so on. Often the commune originated in the federation of various guilds of arts and crafts and sometimes, when it became powerful, the small nobles of the neighboring areas adhered to it with their families.

In France, England, and the Iberian Peninsula the communes never acquired enough importance to block the efforts of monarchs to develop the central power at the expense of local authority. Instead they usually supported the efforts of the king to overpower the quarrelsome nobility. However, in Flanders, Germany, and, above all, Italy they were able to achieve substantial autonomy, and their dependence on the emperor was reduced to a slight and irregular tribute and formal homage.

The political regime of the communes was somewhat similar to that of the ancient Greek and Italic city-state. As in ancient Greece the sovereign organ was the assembly. Thus in the communes, supreme power theoretically belonged to the Great Council, which in legal theory all heads of families attended but where, in fact, the influence of the more authoritative citizens and, above all, the heads of the artisan guilds prevailed.

Another point of contact between the medieval commune and the Greek "polis" was the difficulty both encountered in expanding to the degree necessary to form states of much importance. Even when a larger commune subjected smaller ones, their inhabitants were not considered as citizens but as subjects of the larger commune. As such they were treated like the inhabitants of the surrounding countryside, or of the rural territory of the larger commune itself.

In southern and central Italy, except in Venice and in Tuscany, near the end of the thirteenth century and into the fourteenth nearly all the communes were transformed into *signorie*, another institution with analogies to the not always evil and sometimes necessary *tyranny* of the Greek cities. The *signore* ordinarily was a leader of a political faction and a member of an influential family of his commune. He assumed a kind of dictatorship which he sought to legalize either through a more or less coerced election or by a letter of appointment as vicar for the emperor. But the true base of his power consisted in the support of his party and in that of the mercenary militias. Thanks to their military character and to the mercenaries, the signorie succeeded in enlarging their dominions more easily than the communes, so that some, like that of the Visconti of Milan, achieved the proportions of a modern state of moderate size. A genuine fusion of the dominating city with the dominated cities was never realized, and the latter always retained their aspirations to independence. In addition, few families that acquired the title of signore succeeded in retaining power long enough to obscure the memory of its violent origins. Further, the signore always feared the rivalry of other powerful families and possible betrayal by their supporters and mercenaries.

During the fourteenth century wherever the Italian commune was not replaced by the signoria the commune almost invariably assumed an oligarchic form, as in Venice with the restrictive law of the Great Council and in Florence, a circumstance better seen from the subsequent discussion of the political regime of the principal city of Tuscany in that country.

The Conflict Continues between Church and State. Dante Alighieri, Marsiglio of Padua, and Occam

In the last years of the thirteenth century and the first years of the fourteenth the violent conflict between state and church continued; this time the principal antagonist to the papacy was King Philip the Fair of France. He, seconded by Nogaret, his faithful minister and a grandson of one of the Albigensean heretics against whom the papacy had promoted a crusade of extermination, also wanted the clergy to pay taxes on property. Pope Boniface VIII replied to these demands with three bulls, one issued in 1296 (*Clericis laicos*), another in 1301 (*Ausculta fili*), and a third in 1302 (*Unam* *sanctam*). In them the pope not only upheld the immunity of the property of the church from every type of tax, but affirmed the superiority of the ecclesiastical authority over any lay authority: *Omnem creaturam humanam*—he proclaimed—*subesse romano pontifici declaramus*. The principles proclaimed by Boniface VIII were no different from those advocated by Gregory VII and Innocent III, but the times had changed. The spirit of faith while still profound was no longer so strong, and papal authority had become a subject of controversy. Nor did excommunications produce the effects of preceding times when excommunication had once subjected Henry IV to the humiliation of Canossa. Accordingly it was of little surprise that Philip the Fair answered the pontifical bulls with insolent letters beginning "To Malifacius,* would-be Pope, I wish you little health or none at all," and sent Nogaret to Italy where he, together with Sciarra Colonna, humiliated the pope.

The *Dialogue between the Cleric and the Knight* dates from this same era. In it the cleric advocates the immunity of ecclesiastical property and the knight replies by asserting that property has been bestowed upon the church to aid the poor, and that the clergy, who had accumulated so much wealth, ought not to evade public charges. The author of this dialogue is unknown.

Another exceedingly important work on this subject is Dante Alighieri's *De Monarchia*, written almost certainly around 1310, the age of the invasion of Italy by Henry VII of Luxemburg. The philosophy expressed in this work by the great poet still shows the strong influence of the medieval mentality and it is certainly much less modern than that of Marsiglio of Padua, who wrote his *Defensor pacis* only fourteen years after *De Monarchia*.

In his book Dante begins by affirming, like Averrhoës, that for humanity to develop its *intellectus possibilis*—that is, its potential capacity for progress—peace must reign everywhere, and in order to accomplish this it is essential that some one person govern the world. This single ruler must be the Roman emperor to whom all owe obedience. The universal empire was willed by God, who acted in such a way that the Romans conquered the world and founded the

---

* Malifacius is the contrary of Boniface, the real name of the Pope. The word was an attempt at irony and a play on names. The Pope's real name meant "to do well"; Malifacius meant "to do poorly."—Trans.

empire. Proof of God's will is found in the fact that he wished Christ to be born almost at the same moment as the foundation of the empire. The miracles that the Romans attributed to the gods of paganism were owed instead to the God of the Christians, who helped the Roman people because they had the mission of unifying the world.

According to Dante, the emperor, who was almighty, was above passion and thus could assure peace and justice to the world.

After this argument Dante seeks to disprove the assertions of his adversaries (who compared the papacy to the sun and the empire to a moon which receives its light from the sun). The great poet answers that the moon receives its light from the sun but not its movement, an interpretation consistent with the Ptolemaic system accepted at that time, and that therefore the emperor can be said to receive grace from the pope, but not his authority. The poet supports this same thesis with numerous examples taken from the Old and New Testaments.

Another political writer of the age was William of Occam, an Englishman known as the *doctor invincibilis et subtilissimus*. Taking the side of Emperor Lewis the Bavarian, he upheld the independence of the imperial power as against the church. But if the substance of the thought of this writer sometimes approaches the modern, the form is purely scholastic and thus hostile to the modern mentality.

More important as a political writer was Marsiglio of Padua, who was a contemporary of Occam and lived a little later than Dante. Not everything is known about his life. He was born around 1280 in Padua, a very important scholarly center where it seems that his father had been Secretary of the University. He graduated in medicine in his native town and in law at Orléans, from where he went on to Paris. It appears that he was rector of the university there for three months.

Given the originality of the writer, it is appropriate to seek acquaintance with the intellectual atmosphere in which he lived. After the death of Ezzelino da Romano, the Commune of Padua had adopted a policy that would now be called anticlerical and had initiated open war against the Holy See. The echoes of this struggle must have still been ringing during the first years of Marsiglio's adolescence. Ecclesiastical prerogatives, including exemption from taxes, had been abolished and the conflict had reached the point that murder of a lay person was punished with death and that of a cleric with a fine. Naturally the pontiff had reacted with excommunications, which for a long time failed to modify the political course of the commune.

Even in Paris, in the first years of the fourteenth century during the struggle between Philip the Fair and the papacy, the atmosphere was unfavorable to the demands of ecclesiastical power. Here certainly Marsiglio had contacts with Jean of Jandun, another anticlerical writer. It is difficult to believe, however, that the *Defensor pacis*, Marsiglio's principal work, was written, as some contend, in collaboration with Jean of Jandun.

In this work, composed in 1324 during the conflict between Pope John XXII and Emperor Lewis the Bavarian, Marsiglio's mentality is very different from that which guided Dante's *De Monarchia*. In the *Defensor pacis* Marsiglio is inspired by Aristotle but in certain points departs from and even surpasses him. In fact, the Paduan, among other things, may well be the first writer to explicitly distinguish the executive power from the legislative power. According to him, the legislative power belonged to the people or their natural representatives. On this subject, he affirms that: *legislatorem humanum solam civium universitatem esse, vel valentiorem illius partem.*

Much dispute concerns the meaning of the word *valentior.* According to some, it means the most numerous part, but, according to others, the most prominent. In all probability the latter interpretation is the more exact. It better corresponds to the literal meaning of the word used by Marsiglio, and until the eighteenth century it was generally accepted that the will of the people was expressed through their natural leaders (barons, clergy, heads of guilds, and doctors). According to Marsiglio, it was also the duty of the people to nominate the magistrates who were to execute the laws.

After this section the Paduan then faces the question of relations between church and state. Naturally he advocates the separation and mutual independence of the two powers. He goes even so far as to assert that the state should abstain from persecuting heretics, because their conversion is properly the responsibility of the theologian and not that of the secular arm of the lay authority.

Political Writers in the Second Half of the Fourteenth Century and the Fifteenth Century

In the second half of the fourteenth century and during the fifteenth the great conflict between papacy and empire, which had so impassioned people in the preceding centuries, lost almost all force. After an unsuccessful struggle with Philip the Fair the pope retired to Avignon and little by little he renounced supremacy over all lay princes. Returning to Italy, he aimed instead at creating a direct temporal dominion rather than insisting on his old claims. And in their turn the various houses that had disputed over the imperial title in Germany sought instead to enlarge the direct and hereditary authorities of their families, rather than aim at a position of eminence which had become steadily more nominal, vacuous, and contravened in all the countries of central and western Europe embracing Christian civilization.

Thus, until cultural progress and familiarity with the thought of classical antiquity developed further the critical spirit and capacity for observation, the political writers were few and of little interest. They were, however, not totally absent and some can be recalled who do not deserve to be completely forgotten.

Bartolus of Sassoferrato, who was born in 1313 and died in 1358, was an eminent jurist. He also wrote several political works toward the middle of the fourteenth century. Especially notable is his treatise entitled *De regimine civitatis* in which he claims that monarchy suits large states, aristocracy middle-sized ones, and democracy small ones. For the first he makes a distinction analogous to that adopted by our writers in administrative law who distinguish *atti di gestioni* from *atti d'impero*. According to him, the regime that succeeds tyranny must respect the *acta facta per modum contractus* (*atti di gestione*) and it can annul the *acta per modum jurisditionis* (*atti d'impero*). Following from this distinction, every new government should recognize as valid all obligations contracted by its predecessor that originate in private relationships, including that between a person who has acquired a title of public debt and the state that issued it.

Petrarch, besides being a great poet, was also a political writer, and wrote the *De optima republica administranda* which he dedicated to Francesco Carrara, a signore of Padua. In this treatise he gives advice to rulers on how to govern well. He promises them stability in power if they govern with justice and promote the moral and material well-being of their subjects.

In the first decades of the fourteenth century a famous polemic took place between Pope John XXII and Michele da Cesena, superior general of the Franciscans, who argued that the Gospel denied private property, that clergy should live in poverty, and that consequently the temporal power of the popes was illegitimate.

The Frenchman Nicole Oresme, the teacher of Charles VI, King of France, before he assumed the throne, wrote in the last years of the fourteenth century a treatise entitled *De origine, natura, jure et mutationibus monetarum.* In it he denied to kings authority to alter the monetary standard except with the consent of their subjects; this practice was often resorted to by sovereigns in the Middle Ages. Furthermore, Oresme insisted that royal authority should be limited and he made the customary distinction between king and tyrant, based on the notion that the former governs in the interest of the people and the latter in his own interest.

Concerning this subject, it should be remembered that in 1416 during the Council of Constance the monk Jean Petit upheld the legitimacy of tyrannicide, at least in certain cases, and was refuted by Gerson.

Toward the middle and end of the fifteenth century an entire school of political writers in Italy followed, more or less, in the footsteps of Petrarch. Included were Antonio Beccadelli, called the Panormita, who exhorted princes to imitate the achievements of King Alfonso of Aragon, who took possession of Naples and its country; Platina who wrote the *De principe* and the *De optimo cive* dedicated to Lorenzo de' Medici; Diomede Carafa who wrote the *De regis et boni principis officio,* the title of which explains enough of the contents; and lastly, Francesco Patrizi, not completely lacking in originality and who wrote two treatises, one titled *De regno* and the other *De republica*. In the first, princes are given the customary advice in order to govern well. In the second, in which the author's admiration for Aristotle's *Politics* is apparent, the constitution of Venice is praised and that of Siena, the city of the author, is criticized because it excluded certain noble families from public office forever.[1]

In all the Petrarchan writers, a vision of the conventional political world is presented and it might be said standardized. In these writers there is almost invariably expressed a consistent optimism little in harmony with the customs of the period in which they lived. Machiavelli undoubtedly alludes to them when he refers to certain political writers whose precepts would be useful if one lived as one should live but which are worthless, given the way one actually lives. In the meantime, however, a new mentality was maturing and with the Renaissance the human intellect acquired a keener sense of reality and a greater faculty and accuracy of observation; of these qualities Machiavelli and Guicciardini soon will provide us ample testimony.

---

[1] This Francesco Patrizi of Siena should not be confused with another Francesco Patrizi who was born in Kerso, was a Venetian subject, and was a seventeenth-century political writer.

6

The Renaissance
and Machiavelli

*Political Conditions in Western Europe and
Especially in Italy at the End of the Fifteenth
Century*

As already noted, in the second half of the fifteenth century
a new mentality was affirmed first in Italy and then, more or less, in
all of western Europe. This was the phenomenon, commonly referred
to as the *Renaissance*, that comprehended a greater familiarity with
classical culture, with the intellectual world of the ancient Greeks
and Romans, and a preponderant influence of classical culture on
human thought and, above all, on the philosophy of the ruling classes
and the educated.

At this time the last phase of the Middle Ages, which was to
prepare the Modern Age, began. And if the Middle Ages could not
yet be considered terminated, this was the result of the survival of
some medieval conceptions and beliefs, and of barbarian passions
and instincts still uncurbed by the increasingly feeble religious sentiment.

These changes in the intellectual and moral conditions of
European society were accompanied by a comprehensive modification of political and military institutions in many parts of Europe.
As previously noted, the Holy Roman Empire and the papacy no
longer exerted the unifying action through which, since the eleventh
century, the one had aspired to universal authority over bodies, and

the other to similar authority over souls. Instead, in England, France, and in Spain centralizing and leveling monarchies were continuously expanding their powers, bringing each nationality, constituted on the basis of geographic boundaries and language, into union under a single sovereign power.

Thus in England, after a long period of civil war during which almost all the old nobility of Norman origin died, peace was brought about in 1485 with the advent of the Tudor dynasty, which was to last until 1603. Under the Tudors the old forms of the feudal constitution were maintained, but the authority of the Crown was predominant as the House of Lords, composed almost completely of recently appointed peers, lost its old prestige. Nor had the House of Commons yet acquired the authority it was to achieve in the seventeenth century, because the urban and rural bourgeoisie from which it drew its source of strength was not sufficiently developed.

In France, Louis XI, with an astute and cruel policy but one well-fitted for the ends to be obtained and for the means that had to be adopted to obtain them, succeeded by the end of the fifteenth century in annexing to the Crown almost all the large fiefs. He was also successful in subduing the quarrelsome nobility, carrying forward the unifying and equalizing task that was concluded subsequently by Richelieu, Mazarin, and Louis XIV.

In Spain, thanks to the union of Aragon with Castile and the destruction of the last Moslem realm in Granada, the nation was also unified and the monarchy reinforced. This prevalence of monarchies over feudal regimes was due in large part to the increasingly widespread use of firearms. Until the fifteenth century the decisive branch of service had been the heavily armed cavalry formed by the nobility, and feudal castles could be taken only after long sieges. With the use of the cannon, however, castles were easily seized by assault, and the foot soldier with his arquebus and in pay of the king could overcome the horseman girded with iron.

Different were the fortunes of Germany, where many small and middle-sized principalities tended to become independent from the imperial authority. They were aided, as noted, by the policies of the House of Hapsburg, which looked more to enlarging its hereditary power than to unifying Germany.

Perhaps still more divided than Germany was Italy.

Her two principal islands, Sicily and Sardinia, were united with the Aragonese monarchy in the fourteenth century and the beginning of the fifteenth, and a single dynasty reigned in Aragon and the two islands. But in truth, the union was purely personal and the islands, especially Sicily, enjoyed considerable autonomy. However, after another dynastic union Aragon combined with Castile to form the realm of Spain, and the foreign policy of the two Italian islands was subordinated to that of the Iberian Peninsula.

In the Kingdom of Naples, after three kings of the Angevin dynasty had ruled, a long civil war broke out between the pretenders to the succession and prevented the monarchy from consolidating its position. The turbulent barons supported either one or the other of the pretenders in order to diminish the power of both. In 1442 Alfonso the Magnanimous, King of Aragon, of Sicily, and of Sardinia, achieved power over Naples and the entire Kingdom. Sixteen years later he died, leaving his three hereditary reigns to his brother and the realm of Naples, which he had conquered, to his natural son Ferdinand, who was forced to suppress a plot of the barons aimed at dispossessing him.

North of the realm of Naples was the pontifical state, vast but weak. In the fifteenth century, the popes, abandoning their claims to exercise supreme jurisdiction over all the Christian states, tried, like the House of Hapsburg in Germany, to form a direct temporal dominion.

The nepotism of several pontiffs, however, had led them to grant a number of cities in Romagna and Emilia as fiefs to members of their families. In other cities of the Marches and Umbria local country squires paid tribute to the Holy See only with a formal homage. In Latium itself two old feudal families, the Orsini and the Colonna, commanded mercenary companies and sometimes defied with impunity the power of the Holy See.

Meanwhile in northern Italy almost all the communes had been transmuted into signorie. This did not occur in Tuscany, where the Commune of Florence had subjugated the smaller ones except Siena and Lucca. And Genoa, though troubled by continuous internal struggles between the principal families, was ordinarily governed as a commune. The capture of Constantinople by the Turks (1453) closed off to the Genoese the access to the ports of the

Black Sea where their principal trade had been located; as a result the economic and political importance of the capital of Liguria was by the end of the fifteenth century somewhat diminished.

North of Genoa were the dominions of the House of Savoy and the two marquisates of Monferrato and of Saluzzo. However, none of these states, born out of the transformation of ancient feudal states, had up to that time acquired enough importance to be able to affect seriously the destinies of Italy. Instead, in the Po Valley around Milan, a rather extensive state was formed little by little during the fourteenth century. The Visconti family, after consolidating its power in the city of Milan, had enlarged its territory which extended from Vercelli to beyond Verona, so that the state of the Visconti included almost all of Lombardy and a good part of Piedmont and Venetia.

In 1395 Gian Galeazzo Visconti assumed the title of Duke of Milan, but in 1402 he died. His son Galeazzo Maria succeeded him, but because of his cruelty was soon killed by the enraged people. His other son, Filippo Maria, to recover the duchy, was forced to marry the widow of a famous mercenary captain, Facino Cane; she brought him as a dowry a very great treasure, namely, the signoria of three cities and her deceased husband's company of mercenaries. Having recovered the duchy, Filippo Maria had his wife killed and then for a time carried on war with the three neighboring republics—Florence, Venice, and Switzerland. He ended by ceding to Switzerland a good part of the territory that today forms the canton of Ticino. On Filippo Maria's death in 1447 Francesco Sforza, captain of a mercenary company and husband of a natural daughter of the Duke, had to reconquer Milan, which had rebelled proclaiming the *Aurea Repubblica Ambrosiana*. With Milan he recaptured a little more than half of the duchy, ceding the other half to the Venetians who had conquered all the land up to the Adda River, a day's march from Milan.

Venice thus impeded the formation of a strong state near the lagoons, but, at the same time, cut the strength and halved the territory of the only state in northern Italy that would have been able to face a large foreign state. The Venetian Republic, in addition to the vast territory it held in Italy, dominated almost all the coasts of the Adriatic and the principal islands of the Greek archipelago. She kept a monopoly of the trade with India across Egypt as long as the Portuguese did not overstep the Cape of Good Hope. Furthermore the aristocracy, which directed the destiny of the Republic, established the most stable government then existent in Italy and the only one with nothing to fear from internal factions which in the other Italian states always threatened government stability.

Another plague on the Italian states at this time were the companies of mercenaries. In the twelfth and thirteenth centuries the Italian communes armed their citizens, and citizen militias at Legnano defeated the army of Frederick Barbarossa. Later, however, many communes became signorie and the signori, deeming it dangerous to give arms to the people, surrounded themselves with mercenaries. Other communes followed suit when increasing industry and wealth made it too inconvenient for the citizens to abandon their business affairs to go and fight. Under these conditions, an English adventurer, a certain John Hawkwood, whom the Italians called "Messer Giovanni Acuto," made his fortune. Having come from France with a company of adventurers, he put himself in the pay of one state or another when he was not busy fighting for his own account. His example was rapidly imitated and there soon emerged Italian mercenary companies commanded by such Italians as Braccio da Montone, Attendolo Sforza, Niccolò Piccinino, and so on.

But these were dangerous instruments for the governments who adopted them, for the heads of these companies could, if in the pay of a commune, aspire toward creating a signoria and if in the pay of a signore, aim at replacing him. Because of suspicions of this kind the Count of Carmagnola in Venice and Baldaccio d'Anghiari and then Paolo Vitelli in Florence were killed by these cities. Furthermore, it would seem that the *condottieri*, the heads of the mercenary companies, sometimes artfully prolonged the wars in order to make their profits last longer.

Thus Italy, at that time the richest and most cultured country in all Europe, was at the same time perhaps the most politically and militarily disorganized and, as a result, inevitably became easy prey for foreigners.

Florence in the Fourteenth and the Fifteenth Centuries. The Public Life of Niccolò Machiavelli

If at the end of the fourteenth century and in the fifteenth Italy was the most cultured and richest European country, Florence was at that time the most cultured of the Italian cities. With Venice and possibly Genoa, it shared supremacy in wealth.

Almost two centuries before Machiavelli was born his country had already become a great industrial and banking center and Florentine bankers made loans even to foreign sovereigns. From the age of Dante (1265–1321) a new wealthy middle class, whose members were called *popolani grassi,* had achieved in Florence a supremacy so great as to exclude from public office all those who were not members of their guilds, the so-called *Arti,* especially of the richest and very powerful guilds, the *Arti Maggiori.* Because of this dominance Dante, even though descended from the old feudal nobility, was forced to join the *Arte degli speziali.**

Thus during the fourteenth century and at the beginning of the fifteenth Florentine politics—with two brief interruptions—were directed by the oligarchy of great merchants and bankers who formed the *Arti Maggiori.* The first hiatus took place when Walter de Brienne, Duke of Athens, called to Florence in 1343 to pacify the parties, tried vainly to make himself signore. The second took place in a brief period from 1378 to 1381 when a violent insurrection of the common people overturned the oligarchic government and sought to bring the *Arti Minori* † into the government. As already indicated, neither attempt enjoyed lasting success and the government of the *Arti Maggiori* continued until 1434.

After 1378, however, the influence of a new family not part of the old mercantile oligarchy began to make itself felt. Salvestro de' Medici, the head of this family, during the insurrection which

* The *Arte degli speziali* was the Guild of Physicians and Apothecaries—Trans.
† The lesser guilds—Trans.

occurred that year had behaved rather ambiguously. The wealth, popularity, and thus the influence of the Medici grew steadily thereafter day by day, arousing the jealousy of the old oligarchic families. The result was that in 1433 Cosimo de' Medici, a descendant of Salvestro and a very capable head of the family, was forced into exile. Such a measure was taken too late, for by this time the Medici were very well respected by the common people of Florence and many among the old oligarchs were dependent on them economically. In addition the closing of the many banks and factories over which the Medici exercised great influence produced a grave economic crisis, ended only when Cosimo was recalled from exile. Having thus returned to the country in 1434, he became stronger than before and in turn was able to exile Rinaldo degli Albizzi and other leaders of the old oligarchic party.

In his *Florentine History* Machiavelli, in speaking of Cosimo de' Medici and citing his favorite sentence, "states are not governed with rosary beads," asserts that Cosimo governed Florence always with "liberality."

As historian Machiavelli was accurate because the republican forms were retained almost intact although public offices were entrusted only to those tied to Cosimo either economically or by political solidarity. At times he generously provided his friends with the opportunity to appear in dignity in the various councils, taking upon himself the cost of the *lucco*, or the cloak of red cloth that was the regular uniform for those participating. This is the source of his other favorite phrase, also related by Machiavelli, that "with about three yards of rose cloth an upright citizen was made." In this manner, while remaining in appearance a private personage and continuing to live in the paternal house, Cosimo became in fact master of the city and the princes and republics of Italy negotiated with him whenever they wished to obtain alliance with or avoid the enmity of the Florentine state.

Cosimo de' Medici died in 1464. He left as his successor his son Piero, a good man but a bad politician; in spite of the relationships and alliances that Piero tried to arrange with several Italian signori, the power of the house would soon have been weakened if he had not died shortly thereafter and been succeeded by his two sons, Lorenzo and Giuliano, who continued from the beginning the policy of their grandfather. After a last, vain effort of the old oligarchs to overturn the authority of the Medici, the so-called Pazzi Plot (1478) in which Giuliano was fatally stabbed at the foot of the altar, Lorenzo was able to reaffirm his authority, condemning to death or exile many of his enemies.

From that time on he was absolute master of the destiny of his country and, knowing the aims of all the principalities and of all the Italian republics, he was able to maintain peace among them. He established himself as defender of a policy of equilibrium among the several Italian states, a policy which made him in some ways the moderator of the destiny of Italy until his death in 1492.

But if the authority of the Medici was continually expanded, it must be added that it was openly transformed into a signoria. Cosimo had been the first citizen of Florence but Lorenzo already acted as prince. A great patron of artists and men of letters, he surrounded himself with a true court, composed partly of new men and partly of men from the old oligarchic families who had been drawn into the new regime. From the start of Lorenzo's reign the Medici family was represented in the College of Cardinals and it concluded several alliances, treating as equals the sovereign families of the other regions of Italy.

These events gave more and more irritation to the most hostile part of the old oligarchy and caused discontent among the common people of Florence who had for a long time, from the rise of Salvestro to the Pazzi Plot, considered the Medici to be their defenders and now saw in them the masters of a new aristocratic class.

Even while Lorenzo was still alive a Dominican friar, Fra Girolamo Savonarola from Ferrara, had begun to preach in Florence against the vices of the leading men and had acquired very considerable influence on the common people and part of the middle class. The pulpit at this time took the place of rallies and newspapers, and a famous preacher was well suited for propagating ideas and sentiments, as much so and perhaps more than a modern tribune.

Savonarola prophesied that God would soon punish a city guilty of so many sins. With the arrival in Italy of Charles VIII, King of France, which weakened to a greater or lesser degree all the states of the peninsula and imposed upon the people all the damages accompanying war, many thought that the prophecies of the priest had come true and his reputation grew considerably. The inept Piero de' Medici, son and successor of Lorenzo, knew neither how to fight the king of France, nor how to deal with him. The Florentines witnessed the occupation of several cities of their territory and the revolt of Pisa with French support and were then themselves required to pay to the French a large war indemnity. General discontentment provoked a popular uprising, the members of the Medici family were forced into exile, and the republic was re-established in Florence under a constitution giving preponderance to the middle classes. Fra Girolamo was beyond doubt the moral guide of the new government.

But the Dominican priest had in his turn made many enemies and the influence he exercised over the new rulers constantly created new ones. He had for adversaries the old partisans of the Medici plus many of the old oligarchic families who, after using him to bring down the Medici, unwillingly tolerated his leadership equally displeasing to the many intellectuals and skeptics in Florence at the time who refused to believe in the miraculous virtues of the friar. In addition Savonarola often attacked in his preaching the irregular behavior of Pope Alexander VI who, of course, ended up by excommunicating him.

Choosing their time, his adversaries cleverly opposed him via the preachings of another priest, a Franciscan, who was supported by those in his order. The conflict between Franciscans and Dominicans ended with an appeal to the justice of God. Two champions, chosen by the two religious orders, were to pass between two flaming piles of wood; and the one who came out safe and sound would possess a tangible sign of divine approval. On the day set, a large crowd gathered in the square where the ordeal was to take place but it was delayed by disagreements concerning the procedure. The Dominicans wished the two champions to carry the Blessed Sacrament while the Franciscans refused to accept this proposal. The discussion lasted so long that a strong shower came up making the trial impossible. Savonarola's partisans were disappointed and his adversaries profited from the moment in which his popularity had been diminished to attack the convent of the Dominicans; they seized the friar from Ferrara together with two of his followers and, after one of those political trials in which the sentence is written before the debate has begun, all three died on the stake (1498).

Niccolò Machiavelli was born in Florence in 1469 to an old but rather poor family. He received the usual humanistic instruction which was at that time almost obligatory for young men of his circumstances. He knew Latin rather well and probably some Greek. Certainly he was at least acquainted with some of the Greek classics in the Latin translations prepared by the humanists of the period.

Little is known of the early years of Machiavelli. Undoubtedly he must have witnessed the events that occurred in Florence at the time of the arrival of Charles VIII and the expulsion of the Medici and he must have been present through the period of Savonarola's predominance and tragic end. The character and mentality of Machiavelli were not such as to render him sympathetic to the Dominican friar, and in his letters and works are found rather ironic references to Savonarola. While it is true that in *The Prince* he places Savonarola beside Moses, Theseus, Romulus, and other founders of cities, at the same time he cites him as an example of those who seek to lead the people by trusting exclusively to the efficacy of their discourses, those whom he calls the "unarmed prophets," and who, according to Machiavelli, inevitably end badly.

Not being able to live comfortably on his own income, Machiavelli in 1498 competed for the position of Secretary of the Second Chancery of the Florentine Republic; after winning the competition, he was appointed Secretary of the Council of Ten of Liberty and Peace which, in spite of the title, was concerned also with matters related to war and foreign policy. He held this position until 1512. He must have been particularly appreciated by Pietro Soderini, nominated in 1502 as permanent Gonfalonier, a position comparable to chief of the executive power and president of the republic for life. It often happened that for the sake of appearances Soderini sent as ambassadors to Italian or foreign sovereigns one or two Florentines with famous family names but, at the same time, he sent with these men the modest employee in the Secretariat of the Ten on whose judgment he relied much more. Machiavelli was also sent as commissioner to the mercenary companies that the Florentine Republic hired in order to reconquer the rebellious city of Pisa, a submission only obtained in 1507. The influence of Machiavelli on the Florentine government at this time can be deduced from the fact that Machiavelli, out of his merited dislike for mercenary militias, persuaded the Gonfalonier, the Signoria, and the Ten to create a militia called *Ordinanza fiorentina*. This militia was formed of peasants from Florentine territory, subjects yet not citizens of the Republic, who were enlisted through a type of conscription, had uniform armament, and were obliged to train every Sunday for several hours.

The period during which Machiavelli served as Secretary to the Ten, from 1499 to 1512, was one of the saddest in the history of Italy, for during this time the country was invaded, overrun, and trodden down by French, Spanish, Swiss, and Germans. It was apparent that no Italian state was powerful enough or had a military organization sufficient to expel the foreigners beyond the Alps and the sea. The mercenary companies clearly demonstrated their inferiority to the strong and well-trained Spanish, Swiss, and German infantries and to the French cavalry.

The Florentine Secretary was one of those rare men who became ardently impassioned with their work and who, relying on the results of their experience, think they see, and sometimes really do see, further than those who are in the high ranks of the political and administrative hierarchy. That the misfortunes of Italy were owed to her division into a number of small states and to her military disorganization was so obvious that few Italians contemporary to Machiavelli could be unaware of it. But nearly everybody considered it impossible to undertake immediately the application of the necessary remedies because of two major obstacles: the particularism of the republics and the signorie of that time, none of which would have consented to make spontaneously the sacrifices needed to establish a large state; and the difficulty of organizing within only a few years a national militia sufficiently numerous and strong. Machiavelli possessed the faith the others lacked; in this is found his superiority as a theoretical thinker and, to speak the truth, his inferiority as a practical politician.

In 1512 Cardinal Giovanni de' Medici, who some months later was to become Pope Leo X, obtained from Spain a powerful cadre of Spanish soldiers intended to permit the Medici to reconquer the

Signoria of Florence. The *Ordinanza fiorentina*, tumultuously assembled, lacking good officers, and insufficiently trained, could not bear the brunt of the attack of the experienced Spanish infantry at Prato. Thus Soderini's government fell and the signoria of the Medici was re-established in Florence.

Machiavelli, having remained until the end faithful to Soderini and to the republic, was dismissed from his position as Secretary. After some months in prison on suspicion of participation in a plot against the Medici he was confined to Rocca San Casciano, where he had a house and a small farm.

Here, far away from every political activity, removed from the atmosphere in which he had lived until that time, dismissed from the duties he had performed with interest and passion, he now felt obliged to live the life that he so effectively described in a famous letter to Francesco Vettori. His only solace was in reading the classics and the ideas that he deduced from this reading he applied to the Italy of that time. He became steadily more convinced that with the creation of a strong state and a national army it would be possible to liberate Italy from the barbarians; but it was necessary to find the man capable of realizing this daring project. Such a man he hoped to have found in Giuliano de' Medici, younger brother of Pope Leo X, since the house of the Medici then directed Florence and the papacy and was the most powerful in Italy. Thus he intended to write a type of catechism, a collection of rules, the observance of which could lead to the realization of the desired end. This political code was *The Prince*, dedicated first to Giuliano de' Medici and then—because of his unforeseen death—to Lorenzo de' Medici, nephew of Pope Leo X.

A Condensed Explanation and Criticism of The Prince

The Prince is a short work consisting of twenty-six chapters of unequal length, in which Machiavelli sets forth precepts on the way in which states are constituted, maintained, and extended. It finishes with an exhortation that he who has been assisted by the precepts and has created a strong national army use his powers to liberate Italy from foreign domination. The work can be divided into two parts. In the first section examples are provided, preferably of men who have by various ways succeeded in achieving power and keeping it. In the second part precepts and advice on the art of governing are given, based on the nature of men, and again Machiavelli supports them by examples.

The author begins by saying that all governments that have had authority over men can be divided into republics (a word used perhaps for the first time in its modern sense of a state not ruled by a monarchy) and into principalities, and that these can in turn be subdivided into hereditary, mixed, and new ones. Machiavelli believes it to be easier to maintain the hereditary ones because the people are already accustomed to obedience; and less easy the mixed, especially when the new part does not belong to the same "province" (now one would say "nation") as the old one. In order to overcome the difficulties that arise when the new territory is foreign, he suggests four means: to go to live there, to send colonists, to prevent establishment of another foreign authority in the same country, or to seek to weaken the most powerful states within it and to build up the weaker. According to the author, Louis XII, King of France, lost Lombardy because he failed to practice these precepts.

Nevertheless Machiavelli focuses for the most part on the new principalities that may be founded either by arms, by one's own abilities and those of others, or by villainy. As an example of one who adopted the method of arms and ability he cites Cesare Borgia. As examples of those who have acquired power by treachery he cites Oliverotto da Fermo and Agathocles.

Now Oliverotto da Fermo was certainly a bandit, who achieved power by treacherously assassinating his uncle and the major citizens of Fermo. But Agathocles, who was the tyrant of Syracuse and who was indeed lacking in scruples, as the child of a potter and then as a mercenary soldier knew how to acquire power and maintain it for many years against powerful internal and external enemies, demonstrating extremely remarkable political qualities and uncommon military talents. Cesare Borgia, on the other hand, the son of a pope and equally deprived of scruples, won power over Romagna through the weakness of the signori governing the individual cities and with the aid which the king of France gave him through the intercession of the pope, lost the state immediately after the death of his father.

Machiavelli then speaks of military organization and strongly supports the use of a national militia, advising the prince not to rely on mercenary troops nor on those of his allies. This was one of the subjects that the author of *The Prince* knew best how to examine thoroughly.

In the fifteenth through eighteenth chapters is found the quintessence of Machiavellianism. In these chapters the author presents a parallel enumeration of the virtues and the vices of which the human race is capable. Thus beside liberty he puts avarice. Cruelty is set against kindness, impiety against mercy, lack of faith against loyalty, and so on. Machiavelli asks whether the prince should have the good or the bad qualities and concludes that on occasion it is necessary to avail oneself of wicked qualities, while seeking to appear to be conforming to good ones. Whoever does not act in this manner will surely be ruined, for others will adopt such policies against him.

He then asks whether the prince should be more loved than feared and concludes that it would be best to be feared and loved at the same time but that this is not always possible. It is therefore expedient to be feared rather than loved because gratitude is a very weak bond, given human perversity, while fear arises from a threat of punishment which is always effective.

In the succeeding chapters the writer sets forth the criteria according to which the prince ought to choose his ministers and warns him to beware of flatterers. He believes that fortune is only half responsible for a prince's success or failure and that the other half depends on his conduct and personal qualities.

In the last chapter, that which has, especially among Italians, given major fame to Machiavelli, he exhorts the prince to free Italy from foreigners because "this barbarous tyranny stinks in the nostrils of all men."

In this chapter the Machiavelli of the preceding pages, a cold and pessimistic calculator, is contrasted against an idealist Machiavelli, who wants to attain one of the noblest ends that a statesman can pursue, to free his country from foreign domination. In dramatic style these last few pages reveal Machiavelli's tragic situation, seeking to reach a very lofty aim by suggesting base and repugnant means which were perhaps the most suited to the era in which he lived.

Having thus set forth in summary form the contents of *The Prince*, let us now examine its value.

Aging humanity learns, although sometimes in periods of intellectual and moral decline it forgets what it has learned. Thus it should not surprise us if we, who live in a century much more advanced intellectually than the sixteenth, see easily farther and better than the Florentine Secretary.

With this stated we can begin by saying that the problems that concerned and concern Machiavelli's *Prince* can be reduced to four.

1. Did Machiavelli write his work with serious intent, or did he have the hidden purpose of using it to reveal to the people the iniquities of princes? This thesis was put forth first by Alberico Gentili, accepted by Rousseau, and then repeated by Alfieri and Foscolo. But such a hypothesis must be rejected as unfounded because, contrary to what was claimed by Rousseau, no contradiction is to be found between Machiavelli's thought as contained in *The Prince* and that expressed in his other works. Further, this hypothesis is groundless since when Machiavelli suggests an immoral action he very often justifies it by citing the necessity to act wickedly because others are wicked. Implied is the assumption that if others were good there would be other ways to follow.

2. In politics is it permitted to stand aloof from the precepts of morality? Or, must political life always conform to the rules of morality? On this subject much has been said in the past concerning *The Prince*. Today, however, it may be considered evident that the state, as Cosimo de' Medici said, cannot always be governed with Pater Nosters and that governments must act according to principles somewhat different from those set forth in the Sermon on the Mount. This is not to say that in politics one should systematically ignore the norms of morality, for otherwise the politician would end up by being universally abhorred, which happened to Cesare Borgia and which was one of the causes for his rapid decline. In fact, the art of politics consists primarily of a sense of measurement and a sense of limits; he who does not have this sense is neither a statesman nor a governor.

3. Was Machiavelli the founder of a true political science? Certainly he had great talents to create this science and he possessed two fortunate intuitions on the subject. He saw first that in all human societies there are consistent political tendencies, and, secondly, that these can be identified by studying the histories of various peoples. Guided by these two intuitions, Machiavelli tried to lay the foundation for a political science; but he could not succeed because he lacked the necessary historical materials. Historical criticism had not yet been born and historical events were only imperfectly and partially known, or rather they were known only as set forth in medieval chronicles or in the works of classical writers who naturally referred only to a single period of Greek and Roman history, that directly known to them. Whenever the materials were available to him, the Florentine Secretary knew how to discern fundamental truths, such as the causes of the military superiority of the Romans in the republican era. For this he was able to utilize data offered to him by Polybius and Titus Livy.

4. Did Machiavelli create an art of politics? That is, has he written a useful manual which, with adaptations and necessary improvements, can in all times and all countries serve those who seek either to govern men or to continue to govern them? Even today many reply affirmatively to this question. Others respond negatively and this latter opinion seems to come closer to the truth.

Almost all writers and educated men form their judgments partly on books and newspapers and partly on experience. Nonetheless, according to circumstances one or the other tends to predominate. Now with Machiavelli it appears that the former very decidedly prevailed. Without this tendency it would be difficult to explain his reverence for all that the classical writers had written, or his deep conviction of the complete superiority of the Greeks and, above all, of the ancient Romans over the men of his own times. A reasonable objection to this argument might be that, writing at the beginning of the sixteenth century, Machiavelli was not mistaken in this respect or, all things considered, very little mistaken; but he certainly was mistaken when he thought that it was sufficient to imitate the ancients in order to obtain the same results they had achieved.

And this is an error that he sometimes makes in *The Prince*, but especially in the *Discourses*, where he draws almost continually a parallel between Florence and ancient Rome, demonstrating the superiority of the second over the first without taking into account the great diversity of atmosphere and circumstances between the two.

Consequently, Machiavelli, like all those whose mode of thinking is based especially on books, is above all an idealistic theorist, and, like almost all idealists, sometimes ingenuous. This assertion may seem bold when applied to a man whose name has become synonymous with duplicity and slyness, but we do not think it difficult to supply evidence of its truth.

From books one can learn to know the human spirit generically, but it is practical experience that teaches those with the necessary abilities to know the human individual. That is much more difficult, because each human individual forms a small world for himself and is the result of an ensemble of qualities often internally contradictory. Now Machiavelli certainly excels in the generic knowledge of man, but frequently he is mistaken in his estimation of individuals, and thus his precepts are often generic and of little use in practical cases.

His judgments of men are often incomplete. They illuminate a part of the truth, but not all the truth, because they consider the passions and very complicated sentiments of the human spirit from only one point of view. In life and, above all, in political life incomplete knowledge of truth is at times more dangerous than absolute ignorance, because it causes the man of action to believe that he can deal with varied problems, each with its special characteristics, through a rigid and uniform method.

Thus, for example, it is true that it would be opportune, as the Florentine Secretary teaches, to give favor to men who cannot be destroyed, but it is often impossible to favor some without harming the interests of others, as happens every time an appointment must be made that is coveted by several persons. Often, since it is impossible to reduce to impotence all those who will necessarily be discontented, it is necessary to judge with an astute eye and distinguish among the discontented the most dangerous. And it is also true that men, as written in *The Prince*, are generally "ungrateful, fickle, hypocrites, cowardly in the face of danger, greedy for profit." However, Machiavelli himself admits that not all men are thus and he neglects to add that even those who somewhat correspond to the picture he has painted are at times capable of gestures of altruism and generosity. He fails to teach us how to distinguish the morally superior men, nor does he tell us how the small quantity of loyalty and kindness found even among morally inferior men can be put to good use.

On the art of deceiving men probably no special treatise up to now has been written. It would be timely for someone to publish a study on the subject, for those experienced in deceit would find little that was new to them, and their victims might perhaps learn something. Machiavelli discusses this theme along the way in the sixteenth, seventeenth, and especially the eighteenth chapters of *The Prince*, but it seems that his abilities were inadequate to the difficulties of the task. It could also be that on this subject as on many others the twentieth century is far superior to the sixteenth.

In fact, according to the Florentine Secretary, the prince ought to make it appear that he possesses numerous good qualities, but fundamentally he should instead possess bad ones. In other words, he ought to seem and yet not to be; above all, he need not keep his word and observe his promises if untruth and ill faith can be useful, while always maintaining the reputation of sincerity and loyalty. But the writer does not explain how these two ends, at least in appearance so contradictory, can be attained at the same time. It is necessary not to forget that at that time such an undertaking was much more difficult than it is today, since the world was smaller and deeds capable of attracting attention rarer. Furthermore, no daily press existed to color events in such a way as to excite the passions of the public and offer ready-made judgments to the immense laziness of the majority of human minds.

On this subject Machiavelli might well have added a final chapter to his book and noted that it is one thing to lie and another to deceive, and that the first rule of the art of deceiving consists in using falsehoods as rarely as possible and with the greatest precaution, both because he who lies often is rarely believed and because it is highly dangerous to be caught in the flagrant crime of falsehood. He might have suggested also that it is very useful to mix falsehood with as much truth as possible, in order to make it difficult to distinguish the one from the other.

Further, at the end of such a chapter he might have done well to observe that he who is born with an inclination toward duplicity and falsehood almost never succeeds in refraining from it so much as is needful to acquire a reputation for loyalty and sincerity. He could also have pointed out that, on the contrary, he who is either born with the opposite inclination or who becomes trustworthy and sincere through education and self-control, feels an almost invincible repugnance at consciously telling a lie, even when necessary to do a good deed or to save his country.

Fundamentally, the rules that might guide the able person in defending himself and assist the sly and the *arriviste* in attacking, in public as well as in private life, could be summarized in a few phrases; but the precepts that they contain are in real life rather difficult to apply. In fact, the rule consists of a rapid and exact intuition of the character of the individuals with whom one has to deal, a knowledge of their projects and of the means they possess for accomplishing them, and an ability to penetrate the hearts of others, while keeping one's own counsel as impenetrable as possible. And it is almost superfluous to add that to do this it is necessary always to be cold-blooded, and to maintain complete mastery of oneself without ever permitting one's judgment to be upset by love, hate, vanity, pride, ambition of office, greed for money, or, lastly and especially, by fear of any kind.

Now this art is not taught and cannot be learned from a book. It is a natural gift which, like many others, is improved with worldly practice and practical experience. And it is because of this that *The Prince* is an interesting work, but can contribute little of consequence to the intellectual and moral formation of a politician.

But then one may ask, why has *The Prince*, this small volume, been read and reread and, above all, discussed so much from the second half of the sixteenth century to the first decades of the twentieth?

Several causes have contributed. Some which have been present in certain times and certain countries are temporary, and others which have been in effect in all times and all countries are permanent.

Among the first we can recall the polemics between Protestants and Catholics in the second half of the sixteenth century. Each of the two sides reproached the other for acting according to the maxims of the Florentine Secretary.

The Italians of the nineteenth century, on the other hand, found that Machiavelli had several qualifications meriting their sympathy and admiration. First, he had always been condemned by the priests, especially by the Jesuits, and had sought to show that the temporal power of the popes was a hindrance to the creation of a powerful national state in Italy. Further, he had expressed his hopes that such a state might arise and expel the foreigners beyond the Alps and the sea. In other words, he had drawn the basic outlines of the program that Italian statesmen were able to realize, and even perfect in the nineteenth century, uniting into a single state nearly all individuals who spoke Italian. Therefore, it is easily understood that the Italian generations who realized this program felt a great veneration for the Florentine Secretary and pardoned completely a man who had loved much and, above all, what they themselves loved.

But besides occasional and local causes there have been and are others of a general nature that explain why *The Prince* has provoked so much interest in what are by this time a large number of human generations.

Undoubtedly one of these causes is the impassive coldness with which Machiavelli describes a throng of human miseries and the courage with which he sets forth, without idle circumlocutions and hesitations, the faults and defects of both great and humble, of the common people and of the classes who take active part in political life. Many conventional falsehoods had been written on this subject before Machiavelli's time, and continued to be written after him. Thus it is easy to understand the attraction created by a writer who despises every convention and tries to describe humanity as he really sees it.

It has already been said that the Machiavellian vision of affairs and of men is rarely complete, that often the author of *The Prince* sees only one side of the complex and varied nature of the sons of Adam. But that side he knows how to describe with incisive phrases that strike home to the reader and that, according to circumstance, arouse deep repugnance or great admiration, for often they complete, fix, and embellish a judgment the reader has already sensed without being able to specify and formulate clearly.

In addition, the style is suitable to the contents of the book, spontaneous and thus very effective. Machiavelli in *The Prince* writes under the impulse of conviction and deep passion. Thus he does not waste time adorning his sentences and giving them classic form, as he does, for example, in *The Florentine History*. In *The Prince*, his most famous work, he adopts the Florentine dialect, the native idiom hardly refined, and, above all, tries to express his thought with the utmost clarity and precision possible, caring little about literary form. This philosophy he expresses entirely without diffidence and without sentiment, not caring whether the reader will be favorable to what he writes or whether he will find the maxims disgusting. Thus he never tries to sugar-coat the pill, but only worries about setting forth what he believes to be the truth.

This man, whose claim was that of teaching his fellow men the art of deceiving, of showing them the advantages and necessity of falsehood, was, as a writer, one of the most sincere who has ever lived. He possessed in an exceptional way that professional honesty that consists of expressing to the reader his own true thought, without caring about the success or failure of the book, or the advantage or harm it can cause him. And in this case sincerity contributed to success because it made the contents of *The Prince* more palatable.

In short, Machiavelli was—apart from some small and not uncommon womanly intrigue—honest in his private life, honest as a functionary (because he always served his superiors faithfully), and very honest as a writer. He wished to define the rules of the art of political deception. It was not his cup of tea. If he had really been a sly person and an *arriviste*, given his talent he would have had a much more brilliant career. He would not have died in poverty and, above all, he would have refrained from writing *The Prince*, for truly sly people in all ages and in all countries know well that the first rule of their art consists in not revealing to others the secret of their game.

The Prince is undoubtedly the work that brought most fame to its author, but Machiavelli wrote another work with a political theme, the *Discourses on the First Ten Books of Titus Livius*. It lacks the unity of purpose found in *The Prince*, and it is, therefore, more difficult to summarize. But it can be indicated that in general the author in his work seeks to teach republics the ways in which they can expand and endure. Almost uniformly he supports his precepts with examples taken from Roman history and, as previously noted, takes very little into account the great differences between the time of the Roman Republic and the times in which he lived.

In the *Discourses* Machiavelli presses his recommendation for the institution of citizen militias and he argues that a necessary element for the prosperity of a republic is that the populace not be corrupt.

In the *Dialogues on the Art of War* Machiavelli develops the concepts already set forth in *The Prince* and the *Discourses* on mercenary militias. In order to evaluate Machiavelli's sagacity it would even be appropriate to speak of the *relazioni* with which he informed his superiors of conditions in the countries where he had been sent on diplomatic missions. Some of these *relazioni* do honor to the observer as, for example, that on France. Others are more superficial such as that on Germany, where the Florentine Secretary had been for only a few weeks without knowing the language. The other works, including the *The Florentine History*, have more literary than political value.

Some handwritten copies of *The Prince* circulated in Florence and Rome while the author, who died in 1527, was still alive. The work was published almost contemporaneously in Rome and Florence in December of 1531 and January of 1532. In 1523 a certain Agostino Nifo, a professor at Pisa, had translated *The Prince* into Latin even before it had been published. He altered it a little and published it as his own, cutting out the last chapter and giving it the title of *De regnandi peritia*. He dedicated the work to Charles V.

It appears that *The Prince* was first quoted—by Cardinal Reginaldo Polo—in about 1540. In the second half of the sixteenth century *The Prince*, violently criticized by both Protestants and Catholics, was cited often by those who had read it and not infrequently by those who had not.

Sixteenth-Century Political Writers. Guicciardini and the Practical Machiavellians

Unlike the fifteenth century, the sixteenth produced a rich political literature not only in Italy but also in France, Spain, and, to a lesser extent, Germany. However, in this literature we do not find the unity of direction of the preceding centuries since, for example, the very intense conflict between Protestants and Catholics caused some writers to inquire into the legitimacy of and limits on the sovereign power and the cases in which rebellion and even tyrannicide were justifiable. Other thinkers, following in the footsteps of Aristotle or of Machiavelli, searched for the most preferable among the three classical forms of government or else suggested to princes and republics the best techniques for enlarging the state or preserving it.

This multiplicity of directions was in part owed to the diversity of cultural influences affecting sixteenth-century scholars. These influences partly originated from the writers of classical antiquity and partly were an inheritance from the centuries immediately preceding. The sixteenth century and much of the seventeenth can be considered an era of transition between modern thought and that of the fourteenth and fifteenth centuries.

Even if the writers of the period following the Renaissance no longer compared the pope to the sun and the emperor to the moon, and no longer swore to the absolute infallibility of Aristotle, many of them still took citations from the Bible and from Aristotle to bolster their theses. And though the Italian humanists and then Erasmus of Rotterdam had begun criticism of both sacred and profane texts, and such falsifications as the *False Decretals* and Gratian's *Decretum* had become impossible, the emancipation from the older intellectual chains of custom was still far from complete.

This variety and uncertainty in the political and intellectual currents of the sixteenth century found its parallel in political institutions that were also in transition. The movement had already commenced that by the end of the seventeenth century was to lead to the creation of the absolute state, with its differentiated organs among which a stable bureaucracy and permanent army were foremost; on the other hand, remnants of feudalism were still numerous and the autarchy of the communes remained important.

Against this background we will begin a brief review of the principal political writers of the sixteenth century. In chronological order one of the first among these is Francesco Guicciardini, who was born in Florence in 1483 and died in 1540. He left many works, some of which remained for a long time completely or partly unpublished. One of these was the *Ricordi civili e politici*. Also included among his works are *Storia di Firenze*, *Storia d'Italia*, *Dialogo sul reggimento di Firenze*, and *Considerazioni intorno ai Discorsi di Machiavelli sulla prima Decade di Tito Livio*.

In no work by the author can a systematic statement of his political thought be found but it can easily be deduced from his writings considered as a whole. Guicciardini based his conclusions on observation of facts and of human nature, as Machiavelli tried to do. However, this is the extent of his intellectual contact with the Florentine Secretary because Guicciardini almost invariably reaches conclusions divergent from his famous contemporary.

While Machiavelli at the beginning of the sixteenth century sought the coming of a prince to liberate Italy from the barbarians, Guicciardini, accurately informed as to the true conditions of the period and country in which he lived, was unwilling to support a similar program.

The observations that he makes on Machiavelli's *Discorsi* in the *Considerazioni* and even in the *Ricordi* attest to his very acute sense of reality. He says: "How mistaken are they who cite the Romans in every sentence. They would require a city formed like theirs in order to govern according to that example."

Guicciardini provides a precise definition of political liberty which, according to what he says, consists "in the prevalence of laws and ordinances over the appetite of individual men." It is taken for granted that among these individual men the rulers should also be included. He is not favorable to popular government or, as it is now called, democratic government because he affirms that "the populace is a mad animal."

In his writings it is evident that he preferred a mixed government and wanted a tempered monarchy established in Florence, certainly not because he thought this form of government the best but because he judged it the best among the possible alternatives, given the conditions of the city.

Like many men who have taken an active part in political life, our author is rather pessimistic. In fact, he repeatedly affirms that almost all of those who claim to love liberty, if they found a city where they could rule "they would run post-haste." But his pessimism is not complete for he believes that "in general men love the good and love justice whenever love of their own interest and that of their relatives or fear of the vengeance of others does not pervert their intention."

Another thought worthy of mention is his assertion that "knowledge in weak brains either fails to improve them or ruins them completely." Furthermore, he seems to have been an enthusiast of Martin Luther and suggests that Luther served the papacy faithfully but would have been happy if he had seen the priests reduced to the point "of being without vices or without the means to satisfy them."

Much discussion has centered on Guicciardini's behavior and on the morality and nobility of his philosophy. Generally, the commentaries have been rather unfavorable to him. The truth is that he wanted the good but within the limits that he thought possible, and together with the public good he looked after what he called his "particular good," that is, his personal interest.

As already noted, in the second half of the sixteenth century there were many writers who sought to refute the theories set forth in *The Prince*. Some were Protestant and some Catholic. Among the Protestants the Frenchman Gentillet can be recalled. He attributes the Saint Bartholomew Massacre to the influence of the Florentine Secretary's book and—approaching the truth—notes that the precepts set forth in *The Prince* were more applicable in the small Italian states than in a large, firmly established realm such as France. Among the Catholics, two Jesuits, Father Possevino and Father Ribadaneira enjoyed major fame, but perhaps a small scholastic treatise by Father Lucchesini entitled *Saggio sulle sciocchezze di Machiavelli* (Essay on the Foolishness of Machiavelli), which the booksellers used to call *Le sciocchezze del padre Lucchesini* (The Foolishness of Father

Lucchesini), received greater diffusion. In the same era the Flemish Gaspard Scioppius and Justus Lipsius were cautious defenders of Machiavelli.

Still later toward the end of the sixteenth century and the beginning of the seventeenth other writers were inspired by the principles set forth by Machiavelli and tried to apply them in practice by giving advice to those who governed. One of these was the Sicilian Scipione di Castro, who was born about 1520, according to some in Palermo or, according to others, in Messina. The importance of his works was set forth first by Giuseppe Ferrari in the *Corso sugli scrittori politici italiani.*

Don Scipione lived a rather adventuresome life. He traveled a great deal throughout Italy and spent much time in Milan with Don Ferrante Gonzaga, former Viceroy in Sicily and then governor of Milan and its country. He lived also in the Low Countries and was in London at the time of the marriage of Queen Mary the Catholic to the man who a few years later became Philip II, King of Spain; that is, in about 1553. Lastly, he resided for some years in Rome where he was employed by the popes on works of hydraulic engineering. In London it seems that he was friendly with the Duke of Savoy, Emanuele Filiberto, not yet re-established in his hereditary states. Nevertheless, many points in Don Scipione's biography remain obscure. It is certain that he was in jail twice, the second time at an advanced age for three years and seven months, as he himself wrote this. From his life it would appear that he was more capable of making contacts and acquiring positions than of keeping them.

Scipione di Castro's activity as a writer was great and was almost completely devoted to political subjects, especially practical politics. Worthy of particular mention are *Relazioni degli Stati e governi dei Paesi Bassi, Relazione ed istruzione per lo Stato di Milano, Istruzione ai Principi per sapere ben governare gli Stati,* and lastly, *Avvertimenti a don Marcantonio Colonna quando andò viceré in Sicilia.* The last work, undoubtedly the author's best, must have been written in 1577 and was published for the first time in Milan in the last part of the *Tesoro politico* in 1601. It is appropriate to give a rather extensive account of this work.

At that time Sicily was joined with Spain through a personal union because the same dynasty governing Spain reigned in the large Mediterranean island. However, Sicily maintained a great deal of autonomy. Its Parliament continued to exist and possessed finances separate from the Spanish. The executive power and, in part, the judicial were entrusted to viceroys who were generally Spanish but sometimes Italian. These remained in office for three years and could be reconfirmed. However, their powers, very great in appearance, were partially limited by the secret instructions they received from Madrid through the *Council of Italy,* which was charged with directing them and in case of need keeping them under surveillance.

In his *Avvertimenti a don Marcantonio Colonna* Scipione di Castro begins by reviewing the deeds of all the viceroys who from the beginning of the sixteenth century had been sent to govern Sicily. The author of the *Avvertimenti* asserts that almost none were successful, given the great difficulties that they encountered in carrying out their duties. He supports this statement with numerous and, in truth, not always suitable examples, for in several cases the failure was due not to the difficulties that the office presented but to the defects or faults of those who filled it.[1]

Our author, in enumerating the various obstacles facing the viceroys of Sicily, reduces them to ten: the nature of the inhabitants, the influence of Parliament, the power of the feudal "signori," the exemptions of Messina, the cunning of the bureaucrats, the intrigues of the apostolic legate, the decisions of the tribunals, the self-interest of the servants, the jurisdiction of the Holy Office, and the right of ratification insisted upon by the king.

In setting out the nature of these difficulties Di Castro displays a remarkable power of observation. His description of the character of the Sicilians is very pessimistic, but from many points of view approaches the truth. In order to reduce the other difficulties he suggests that Parliament be convened in winter and in uncomfortable places and that it be selected in such a way that corrupt people who could be bought or intimidated would enter the Parliament. He provided other suggestions of the same type which, alas, were of little use to Don Marcantonio Colonna, who because of his irresponsibility had his misfortunes also.

[1] For example, the Duke of Medina Celi was deprived of his authority because of the timidity and cowardice that he displayed in an expedition against the island of Gerba. However, Di Castro himself says that he would have been able to keep a good reputation if he had never governed.

Another writer of the same school is the Frenchman Gabriel Naudé who toward the end of the sixteenth century wrote a treatise entitled *Considérations politiques sur les coups d'état* and published in 1639. Clearly Naudé aimed to pass for an unbiased man and thus tries to impress the reader with his paradoxes. He affirms, for example, that the Saint Bartholomew Massacre merited censure because it was incomplete since not all the Protestants were killed. His advice also is often generic and of little practical value such as his teaching that one must never attempt an action if he is not sure of carrying it to a successful end. However, he does not explain how one foresees surely whether a stratagem will succeed or not.

If Di Castro, while knowing human nature, displays an elegant cynicism, and if Naudé exaggerates his amoralism to impress the reader, the same cannot be said for the writings of an anonymous Venetian, who probably was Fra Paolo Sarpi. This writer draws the basic outlines of a systematically amoral government with a sure hand and with keen wisdom. His work was probably written about 1610. It was published in 1683 and translated into French in 1725. Its title is *Opinione del come abbia a governarsi internamente ed esternamente la Repubblica di Venezia per conservare il perpetuo dominio.*

Sarpi begins with the assertion that the basis of every government ought to be justice, but since the first justice consists in conserving ourselves, he will teach in what way the Republic of Venice can maintain its regime and its independence forever. The behavior appropriate to attain this end will vary according to whether the question concerns the capital town, the Italian territories on the continent, or the colonial dominions.

So far as the capital is concerned, the author finds it necessary to restrict further the already oligarchic government, reducing the authority of the Great Council which is too numerous and "too popular," and augmenting the power of the Ten and of the other limited bodies. To realize this aim he suggests that it would be desirable to disgrace the *Avogadori*, the magistrates assigned the duty of denouncing violations of the constitution, by filling the office with incompetent and discredited men who could not prove dangerous. Above all, he recommends that the prestige of noble blood should be maintained by never openly condemning a noble person, eliminating the obnoxious with dagger or with poison. He does not fail to note also that it would be opportune if members of the Venetian nobility married heiresses from the mainland.

As for the continental Italian territories the author suggests that the rivalries between the noble houses be kept alive and that this should be done in such a way that their possessions pass by marriage or by purchase into the hands of Venetian nobles. For this reason he deems fatal the privilege accorded to Brescia by which the lands of its territory could belong only to Brescians. As for the colonial dominions the anonymous writer believes that they are best conserved by using rigorous and occasionally cruel means. Finally, in Venice as in the cities on the mainland and in the colonies the government must be certain that the people lack neither holidays, nor bread, nor, in case of need, gallows.

However, at the end of this treatise the author does not neglect to add that because of the "natural instability of human affairs no power can be perpetual and the life of a government cannot be prolonged when its ruling class loses energy." This the Venetian Republic was to discover at the end of the eighteenth century.

7

The Early Modern Period

Thomas More and the Communist Movements in Germany in the Sixteenth Century

After Machiavelli, the most famous political writer of the beginning of the sixteenth century was Thomas More. He, as much as the Florentine Secretary, enriched the language of the European peoples with new words. To Machiavelli is owed, of course, the noun *Machiavellianism* and the adjective *Machiavellian* and to More the word *utopia* with all its derivatives.[1]

Thomas More was born in London in 1479 into a family most probably of Venetian origin, which had already resided in England for some generations. His father, a judge in the service of the king, belonged to the nobility but was not among the oldest and most illustrious. Thomas studied at Oxford, where he knew Erasmus of Rotterdam and mastered the classical languages to such an extent that he was able to translate Lucian's *Tyrannicide* from Greek into elegant Latin. At the age of nineteen he conducted a series of conferences in London on Saint Augustine's *City of God*. Soon after he entered a Carthusian monastery and stayed there for four years but without ever deciding to take the vows. Divesting himself of his religious garb, he married and carried on the profession of a lawyer.[2] Later he was elected to the House of Commons at a time

[1] Naturally *Machiavellianism* and its derivatives were not invented by Machiavelli, but by his followers and, above all, by his opponents, while the honor of having invented the word *utopia* and its derivatives belongs to Thomas More.

[2] In Thomas More two tendencies appear in conflict: a mystical tendency which held him closely to a rigorous Catholicism, and another much broader one

when the influence of the Crown was predominant. At times he demonstrated his ability to resist the royal will and this may have contributed to making him appreciated by Wolsey, Henry VIII's Lord High Chancellor, who brought him into the King's service and gave him access to the highest state offices. He was nominated a member of the Privy Council in 1515, sent to Flanders on a diplomatic mission the following year, and afterwards appointed Chancellor of the Exchequer and included in the number of functionaries who in 1520 accompanied the King of England to France. He was finally elevated to the eminent post of Lord High Chancellor in 1529 just before the conflict broke out between the Crown and the papacy. In this disagreement the unshakable firmness with which he defended the position dictated by his conscience led him to execution, which he faced fearlessly in 1535.

Utopia, whose first publication came not later than 1518 or earlier than 1516, was not something pondered upon and written by Thomas More in the last years of his life, but was prepared certainly during his mission in Flanders. In this work are evident both the memory of Plato's *Republic* and the influence of the work, *Praise of Folly*, by Eramus of Rotterdam, in which he shows that in society there are many unreasonable things.

The *Utopia* begins with a description of the conditions of English society at the beginning of the sixteenth century. The times were far from prosperous, for there still remained the consequences of the long period of bloody civil wars, which had impoverished the country in the second half of the fifteenth century and which ended only in 1485 with the advent of the Tudor dynasty.

The civil wars and the tortures inflicted upon the conquered by the victorious had brought the decline of many of the old noble families of Norman origin, while other families, humble at first, had increased in influence, as always occurs when a long period of confusion makes possible rapid changes of fortune and sudden gains.

On the other hand, many people had become habituated to making their living from arms rather than work, and when the wars ended many became brigands, who made roads and private property

which allowed only a vague deism. The struggle between the two tendencies explains some of the contradictions in his writings and life, at the termination of which the former tendency prevailed.

unsafe, or who entered the service of the barons as men-at-arms, charged with guarding their estates.

Further, many lands once cultivated in wheat had been turned into pasture. This occurred because of the increased export of English wool to Flanders where the woolen cloth industry flourished. This transformation enriched the proprietors, but caused the price of bread to rise and augmented the number of unemployed. It thereby diminished the wage level, perhaps only temporarily, but for the moment very painfully. Legislation sought to remedy these disorders through strict repression and capital punishment was prescribed for highway robbery, even when not accompanied by wounding and homicide.

In the second part of his work More pretends that a certain Captain Raphael Hythlodaye, who had sailed with Amerigo Vespucci, discovers the island of Utopia, where arrangements exist to render all the inhabitants equal and happy. There all the injustices and afflictions which the author has so effectively described disappear. The most radical of these arrangements is the abolition of private property, so that lands, houses, factories, and supplies of raw materials all belong to the state. Money relations and contracts between private individuals are abolished and all the inhabitants are employed in rotation in agriculture or in the mechanical arts. But, since there are no idlers in Utopia, who would have been, according to Hythlodaye, the soldiers, bravos, brigands, servants, bankers, and those who live on income, six hours of work daily is enough to provide abundantly for the needs of all. In fact, the authorities responsible for the production and distribution of useful things leave to the discretion of the Utopians the acquisition from the public warehouses of that quantity of foodstuffs that each family judges necessary for its own consumption. Such freedom did not increase consumption since articles of luxury were unknown and hoarding pointless when everyone knew that he would never lack necessities.

The political and administrative organization of Utopia is essentially democratic. Every thirty families elect a *phylarch*, and every ten phylarchs elect a chief phylarch. At the head of the hierarchy is a supreme chief chosen by the phylarchs from among four candidates nominated by the entire populace. He remains in office for life, but can be deposed if he aspires to tyranny. However, the phylarchs, chief phylarchs, and supreme magistrate at the head exercise what could be called the executive power, because their principal function consists in applying the laws and supervising the work done by the citizens, whereas the duration of work, the manner in which it is to be distributed, the calculation of the quality and quantity of products necessary for the society, and the establishment of norms concerning their distribution, are entrusted to an assembly elected by all the citizens of Utopia. It is worth recalling that, besides the citizens, there were slaves on the island employed for the most humble and repugnant tasks. Some of these were citizens who had committed crimes that carried the punishment of temporary servitude. Others were prisoners of war and, finally, some were foreigners who preferred slavery on this happy island to liberty in their own countries.

As opposed to Plato's *Republic*, More's Utopia maintained the family so that the institution of marriage was retained and adultery and concubinage punished. However, divorce was permitted for incompatibility of character, and when there were too many children in one family the magistrate could compel the parents to give some to another family without them. Each family had its own dwelling, but every ten years was required to move to a new home determined by lot.

For the time in which More wrote, the views that he sets forth in the last part of the book are profoundly original. These concern the religious and foreign policies of the Utopians.

All religions are equally tolerated in Utopia, and even atheists and those who deny the immortality of the soul face no penalty, although they are deemed incapable of exercising any magistracy. But the religion followed by the majority of the Utopians is a pure deism, interpreted in a manner so broad that the followers of all the other religions can participate in its ceremonies. Religious intolerance, insults against other cults, and assertions that salvation requires that the precepts of some one religion be followed, are all prohibited and punished with exile. As can be seen, it would appear that, in writing the *Utopia*, More thought more often of Lucian's *Dialogues* than Saint Augustine's *City of God*.

It is with great surprise that the modern reader reads of the principles guiding foreign policy of the Utopians, since he finds in them a description of the foreign policy followed by England from the time of Queen Elizabeth down to the nineteenth century and perhaps even, with some modifications, into the twentieth century. The island of Utopia was, in fact, close to a large continent and the policy of the Utopians aimed at so acting that the hegemony of no single state over all the others could be established. To realize this objective the Utopians always tried to ally with the weakest states against the strongest and to sow the seeds of internal dissensions in those states aspiring to subject the others. If war was declared, the Utopians principally aided their allies with money; to do this, although the use of money was prohibited in internal relations, they maintained large reserves of precious metals for commercial and political relations abroad. But, at the same time, they contributed to the common victory by sending to the continent the smallest possible number of their own soldiers.

In conceiving the sociopolitical system in effect in Utopia, did Thomas More hope to realize practical results? That is, did he really believe that the state of affairs described in his work could be put into effect or not? We can find an answer to such a question in the conclusion he reaches at the end of his book. In fact, More affirms that the example of Utopia certainly cannot be blindly imitated. Nevertheless, much could be learned from it to modify the imperfections and defects in the social and political conditions of Europe. To objections and doubts about the possibility of accomplishing an egalitarian and communist regime, More, with subtle British humor, makes Captain Hythlodaye answer that the institutions of the Utopians do not give rise to any inconveniences and that if anyone retained doubts on the subject he could go himself to Utopia and ascertain the truth of what was reported in the book.[3]

Thomas More's work had a considerable influence on the formulation of communist theory, especially in the second half of the eighteenth century. In addition, it presumably was influential much closer to its own time, since it was certainly not unrelated to the formation of the mentality of the leaders of the socioreligious movements manifested in Germany in the sixteenth century. It is wise to give a brief account of these movements.

[3] *Utopia* is a word derived from the Greek and literally means "nowhere"; that is, a country that does not exist.

Luther had already affirmed that the basis of Christian beliefs was free interpretation of the Bible by every true believer according to his own conscience. With such an affirmation he struck a fierce blow at the Catholic Church which had for many centuries taken for itself the exclusive right to interpret the word of God. Furthermore, in the countries where the Lutheran reform prevailed the lay princes took possession of almost all ecclesiastical property. Nicholas Stork, a follower of the Lutheran reform, surpassing Luther, asserted that if the Bible were correctly interpreted every social hierarchy should be destroyed including also every economic inequality, because both were in complete conflict with the spirit of the Gospel. Stork's followers called themselves Anabaptists because they maintained that the baptism conferred on newborn children was not valid and that it was necessary therefore to rebaptize adults. But, while Stork limited himself to theory, Thomas Münzer, a man of action and a follower of Stork, succeeded in realizing a communist regime in Mülhausen, a city in Saxony. Meanwhile in Germany another movement arose, that of the peasants against the feudal lords. Münzer believed he could link this movement to the Anabaptist cause, but before he could join the insurgent peasants he was defeated by the troops of several German lords and put to death. Nevertheless, the revolt of the peasants continued for some time and was led by a nobleman, the famous Götz of Berlichingen, called the Baron with the Iron Hand, who gave the movement a cruel character until in 1526 he was finally overcome.

But the Anabaptist movement was like an immense fire which, put out in one place, started to blaze in another. Small insurrections took place in German Switzerland, in Alsace, in Thuringia, and all along the Rhine. In 1535 the revolt flared fiercely in Münster in Westphalia where John Matthias, having seized the city, installed a communist regime. Matthias, killed in battle, was succeeded by John Bockelson, better known by the name of John of Leyden, who, claiming to be inspired by God, became the dictator of Münster. The movement degenerated into a frightful riot until the city, exhausted from hunger, was taken and John of Leyden, having become a prisoner, lost his life on the scaffold.

This was the last of the violent manifestations of the Anabaptists in Germany. Many Anabaptists emigrated to Moravia where they colonized lands at that time deserted, but even there their communities in time dispersed or adopted individual ownership.

Girolamo Vida. The Monarchomachs. Bodin and Botero

Girolamo Vida was an original writer who cannot be classified as belonging to any given school. Toward 1550 he published a work entitled *De optimo statu reipublicae*, written in the form of a dialogue between the humanist Flaminius and an interlocutor, which the author pretends took place during the Council of Trent. The ideological content of this work by Vida is praise of the simple, tranquil, and natural life of the country as opposed to the artificial and tumultuous existence of the city. According to Cardinal Flaminius, all governments originate from cunning and violence, for it is not possible that men of their own free will have given up the free and tranquil life. Therefore, no government is legitimate but all are based on force and all are to be condemned. The answers that the interlocutor gives to the Cardinal are weak and unconvincing and are based on the utility of governments and the injurious consequences of anarchy. Thus the impression remains that Vida approves of the ideas that he has Flaminius set forth. Certainly for the period these ideas were quite original and bold, but it would be excessive to consider Vida a teacher of Jean Jacques Rousseau. In his work the Italian writer insists much on the contrast between the life of the country and that of the city and on the violent origin of political organization. However, he does not develop the theme to the point of reaching the same conclusions arrived at in the eighteenth century by Rousseau.

In the second half of the sixteenth century monarchy grew continually stronger, especially in France and Spain, as the authorities between the supreme ruler and the single individual were consistently weakened. Previously these authorities had hindered the transformation of the old feudal structure into an absolute, unitary, and bureaucratic state.

One strong intellectual current of the time was opposed to

this transformation. As a result of their common opposition to absolute monarchy this group of writers came to be called *monarchomachs*.

Among these the first chronologically is probably François Hotman, a Frenchman who in 1573 published the book *Franco-Gallia*, which was widely circulated even in later times. In this work Hotman demonstrated that the older French monarchy had never been absolute because the authority of the king was tempered by the privileges of the nobility, the clergy, and the communes, and by the assemblies in which the barons, the clergy, and the communes were together represented. This thesis corresponded historically to the truth, but the author gave no consideration to the fact that the conditions of French society, especially after the reign of Louis XI, were very much changed. Nor did he foresee that they would be modified more and more in the very near future.

Another monarchomach was the author of the *Vindiciae contra tyrannos*, published under the pseudonym of Junius Brutus and until recently attributed to Hubert Languet. However, according to later studies, it appears to have been written by Du Plessis-Mornay. Whoever the author may be, it is obvious that he was a French Protestant who was very familiar with the Bible. With arguments taken in large part from the Old Testament he maintained that political constitutions are based on two pacts: a three-way pact between God, the sovereign, and the people, and a two-way pact between the sovereign and the people. He adds that in the absence of the sovereign's adherence to the first or second of the two pacts, the people are permitted to rebel; to illustrate he cites the removal of King Saul through the efforts of Samuel. Finally, he concludes that sovereignty belongs to the people, not, of course, to the people considered as a numerical majority, but through its natural representatives (ephori, selecti*), barons, doctors, and leaders of the communes.

In Scotland the monarchomachs were represented by George Buchanan, who was born in 1506 and died in 1582. In 1579 he wrote the work titled *De jure regni apud Scotos*, in which he argued that the sovereign should not govern with absolute power but that his action should be limited and controlled by the assembly of the rep-

* i.e., elected representatives who were overseers—Trans.

resentatives of the people, again ordinarily constituted of the natural leaders.

In Germany also we find a monarchomach writer. This was Althusius, who in the very first years of the seventeenth century wrote the *Politica methodice digesta.* In this work Althusius upholds ideas that some people have erroneously deemed precursors of Rousseau's *Social Contract.* In reality, the conception of the German writer is the usual one of writers of his period, since he supports popular sovereignty but believes that the natural representatives of the people should be the elders. Only in the eighteenth century did the idea prevail that the *people* was understood to be the numerical majority of citizens.

Even the Order of the Jesuits had its monarchomachs. Some consider Suarez a monarchomach. In 1603 he wrote a treatise titled *De Legibus.** In it Suarez acknowledges popular sovereignty, but he believes that once the people have transferred their sovereignty they have lost the right to exercise it and must permit themselves to be governed by the sovereign whom they have chosen. Thus he justifies rebellion only when the sovereign becomes a tyrant.

More explicit is another Jesuit, Mariana, who in his treatise *De Rege,* published in 1599, even comes to justify regicide. He depicts the tyrant as a ferocious beast who must be suppressed at all costs. He expresses doubt only concerning the propriety of using poison to kill him.[1]

Two additional writers, one French and the other Italian, enjoyed at the end of the sixteenth century a fame that cannot be called undeserved, Jean Bodin and Giovanni Botero.

Bodin wrote in French a thick and voluminous work of six books entitled *De la République.* Then in 1586 the author translated it into Latin. It is superfluous to recall that the word "république" was used in the older Latin sense of "state." Clearly the author wished to imitate Aristotle's *Politics,* adapting it to his times. His books follow the order and outline of the *Politics.*

* Evidently, *Tractatus de legibus ac deo legislatore,* 1612—Trans.

[1] On this subject, it is necessary to remember that the Jesuit Order has often been accused of advocating the theory by which regicide would be justified in certain cases. We must recognize that in fact the Order as such has never supported such a theory, which has been advocated only by some of its members.

Like Aristotle, in fact, he begins by discussing the family, but on this subject his ideas are more backward than those of the Greek philosopher, since, following the Roman concept of *pater familias,* he gives to the father an unlimited authority over all members of the family. However, concerning slavery he is more modern than Aristotle, for he reprimands the governments that tolerate it whether in Europe or in the colonies. On the subject of property, he is in agreement with the Greek philosopher; he believes that property is necessary and beneficial because it gives men the impulse and interest for work and production.

He then speaks of the attributes of the sovereign power, which would be the legislative and executive power earlier identified by Marsiglio of Padua, as involving the making of treaties with foreign powers, of settling disputes (the judicial power), of coining money, and others. He discusses also the advantages and disadvantages of the three classical forms of government: monarchy, aristocracy, and democracy. He points out that the prevalence of one of the three forms over the others is not accidental but depends in part on the climate, an idea later developed by Montesquieu. However, fundamentally he displays his preference for monarchy, which he considers to be the most appropriate form of government for France. He is not favorable to the mixed governments in which the three classical forms are fused and tempered, for he thinks that such combinations rapidly degenerate and are transformed either into pure monarchies or into democracies.

The six books of Bodin's *De la République* were very famous at the end of the sixteenth century and the first half of the seventeenth. Today they are almost completely forgotten, although their author at times expressed views in advance of the times in which he wrote.

Giovanni Botero was born in Bene Vagenna in Piedmont. The date of his birth cannot be specified exactly, but is between 1530 and 1540. He took holy orders and in his youth was a Jesuit novice. He then held an appointment as secretary to Saint Carlo Borromeo, Archbishop of Milan.

To appreciate adequately the influence that this appointment must have had on Botero one must remember that Saint Carlo was one of the most valiant champions of the Catholic Counter-

Reformation, that his influence was predominant in the second phase of the Council of Trent, and that his leadership was of great importance in all the countries where the Catholic Church was in combat with the heresies of Luther and Calvin. It is hardly necessary to add that to Saint Carlo is owed in good part the restoration of discipline and a more rigid morality for the Catholic clergy, both of which he had advocated within and outside his diocese. With his sometimes excessive severity against heretics he also coupled great pity for the poor, which he demonstrated especially during the pestilence that broke out in Milan in 1576.

Botero wrote many works of a religious or, more accurately, an ascetic nature. In addition to these he wrote three books closely connected with the study of politics, *Ragion di Stato*, *Le relazioni universali*, and *Delle cause della grandezza e magnificenza delle città*. Beyond a doubt the history of political theory must concern itself with the first of these in particular, published for the first time in 1589.

Botero begins by affirming that the *Ragion di Stato* (Reason of State) ought to teach governors the most suitable means of keeping power since, as he says, it is more difficult to maintain political supremacy than to acquire it, given the innate fluidity of human affairs. This is a thought not lacking in depth and in large part corresponding to the truth. The author, a deeply religious man, advises the prince to establish a Council which he may consult whenever a doubt arises that a given action conforms to Catholic morality. He then adds that it is natural for a prince to trust the nobility, but not blindly. Otherwise he would lose the favor of the people, which is no less necessary to him. Agreeing with Machiavelli, he further advises the prince to form a national army, not depending on mercenary or foreign arms. This advice was in fact followed by the Duke of Savoy for whom it appears the book was written.

Although more scrupulous than the Florentine Secretary, Botero still is not entirely averse to suggesting the adoption of means not completely conforming to evangelical morality, especially when it is a matter of fighting heretics. He says that heretics should first be led to the true faith by attracting them with rewards, but that it is necessary to adopt violent methods if cajolery and favors are unsuccessful.

Botero is truly original and profound in the economic aspects of his work. Economic considerations are almost completely lacking in the works of Machiavelli. On this theme Saint Carlo Borromeo's secretary has thoughts denoting an intellect superior to his times. With more precision than that found in the economic theories of Serra, touted as the precursor of Adam Smith and Ricardo and also later than the Piedmontese writer, Botero notes that national wealth does not consist in the abundance of precious metals, but in the quantity of useful things that a country produces. Therefore, when a nation produces goods of universal value, it will be able to procure the precious metals necessary for its needs through trade with foreign countries. If one recalls that we are still discussing the end of the sixteenth century—that is, an economic era of narrow mercantilism in which gold and silver were considered the only riches —these perceptive observations confirmed by modern economic science ought to be highly appreciated. As a practical example of his observations the author cites the case of Spain which, even possessing the gold and silver mines of Mexico and Peru, was at that time still a poor country. Its industry was almost nonexistent and its agriculture unproductive because of the scarcity of labor aggravated by the expulsion of the Moors.

In the *Cause della grandezza e magnificenza delle città* Botero with equal acumen attributes the absence of population growth in large cities to the rise in living costs originating in the difficulty of supply, a difficulty that increases with the growth of population. All this was true in the time of Botero, although today railroads and steamships, reducing greatly the costs of transportation, allow large numbers of people to receive supplies easily. This makes possible in turn the creation of the numerous metropolitan areas with their millions of inhabitants and thus becomes one of the principal causes for urban growth. Lastly, *Le relazioni universali* is a very accurate treatise on political geography, given the period in which it was written.

Campanella, Paruta, Boccalini, and Grotius

Tommaso Campanella is separated from all of the preceding writers by the originality of his concepts, although in reality this originality sometimes degenerates into the bizarre. His life was highly adventurous and many of its details still remain obscure. He was born in Stilo in Calabria. When fourteen years old he went to Naples where, according to legend, as soon as he arrived he happened upon an academy where philosophy was being discussed. He took part in the discussion amazing those present with the fire of his eloquence and the acumen of his argument. Afterward, having entered the Dominican Order, we find him in Venice and Bologna where he aroused the suspicions of the Inquisition. Returning to Naples, he was judged dangerous by the Spanish government and was compelled to retire to a monastery in Calabria. But not even there did the feverish activity of the friar halt. With others he contrived a plot against Spanish power which failed and led many of the plotters to the gallows. Taken to Naples, Campanella was tortured, prosecuted, and thrown in a prison where he remained for a long twenty-seven years.

Campanella's imprisonment has something strange about it that is difficult to explain. On the one hand, according to the friar, never was a prisoner left in more miserable condition than he. His laments are heart-rending and full of grief. (Evidence of this is found in his poetry.) On the other hand, he wrote incessantly, exchanged polemics with his opponents, and his writings were propagated through half of Europe. In these twenty-seven years his notoriety grew day by day and the glance of many influential men of the world fell upon the humble frair who groaned in a Spanish dungeon. The Duke of Ossuna, Viceroy of Naples, descended into the jail to speak with Fra Tommaso; the Fugger brothers, powerful German bankers, also became interested in him. After many years Campanella, accusing himself of heresy, probably by agreement with Pope Urban VIII, was brought to Rome to be judged by the Holy Office, thus escaping from the hands of the Spanish. In Rome, however, the common people rose in tumult against a friar thought to be a heretic and a wizard, necessitating the intervention of the French ambassador who, in the name of the king, asked the pontiff to free the friar. Having obtained his liberty, Campanella went to Paris where, pensioned by King Louis XIII, he aroused strong sympathies and received powerful protection. Thereafter, the last years of his life might have passed in tranquility but his restless spirit never settled and until his last days the friar, by then a septuagenarian, continued to write and argue. Believing in astrology, he drew up the horoscope of the life of Louis XIV and with relative accuracy described the character of the future monarch and predicted the events of his reign. And in this horoscope he who cares may find a foreboding, vague and uncertain though it be, of the revolution of 1789.

Particularly characteristic of the thought of Campanella is his opposition to Aristotelian philosophy, owed certainly in part at least to the influence of Bernardino Telesio whose works Campanella had read and pondered. With the temperament of a polemicist and a fighter, he showed an exceptional fecundity. Of his works we will note only those having some relation to political science.

Chronologically, perhaps the first among Campanella's political works was the *Monarchia ispanica*. In it the author advocates Spanish imperialism. He observes that there has always been a people who have exercised supremacy over others; first in the east the Assyrians and then, going always from east to west, the Greeks, the Romans, and lastly, the Spaniards. In order for these people to maintain their authority it is essential that all become militarists, while naturally supporting also the Catholic Church, but leaving to others the cares of agriculture and industry.

It has more recently been discovered that in this work by Campanella some pages from Botero's *Ragion di Stato* are repeated word for word. Professor De Mattei, discoverer of the plagiarism, explains the fact in this way: the *Monarchia ispanica*, written by Campanella in jail, was consigned handwritten to Tobjas Adam, a German who arranged for its printing in Germany sometime around 1620. Because the Thirty Years War between Protestants and Catholics had just begun Adam believed it would be opportune to insert in the work some pages from Botero, thinking to better render service to the Catholic cause.

In the *Monarchia delle nazioni,* written while Campanella was in France, the Calabrese philosopher recognizes the ineptitude of Spain, then already showing evidence of the decline of its primacy in the world, and suggests that France would have been better suited to the task of leadership. In the *Monarchia Messiae* he maintains that all lay principalities should be subject to the pope. One can also recall the *Atheismus triumphatus,* in which the author refutes atheism with such arguments as to cause some critics to affirm the work could have been more coherently entitled *Atheismus triumphans.*

But the work to which Campanella largely owes his fame is the *Città del sole* (The City of the Sun), published after the death of the author in 1643. Like More's *Utopia* it is in dialogue form but in many other points it differs from the *Utopia,* taking its inspiration more from Plato's *Republic* and from the Catholic monastery.

In the *Città del sole,* a place on the island of Taprobana or Ceylon, a communist republic is in effect such that the production as well as the distribution of commodities necessary to life are the responsibilities of the state authorities. On the island lazy people do not exist because the governors do not tolerate them; thus four hours of work daily for each inhabitant are sufficient to provide for the needs of everyone.

The chief of state is called the Great Metaphysician, the wisest man in the republic. His appointment is for life but if during his lifetime he comes upon some citizen wiser than him, this citizen can replace him. The Great Metaphysician nominates three ministers as his collaborators: Wisdom, who looks after public education; Power, who provides for the defense of the state and military organization; and Love, who is concerned with sexual unions, births, and the betterment both of the human race and of animals. In turn, the three ministers nominate other magistrates subordinate to them. As portrayed, the Solarians [inhabitants of the City of the Sun] possess a constitution that lies between the autocratic and the democratic, because the supreme chief of state is elected by universal suffrage while all the other magistrates, beginning with the most elevated, are nominated by him. Unlike Thomas More, Campanella anticipates that there may be frequent infractions of the laws and believes that he finds a remedy for this problem in an entire system of penalties of which the punishment inflicted on the lazy is characteristic. Their punishment consists of depriving them of relations with women. In the City of the Sun the family does not exist because Campanella believes that only by abolishing the family can private property be abolished. Nevertheless, in the *Città del sole* free love does not replace the family because temporary marriages are prearranged by the governors. As in Plato's *Republic,* the education of the children is left to the state and the offspring do not know their parents. Finally, a spying system is in force, exercised through a type of oral confession.

Before the chapter is closed it is important to make mention of a few writers who enjoyed a degree of fame and published their works in the last decades of the sixteenth century or in the first years of the following one.

An author who enjoyed much notoriety during his lifetime and also for a while after his death was the Venetian Paolo Paruta, who was born in 1540 and died in 1598. In 1579 he published a book titled *Prefazione della vita politica,* in which opportunely he observes that wisdom does not consist in standing aloof from the world but that the wise and patriotic man must instead put his activity at the service of his country. According to the author, among all the forms of government the best was that of his native city, Venice, and this same notion was professed at the time by several other writers. In another book narrating the history of Venice Paruta again exalts his city, the queen of the lagoons. But fundamentally, he was a writer inferior to the fame that he enjoyed and one would search in vain through his works for profound and truly original views.

Traiano Boccalini, a contemporary of Paruta's but very different from him, was born in the Marches in 1556 and died in 1612 in Venice, where the year before he had published the *Ragguagli di Parnaso* (Dispatches from Parnassus).

This work is a frequently witty and sometimes violent satire on men of letters and governors both contemporary and prior to the author. To convey an idea of the work it is enough to recall the episode of Aristotle who, residing on Mount Parnassus next to Apollo, is attacked by a number of rulers and governors contemporary to Boccalini. They rush upon the Stagirite because his description of the tyrant corresponds exactly to their behavior. To avoid the worst, therefore, Aristotle is compelled to declare that the tyrant was a monster who lived in a remote age but disappeared in more recent times. More satirical is the description of a meeting of some wise men and governors who, having assembled in order to devise the most apt methods of removing the gravest inconveniences from the world, in the end succeed in agreeing upon a project to reduce the price of cabbages. Not entirely unjustly Boccalini has been labeled by some as the precursor of modern humoristic journalism. Several of his contemporaries believed that he was killed by order of the Spanish authorities against whom he had directed his darts with ease.

Finally, it seems appropriate to recall a famous writer of the beginning of the seventeenth century whose works have some connection with political science, although they have very great importance in the history of public law and, especially, international law.

The writer referred to is Hugo Grotius, a Dutchman, who was born in 1583 and died in 1645. Caught up in the political vicissitudes of his country, he was arrested and condemned to prison for life. He succeeded in escaping and went to Paris and later to Sweden. Appointed as ambassador by the Queen of Sweden, he returned to Paris and died ten years later while crossing Germany on his way back to Stockholm. As already noted, his most famous works are in the field of international law; among these to be noted especially is *De jure belli ac pacis*, in which he formulates the theory of natural law, already partially conceived by Greek and Roman philosophers. In this work he asserts that private ownership of property did not exist in early times and that it originated in conquest, although he recognizes its necessity. He even claims that sovereign powers originally belonged to the people but admits that the people may legitimately transfer them to others. He justifies slavery when it is voluntary or involves prisoners of war.

8

The Development of English Parliamentary Government

The Magna Carta and the Development of the English Constitution Up to the Advent of the Stuarts

Until recently the belief was widely held that the seventeenth century contributed little to the history of human civilization. However, such an opinion does not correspond to the truth. The work of a century can be judged by comparing it to the preceding and subsequent ones; if we make this comparison, we can easily ascertain that the advances realized in the seventeenth century were many and great. It was this century that really put an end to the Middle Ages and if, at its outset, we still find distressing and infantile prejudices, such as the officially sanctioned belief in the existence of anointers and sorceresses; if the scourges owed to ignorance, to the scarcity of means of communication, and to imperfections of political organization still persist; and if, therefore, pestilences, famines, and undisciplined armies still too often torment the populations of central and western Europe, we must remember that all this was a passive inheritance from preceding centuries. This legacy the seventeenth century did not in turn bequeath to the subsequent one, and therefore the eighteenth century could not have accomplished its vast program of reforms if the preceding one had not cleared the ground and prepared the way.

In science the seventeenth century gave us Bacon, Galileo, Newton, Hobbes, and Locke. The last two were, in a significant way, the precursors of eighteenth-century political thought. So far as political institutions are concerned the absolute state, which then in turn made possible the birth of the modern representative state, was formed in that century on the European continent. Still within the same century, in England the old medieval constitution was transformed after long conflict into a political regime in which the fundamental lines of the modern representative system were drawn.

Before we discuss the English constitution it will do no harm to recall that in Sicily the old medieval constitution, restored after the victorious insurrection of the Vespers, also developed in such a way as to approach the modern representative constitution, and was maintained in this form until the first years of the nineteenth century.

The Sicilian Parliament was composed of three *Bracci* or chambers, the Chambers of the Nobility, of the Clergy, and of the Communes. Remarkably enough, it was convened regularly every three years, voted the taxes which came to be called gifts, and nominated a committee called *Deputazione del Regno,* which exercised control over expenses and verified whether the funds appropriated were actually spent for the purposes they had been requested for.

But after the end of the sixteenth century the development of the Sicilian constitution was arrested because one of the indispensable conditions for a modern representative regime, the formation of a middle class independent of government, aristocracy, and clergy, was lacking in Sicily. Instead, on the island, at that time and in successive years, the only career to which a plebeian could rise was that of a lawyer. Since the lawyer's clientele was made up of nobles and clergy, this limited in practice in a very important way the independence of the attorneys, the most famous of whom were ultimately nominated as magistrates and raised to the ranks of the nobility. Under the influence of liberal English ideas a constitutional reform was attempted in 1812 which was observed by the Bourbons for only three years. In 1816 Sicily lost her autonomy and was promptly united with the realm of Naples. Thereafter, except for the brief period between 1848 and 1849, it was governed by an absolute monarchic regime until its union with Italy.

With this rapid glance at the old Sicilian constitution, we will now set forth the principal events in the constitutional history of England.

The Roman Empire, which from the time of Caesar and Augustus had conquered all southern and western Europe up to the boundaries marked by the Rhine and the Danube, began the conquest of Britain late and only under the Emperor Claudius. The conquest was never completely realized. In the fifth century A.D. the Roman garrisons were recalled, and Britain, which had been Romanized only in the cities and there imperfectly, suffered the inroads of Picts and Caledonians, northern barbarians coming from Scotland. In order to defend himself against these barbarians, one of the leaders of the Britons asked the help of the Angles and the Saxons, Germanic peoples living near the mouth of the river Elbe. However, after driving the Picts and the Caledonians back to the mountains, the Angles and Saxons conquered the country for themselves, expelling the indigenous population in Wales and compelling it to emigrate to French Brittany.

Within England the Angles and the Saxons founded, according to the most reliable version of history, seven kingdoms which formed the so-called Saxon Heptarchy. After the invasion of the Angles and the Saxons England became a country populated by the Germanic race. Christianity, previously accepted by the indigenous population while under Roman domination and then extinguished by the German invaders, was again introduced in the island at the end of the sixth century by missionaries sent by Saint Gregory the Great. By the middle of the seventh century Christianity had once again become the dominant religion.

In the ninth century and later, new invasions by still heathen Danish pirates occurred. Toward the middle of the ninth century, the better to resist the invaders, King Alfred fused the seven kingdoms into one.

Some writers have sought to trace the origins of the English constitution back to the epoch of the seven Anglo-Saxon kingdoms. But, in reality, nothing known about the political organization of that remote period permits us to believe that it had any special character. In each of the seven kingdoms there was naturally a king who had military command, administered justice, and was obliged in serious cases to consult the Witenagemot, or council of elders, and in very serious cases the assembly of all the warriors, or Folkmoot. These were political arrangements conforming to those in which all peoples find themselves when the tribe is not yet developed to the point of forming a state of some importance.

With the fusion of the seven Anglo-Saxon kingdoms into one, the English political order acquired a more aristocratic character since it was impossible in one state, already so vast, to convene an assembly of all the warriors; thus the king governed with the assistance of the most influential leaders. These characteristics endured until 1066.

In that year events occurred that contributed greatly to changing the course of English history. In the part of France bordering on the English Channel, Scandinavian pirates had founded in the tenth century a duchy which, taking its name from the conquerors (the Normans), was called Normandy. The Scandinavians fused with the rest of the population, adopting the language, customs, and French political arrangements—i.e., the feudal regime—without however losing the spirit of conquest they had inherited from their forefathers. There, in 1066, William the Conqueror, who claimed rights to the throne of England, was Duke of Normandy. He assembled a large mercenary company, composed in part of his Normans and in part of French adventurers from other regions. Heading this army, he landed in England where at Hastings, on October 14, 1066, one of those battles took place that decide for centuries the future of a people. In the fighting the invaders were victorious and Harold, the last Saxon king, perished with a large part of the Saxon nobility. After this defeat the entire country fell into the power of the Norman conquerors.

The lands of all the Anglo-Saxons who had fought against the invaders were confiscated and granted in feudal domain to the followers of William the Conqueror. However, the feudal system introduced at that time in England had from the beginning certain special characteristics differentiating it from that of the nearby continent. Thus, while in France and elsewhere the small feudatories depended almost always on the larger feudatories, in Great Britain many small feudatories depended directly on the king. This it seems was the origin of the class of knights which in the thirteenth century began to assume considerable political importance.[1]

The Norman Conquest was not accomplished without strong Anglo-Saxon resistance, which continued at intervals until 1070 and was protracted even thereafter in the form of a brigandage that rendered unsafe the lives and possessions of the victors. For this reason in the years immediately after the Conquest the new nobility seldom sought to weaken the strong discipline to which William the Conqueror and his immediate successors subjected it. Later, the frictions further abated; conquerors and conquered fused into a single population and adopted a common language, English, born out of the fusion of the French of the victors and the Low German of the conquered. Subsequently the nobility began to sense more sharply the effects of the arbitrary power that the king exercised over it. In consequence a rebellion against the authority of the monarch came about as soon as a favorable occasion presented itself.

In 1189 Richard, called the Lion-Hearted, ascended the throne of England. In 1191 he left with an army for the Holy Land in order to liberate Jerusalem, which had been taken by Saladin. In the Holy Land he distinguished himself highly in tournaments and battles, but encountered difficulties with the King of France and the Duke of Austria, and was unable to rescue Jerusalem. In 1194, returning to England, he imprudently crossed the territories of the Duke of Austria where, once recognized, he was taken prisoner and delivered by the Duke to the Emperor of Germany, who before freeing the King demanded a large ransom. Under feudal custom the barons were required to pay the ransom of the prisoner king. Thus the English nobility had to lay out a very large sum. Richard the Lion-Hearted died a few years after and his brother John Lackland succeeded him. He possessed all of Richard's defects—principally that of always asking the barons for money—without having those merits that

[1] According to William Stubbs, author of a study of the constitutional history of England, the knights were the descendants of those Saxon *thane* or *thegn*, who, not having taken arms against the invaders, maintained their possession of landed property and assumed the role of the feudatories of the king, being obliged to pay homage to the new sovereign with their lands and to offer him military service. According to other writers, the ancestors of the knights were the French or Flemish volunteers who had individually enlisted in the great mercenary company of William the Conqueror. It may be that both the one and the other version are partially correct.

had rendered his predecessor popular. After some vicissitudes and after John had been defeated by the king of France and excommunicated by the pope, the English barons rebelled and forced the king to swear to a pact establishing the rights and reciprocal duties of the king and his feudatories. This pact, the Magna Carta, was written in 1215.

In truth it cannot be affirmed that the Magna Carta, written in a rough Latin mixed with French and using English expressions imperfectly Latinized, and defined as *fundamentum libertatis Angliae,* contains the main points of a modern constitution. Rather it was one of the many pacts between barons and kings that were common enough during the feudal regime and that were rendered possible by the nature of the regime.

For example, an article of the Magna Carta removed from the king his right to extend protection to barons not yet of age, a right that had made possible abuses and waste on the part of the king to the damage of the barons. Article Two established that the nobles and clergy were required to pay contributions only after they had approved them in assembly. Article Three established that no noble could be dispossessed of his fief, banished, or imprisoned by the sovereign without a judgment by his equals. This meant that if the accused was a knight, he had to be judged by twelve knights, if a baron by a council of twelve barons, and if a lord by an assembly of lords, that is, by the Upper Chamber.

The nature of the treaty between the local lords and the king stands out much more in the final articles of the old English feudal constitution. In fact, in them it was established that if disputes arose between the king and a feudatory concerning the interpretation of some article of the pact sworn to and ratified by the king, the judge of this dispute was to be a board of arbitrators formed of twenty-four of the greater barons plus the Lord Mayor, head of the guilds or corporations of London, the only commune at that time possessing any importance. If the judgment of the board of arbitrators ran contrary to the king and he did not observe it, the arbitrators were bound to declare war on the sovereign who broke the pacts and to occupy his castles.

This right of resistance, or more accurately, the right of rebellion, which the king accepted, corresponded to the power that

the local lords possessed everywhere to fight in certain cases against
the head of their confederation, and it was a consequence of the
feudal arrangement, according to which every baron had the material means to resist the sovereign. It goes without saying that the
forces of many barons united would be superior to those of the king.

It cannot be asserted that the first successors of John Lackland all scrupulously observed the Magna Carta. Weak kings, lacking
in support, were compelled to observe it, but the shrewd and artful
ones, who succeeded in finding allies among the most powerful barons, in reality often violated it.

The evolution of the Magna Carta began at once. In 1254 it
established that, since the small feudatories directly dependent on
the king, i.e., the simple knights, did not attend the *commune concil-
ium regni*, then called *Parliamentum*, the knights of every county
would charge two of their number to represent them. Some years
after, in 1264, those communes that had acquired importance also
were invited to send their representatives to the assemblies that
approved the money grants that all the local bodies conceded were
due the head of their federation.

Still more important was the development of English institutions in the fourteenth century. During this century the division
of Parliament into two houses took place. It is very difficult to establish the precise year in which this occurred, because it seems that it
was accomplished by the prevalence of a custom by which the bishops and the greater feudatories met and deliberated separately from
the representatives of the minor feudatories and the communes. It
even appears that the great difference in social condition between
the members of the two chambers was the true cause of their separation.

Of the two houses it was the Lords that until the fifteenth
century maintained greater authority and prestige. During this period
the Parliament acquired by prescription a broad participation in the
legislative power. At this point, it is necessary to note that the concept of the distinction and separation of powers was very obscure
in the Middle Ages; a statement of this theory begins to emerge, as we
have seen, only in Marsiglio of Padua. Thus, the king of England,
who would not have been able to impose on the barons and communes new burdens without their consent, retained the power to

issue ordinances regulating his subjects which would now be considered as only within the competence of the legislator. This power of the king, however, was recognized only in theory, for the effective execution of royal orders was then entrusted, in large part, to the good will of the local sovereigns.

In order to ensure their cooperation the kings introduced the practice of making solemn declarations of the arrangements which they wished to make obligatory before the legal representative for the local bodies; that is, in front of Parliament. But this habit soon produced another. In the assemblies of the barons and of the representatives of counties and communes the members began to invoke, by means of petitions addressed to the sovereign, dispositions of a legislative character. Therefore, in a solemn assembly at the end of each session the king listened to the petitions directed to him by *his noble Lords and his faithful communes,* and if he responded with the affirmative formula *le roi le veult,* the petition immediately acquired the force of law, which did not, however, occur if the formula was negative or suspensive, for example, *le roi avisera.**

In this way the institution of royal sanction was born, which even in modern monarchies is indispensable for the validity of a law. And so it was that the English Parliament achieved a kind of participation in the legislative power, so that the sovereigns themselves found it practical and opportune, when they wanted to take some important measure, to have it proposed and approved first in Parliament.

Toward the end of the fourteenth century the Parliament acquired new prerogatives. In 1399 the king ratified a petition through which was obtained the inviolability of the Members of Parliament during sessions, unless criminal prosecution had been authorized by the House of which the accused was a member. In the conflicts of that century and the beginning of the next between the Crown and the Parliament the kings often had to give way. This progressive development of the Magna Carta, which after a fashion came to approach a modern constitution, was interrupted toward the middle of the fifteenth century by that atrocious civil war, called the War of the Roses. Two dynasties had claims on the legitimate succession to the throne, the Yorks and the Lancasters: the first held for armor-

* "The king so wishes" and "the king will take it under advisement"—Trans.

ial bearings a white rose, the other a red rose. Thus, for a while, co-existed two pretenders to the throne and two Parliaments, each calling itself legitimate and charging the other with being a usurper. The War of the Roses lasted until 1485 and was a period of savage violence and very serious civil war, during which the country was exhausted and impoverished and almost all the old nobility of Norman origin, which up to this time had formed the preponderant social class, perished in battle or under the executioner's axe.[2]

Therefore, when in 1485 peace was restored under the dynasty of the Tudors, formed by a fusion of the two rival families of York and Lancaster, the House of Lords, which in previous centuries had been the chamber that principally had faced the Crown, found itself composed almost exclusively of new elements owing their appointment to the kings of the new dynasty. They possessed neither the authority, nor the prestige, nor the material strength of the old Lords.

And on the other hand, no true middle class, composed of wealthy gentlemen of the counties and wealthy businessmen and industrial men of the cities, had yet come into existence which, represented in the House of Commons, might have been able to assume the political direction of the country. The consequence of this state of affairs and of the general weariness of the nation was the predominance of the royal authority during the dynasty of the Tudors, that is, from 1485 to 1603. This was a state of affairs very well described by Botero in his *Relazioni universali* when he said that, even if the king of England continued to convene Parliament frequently, he was in reality no less absolute than the king of France.

In fact, to be exact, the English Parliament continued to be convened at not infrequent intervals and continued to vote the allowances and to approve the laws; but in reality the kings of that period obtained from the Chambers almost everything they wanted, and the most important acts of English political life were then completed on the impulse and initiative of the Crown. The separation of England from the Church of Rome was primarily due to the initiative of Henry VIII, even though the King had rejected the doctrines of Luther

[2] One measure of a constitutional character that can be recalled as introduced in the fifteenth century was the statute of Henry IV, who ruled from 1423 to 1471, which withdrew the right of participation in the elections of deputies for the counties from all those who did not have the free ownership of a country property with an income of forty shillings yearly.

and had even written a book to refute them. During the years when Edward VI was a minor his guardians adhered in large part to the doctrines of Calvin, thus bringing the Anglican Church steadily nearer to Protestantism. It was also at this time that the country accepted this profound religious change. With only a few exceptions, it remained equally passive in 1553 when Queen Mary re-established Catholicism without, however, restoring to the Church the property that had been confiscated. With Elizabeth, who ascended the throne in 1558, Protestant Anglicanism was definitively reinstated.

In truth, apart from the difference noted by Botero, there were other differences of a political and social nature between the two countries on opposite sides of the Channel. In France the nobility had lost their sovereign prerogatives little by little and had yielded the land inch by inch. In England the War of the Roses had in the fifteenth century caused almost all the old and powerful feudal families to perish, so that it was easy for the Tudors to replace the old baronial jurisdictions with functionaries of royal appointment; but, for reasons of economy and in order not to abuse too greatly the customs of the people, almost all the local functionaries were chosen from among the wealthy and influential persons of the counties and villages where they exercised jurisdiction. This system of appointment made it possible to avoid paying them. From this originated what then was called English *self-government;* that is, a customary obligation which at the same time was a prerogative. In this fashion a large part of the offices of the public, administrative, judicial, and police services in the counties and cities came to be fulfilled gratuitously by the gentry. This class included all the families who, in the country and the cities, combined with well-being a certain sense of decorum, which morally obliged them to maintain and increase the splendor of the family name.

A comparable system was adopted by the military establishment, and militia units, recruited from the artisans of the city and the large and small proprietors in the country on whom was imposed the obligation of military service, were created. This system was undoubtedly more economical than that adopted by the princes and the republics on the continent, which in the sixteenth century had begun to create permanent armies composed of professional soldiers. However, militarily it was less efficient, and England was enabled to retain it so long only because her insular position made invasion by large foreign armies difficult.

In point of fact, the English militias were composed of peasants and artisans, who trained with arms on their holidays, rarely went more than a few miles from their homes, and were concerned ordinarily with their own professions and trades. Their officers were also chosen by the king from among the gentlemen in the area and although they had, especially in the country, a greater familiarity with arms and with horses, nevertheless they did not possess any real military preparation.

It is easily understood that a class of civil and military functionaries of the type described could offer very little secure protection to the royal authority if it wished to oppose the general sentiments of the country, a thing which in any case the Tudors carefully refrained from pursuing. It is not, of course, with indigenous and unpaid functionaries that general currents of public opinion can be restrained, nor could force be easily adopted in this case. The armed forces were made up of a mercenary militia, which lack *esprit de corps* and which not only came from the country but signified the country itself.

In conclusion, therefore, the kings of England in the sixteenth century exercised an almost absolute power, but neglected to prepare the necessary instruments to make durable their absolutism; that is, a regular bureaucracy and a professional armed force. Instead they retained the Parliament despite the fact that it would provide a very effective instrument of opposition to the royal authority in case public opinion turned against the monarch.

The First Stuarts and Cromwell's Dictatorship

The beginning of the crisis through which the English constitution, still with prevalently medieval characteristics, was gradually transformed into a constitution very similar to that of a modern representative state can be traced back to 1603.

In that year Queen Elizabeth died and was succeeded on the English throne by the son of Mary Stuart, whom Elizabeth had condemned to death, James VI, King of Scotland who became James I, King of England. For the first time the three crowns of England, Scotland, and Ireland were united under the same leader, but conditions in these countries were very diverse.

England was a relatively wealthy and civilized nation. During the reign of Elizabeth, English literature had achieved one of its most brilliant periods. The country was relatively rich because it had not experienced wars on its own territory and because the Tudors, not having created a large, permanent army or an excessively large salaried bureaucracy, restrained taxation within rather modest limits. Furthermore, trade with America and Russia had begun. In the cities a wealthy middle class developed and in the country a class of middling proprietors who had realized substantial profits from the acquisition of lands confiscated from the religious orders.

The middle-class individuals of the cities with those in the country, who were called Cavaliers, formed the new ruling class. However, the temperaments of each element were somewhat different.

In the country the Cavaliers clearly desired the preservation of the old English constitution because they understood it as necessary to prevent arbitrary increases in taxes and fully realized that the existence of self-government was closely linked to the existence of the House of Commons. As for the others, they retained much devotion to the royal power because the king was at the same time the traditional political leader and the supreme head of the Anglican Church, of which they were followers. On the other hand, among the bourgeoisie of the city a pure Calvinism, which did not accept the religious supremacy of the king, was propagated, and within this class the discussion of religious subjects, based upon diligent reading of the New and Old Testament, passing from religion to politics, often brought about the acceptance of theories contrary to the royal prerogative. These theories readied the people to adopt concepts that would now be called republican.

Very different and much less favorable were the conditions of Scotland, a poor country still semi-barbaric in its mountainous regions. Its ruling class was formed in part of a poor and restless nobility, which frequently augmented its scarce income with brigand-like raids upon the northern shires of England. In part, it was formed of Calvinist pastors who, having much influence on the common people, feared above all that Anglicanism would be introduced even into Scotland with the inevitable consequence of requiring obedience by the pastors to the bishops and the bishops to the king.

Still more serious were the conditions of Ireland which, untouched by the animating spirit of Rome, had remained for many centuries cut off from European civilization. Beginning in the twelfth century some English barons began a conquest, identifying themselves as vassals of the king of England, but their progress was very slow, so that only during the reign of Elizabeth was the last native, independent leader subject to the English crown. In that unfortunate country the three differences that divide men from one another— language, religion, and social class—were, so to speak, massed, for the natives had remained Catholics and the English colonists were Protestant. The former spoke a Celtic language very different from English and had been finally dispossessed of their lands which were then allotted to the small population of English or Scottish origin. Thus an incurable hate was born that divided the conquerors from the conquered, the owners of the soil from those who cultivated it.

James I, a scholar and a respectable connoisseur of Latin, was also very interested in the works of the most famous political writers of that time; it can be easily understood that, being king, of all the doctrines he examined the one he found most appealing was that of royal absolutism. And, although the disposition of the English nation was hostile to such a conception, he did not refrain from supporting it publicly even with messages directed to Parliament. He asserted that if, through ancient usages, the king tolerated old parliamentary prerogatives as being from God, he still retained the authority to abolish this participation in the sovereign power whenever he deemed it convenient. The House of Commons was at first silent but then reacted by affirming that, on the basis of the constitution in effect for many centuries, the royal power was limited by parliamentary prerogatives.

If James I had been a prudent statesman he would have concealed his political ideas and would rather have prepared the only instrument qualified to achieve their triumph, that is, the creation of a permanent army devoted to him. But since he was eminently peace-loving he did not care at all for the formation of an armed force directly dependent on him. And already in the last years of his reign he could recognize how much the prestige and authority of Parliament had increased and how much that of the Crown had decreased. In fact, Francis Bacon, an illustrious man in the history of science and Lord High Chancellor of the King, was accused, it seems with reason, of corruption by the House of Commons and sentenced by the House of Lords to a high fine and imprisonment without the king daring at once to pardon him.

On this occasion Parliament adopted one of the two procedures that had been used during the period of civil war—that is, the War of the Roses—and that had then served the Tudors to rid themselves of their adversaries. One, employed against Bacon, was impeachment, which is an accusation originating in the House of Commons and on which judgment was made by the House of Lords. The other, used a short time later against a minister of James' successor, was the bill of attainder.* This consisted of a law having retroactive effect. An act in itself not a crime committed by the accused was made a crime. A penalty could thus be established which was, almost always, capital punishment.

James I died in 1625 and was succeeded by his son Charles I, who was also convinced that the exercise of absolute power was not only the right but the duty of the king. More active and more energetic than his father, he wanted to realize his program for rendering illusory the prerogatives of Parliament. Still he well understood that to establish royal absolutism a permanent army was necessary. Very skillfully he conceived that nothing would be more opportune to build this army than to begin a war, a popular war approved by the nation, which might be one in aid of the French Protestants against the king of France.

With the Edict of Nantes, Henry IV, King of France, had assured the French Protestants full liberty of conscience and in guarantee of this had left in their power some of the fortified towns of the kingdom. When his son, Louis XIII, ascended the throne Cardinal Richelieu, his Prime Minister, who had tried to destroy everything that restricted full royal authority, was unable to accept that the

---

* It should be noted that throughout this chapter Mosca speaks of a bill of attainder but the definition he offers is really for an *ex post facto* law, not a bill of attainder.—Trans.

French Calvinists, called Huguenots, should retain possession of fortified towns which were part of the kingdom. He therefore undertook a campaign to recover them. When Charles I ascended the
throne only the Huguenots of La Rochelle still resisted the troops of
the king of France and since at that time religious sentiments prevailed over patriotic, they asked the Protestant king of England for
help. For the reasons noted, he received their appeals favorably.

War with France was declared and Parliament granted funds
that were believed sufficient to aid the besieged city. But whether
they were insufficient, or whether the contingent was poorly directed,
it is certain that the English fleet with its Royal Marines was compelled to return to England after several battles with unfavorable
outcomes. The Huguenot defenders of the strongholds, coerced by
hunger, were forced to come to terms.

As happens in such cases the parties sought to shift the responsibility for the failure on one another inasmuch as twice already the
king had been compelled to dissolve the House of Commons because
of the violent opposition he encountered there. A third Parliament
granted large subsidies to continue the war, but first demanded that
the king approve an act, called the Bill of Rights, which contained
the following provisions.

1. The king could not impose taxes without the consent of
Parliament, even in the form of loans, favors, gratuitous gifts, etc.

2. No one could be persecuted or prosecuted for failing to
pay taxes not agreed to by Parliament.

3. No one could be taken away from his regular judges and
that exceptional and extraordinary tribunals, whether civil or military, could not be instituted.

4. The king could not quarter soldiers or marines in the
homes of private citizens.

The first provision expressly prohibited the practice introduced under the Tudors of raising more or less spontaneous contributions, which were said to be voluntarily offered by private individuals, and which thus were not considered as duties and were not
approved beforehand by Parliament. The second was intended to remove the means by which the kings sometimes coerced those who
refused to pay the so-called voluntary contributions by forbidding
any judicial proceeding on the subject. The third sought to prevent

the sovereign from referring those charged with political crimes to magistrates on whose servility he was able to count, protecting them from the judgments of those tribunals that had been earlier established by law or by custom. The fourth aimed at rendering impossible the creation of a permanent army without the consent of Parliament, removing from the king the means to maintain troops for which Parliament had not granted the necessary funds.

Charles I gave his sanction to the Bill of Rights. He did not neglect to collect the subsidies voted by Parliament and immediately thereafter he dissolved the House of Commons. He made peace with France and in a span of eleven years governed as an almost absolute sovereign, never again convening Parliament, exacting some taxes that Parliament had not approved, and even instituting exceptional tribunals. And yet the serious discontent aroused by this behavior might not have been sufficient to provoke a revolt in England. In fact, it is necessary to bear in mind in that period the absolutist program of Charles I did not seem absurd, for absolutism had triumphed almost everywhere on the neighboring European continent. Instead, the insurrection began in Scotland, at that time a poor and restless country, to which Charles I, on unsound advice, wished to introduce a royal supremacy on ecclesiastical matters and discipline. The Calvinist pastors incited the people to open and violent rebellion. Masters of Scotland, the rebels did not delay in invading England, and the discontented English militias fought halfheartedly or not at all. To repel the invasion it was necessary to convene Parliament in order to have the means of recruiting more substantial armies.

But Parliament, as soon as it was convened, considered it more urgent to fight the absolutist program of the king. Charles I dissolved the House of Commons hostile to him, but then had to face a still more contrary one. This Parliament began by accusing the Viceroy of Ireland, Lord Strafford, and bringing him before the House of Lords on the charge of having violated the Bill of Rights while minister of Charles I. Strafford defended himself by saying that he had obeyed the king's orders, and that obedience to the king's illegal orders was not a misdemeanor. But the House of Commons changed its impeachment into a bill of attainder, that is, into a law that, as we have just noted, possessed retroactive effect; on that basis obeying the king's illegal orders was a crime liable to capital punishment.

Charles I did not have the courage to deny sanction to the bill of attainder nor to pardon Strafford, who faced his fate with dignity and courage. Perhaps the king thought he could calm the revolutionary ferment by abandoning to it an illustrious victim. Instead Parliament became more arrogant and not only continued to deny the taxes the king had requested, but the House of Commons refused to dissolve itself when the king ordered its dissolution. Then the king, abruptly passing from timidity to audacity, entered the House of Commons with his guards to arrest the leaders of the opposition. His intent was not realized. The same evening open revolt broke out in London and the militia of London refused him allegiance in order to assume the defense of Parliament. The king lost the capital in a single day.

However, the prestige of the Crown was still so great that despite the many errors committed by Charles I, as soon as civil war broke out, half the nation declared itself in favor of the Crown. In fact, the country militias, led by the rural proprietors, who, as we have already said, were usually referred to as Cavaliers, almost without exception sided with the king and at first reported notable successes over the city forces who defended the Parliament. But Parliament, profiting from the greater financial resources that it commanded through its power to levy taxes paid by the cities, did not delay in building a permanent army. This decision was made primarily on the advice of Oliver Cromwell, a politician of exceptional ability, who had embraced the cause of the parliamentary party.

Having defeated after some years of fighting the party of the Cavaliers, Cromwell, who had formed his army by recruiting from among the most ardent Calvinists—that is, the Puritans—came into conflict with the House of Commons when it wished to bargain with the king. Betrayed by the Scots with whom he took refuge, the king was made a prisoner. Cromwell then interrupted the negotiations and committed the judgment of the king to a council of officers. Charles I was condemned to death, which he courageously faced on January 30, 1649.

After the death of Charles I, Cromwell had to repress the party of the Levellers which, leaning on the Bible for authority, wanted to establish an absolute equality that would be not only political but also economic. Cromwell then went to Ireland; here, taking advantage of the disorders that had already broken out in England, the natives had in November of 1641 massacred a large part of the English settlers. The repression was rapid and cruel. Next came Scotland, which had attempted to separate from England and had recognized as king the eldest son of Charles I. The Scots were overcome in two bloody battles and Scotland was militarily occupied. Returning to England, Cromwell violently dissolved the House of Commons which, though purged of the element favorable to the monarchy, did not wish to recognize Cromwell's dictatorship. Afterwards he took the title of Lord Protector of the English Republic. Forming another House of Commons from people whom he thought he could trust, he also found problems with it and then even in a third house. In 1657 the title of king was offered to him which he had to refuse because of the opposition of his officers. However, he continued to be the absolute master of England.

His government was a military dictatorship, a regime until that time unknown in England. It is necessary to note that his foreign policy was as daring as ever and farsighted and that in a war in the Netherlands, the English fleet and even the Royal Marines achieved remarkable successes. Internally, the military regime ensured order and prosperity by adopting rigorous but effective means. At times the nation tried to resist, but it lacked the capacity to overcome the pressure that burdened it and that manifested itself also in the form of an extreme, puritan rigorism: prohibition of balls, too luxurious dress, and everything implying worldliness.

Thus, in spite of the internal peace and the military glory, the dictatorship of Cromwell left unhappy memories, and the English developed an intense repugnance for the permanent army, which was the instrument through which Cromwell was able to maintain absolute power for more than ten years.

Events under the Last Stuarts and William of Orange

Upon Cromwell's death on September 3, 1658, his power was so complete that his son Richard was immediately proclaimed Lord

Protector by the army as if the monarchic system of succession in direct line had remained valid even in the English Republic. Fortunately for English liberties he was an inexperienced, good young man, but absolutely incapable of ruling the quarrelsome temperaments of the principal officers of the army. Among them several aspired to succeed Cromwell, but no one had the ability and prestige to outshine his competitors. When the rivalry between the various generals threatened to degenerate into bloody conflict, England risked being subjected to something worse than military despotism, that is to military anarchy.

The overwhelming majority of the country, which had submitted to the tyrannical but stable government of Cromwell, desired to return to the old monarchy, for they saw in it an escape from military anarchy and a restoration of normal political life. One of the generals in Cromwell's army, George Monk, more clever than the others, understood the wisdom of seconding the decision of almost the entire nation.

Thus he came to London with the army corps that he commanded and that was stationed in Scotland. The remnants of the old Long Parliament, convened by Charles I in November of 1640 and dissolved by Cromwell by force in 1653, assembled there. Monk wanted to readmit all those deputies who had been expelled because they were favorable to the Stuarts, and the Long Parliament thus dissolved itself, calling a Convention to decide on the form of government that England was to adopt. Monk gave assurance that with his soldiers he would respect the decision of the Convention, which, responding to the almost unanimous vote of the country, re-established the old constitution and recognized, as king, Charles II, oldest son of Charles I (May, 1660).

The only adversary that could effectively oppose the vote of the Convention and the aspirations of the country was Cromwell's old army, but the numerous generals were not in agreement and, in part, were bought out by the new regime. The soldiers were first dispersed in small groups throughout all of England and then easily disarmed and discharged.

If Charles II had been only a mediocre king, it is probable that the first English revolution would have been the last and that the constitutional development of England would have been, at minimum, retarded a great deal. In fact, the English ruling classes were content with the restoration of their old liberties, the security of not submitting to taxes not approved by Parliament and, above all, with not having to submit to an absolute and arbitrary power supported by military force. Furthermore, the country had experienced the scourge of a long period of civil wars and had for many years faced the bigoted tyranny of the most fanatic faction of the Calvinists—the Puritans—so powerful under Cromwell; now it aspired to internal peace and wanted to avoid new upheavals.

But the very least that can be said of the new king is that he did not understand nor feel the dignity of his position. Frivolous, luxurious, and skeptical like his father, he did not aspire to absolute power, but made frequent requests to Parliament for money which he used to support the pomp of a sumptuous court and to enrich courtiers more than to maintain public services. In a war against Holland, which broke out in 1665 for commercial reasons, after various vacillations the Dutch prevailed. The funds approved by Parliament had been squandered on the maintenance of the crews and thus many English warships were left disarmed. Afterwards, by means of a secret treaty with Louis XIV, King of France, Charles accepted money that the French king offered him on condition that the foreign policy of England be subordinate to that of France.

The prestige of the sovereign began to decline and his behavior did not fail to arouse widespread distrust on the part of Parliament and the country. This sentiment had beneficial effects on constitutional legislation because it contributed greatly to the approval of several laws aimed at curbing the will of the king and the court. In fact, the custom was adopted whereby Parliament, for every new concession of money to the king, in exchange asked that he sanction a bill that reinforced the authority of the legislature and diminished the royal power. And the king, in order not to incur greater unpopularity and to have new funds, authorized the laws approved by the Parliament.

Among these measures the one called *Habeas Corpus* had capital importance. It was approved in 1679 and today still protects English citizens against arbitrary arrests and long detentions pending judgment in such a practical and efficient way that it has not been possible to better its provisions in any other country.

In substance, the Habeas Corpus Act provides the following.

1. Within twenty-four hours after his arrest, a citizen has to receive communication in writing of the type of accusation with which he is charged.

2. Except in cases of felony, high treason, or other very serious crime, any arrested person can obtain provisional liberty through bail.

3. Within twenty days from arrest the accused has to be brought before a grand jury, which will ascertain the existence of the criminal deed and will judge if there is sufficient evidence to continue penal proceedings.

4. Every police officer, magistrate, and jail-keeper who violates the Habeas Corpus Act in any way must pay five hundred pounds sterling to the injured party.

It is to be noted that the presence of the jurors during the preliminary actions was already in force in English penal proceedings, and therefore the third paragraph of the Habeas Corpus Act only established a period during which this participation had to take place. Furthermore, the provision contained in the fourth paragraph, which establishes the direct and pecuniary responsibility of public officers, has always seemed to be a very efficient instrument for the protection of individual liberty.

Charles II had always treated religious questions very lightly. On this subject, he appeared indifferent and skeptical, but the intimates of the king knew that, in the rare moments during which he spoke seriously, he manifested a certain inclination toward Catholicism. Naturally, this could not help him in a country that now practiced Protestantism zealously and where the king was the supreme head of the reformed national church. When the king died in 1685 he confirmed the suspicions of the populace by calling a Catholic priest to his bedside for confession.

His brother James II succeeded him. He was a declared and fervent Catholic who in addition held the views of James I and Charles I on royal power, thus leaning toward absolutism. Nonetheless, despite the fact that these sentiments of the new king were known and that he, the head of the Anglican Church, showed open favor to all who by design or flattery embraced Catholicism, the English ruling classes regarded revolution as so repugnant that it probably would have been avoided. The king was in fact advanced in years and his two daughters from his first marriage were Protestants and married to Protestant princes. Furthermore, his second wife, a Catholic princess from the House of Este, had borne no children.

But when James had a son by his second wife, excluding the sisters from the throne, and when his son was baptized according to the Catholic rite, then the danger became apparent that an absolutist dynasty of Catholic princes might be established in England. Accordingly the leading politicians in the English Parliament sought to contrive the best way to rescue the nation from this risk with as little violation of legality as possible.

They secretly came to an agreement with William of Orange who had married Mary, eldest daughter of James II. William was Stadtholder of Holland, an office equivalent to that of president of the Dutch Republic. The Prince of Orange disembarked in England with an army composed of Dutch and English political fugitives, saying that he had come to restore abused constitutional liberties and the damaged Protestant religion. James, who had administered the treasury of the Crown in a more careful fashion than his brother, was able to equip a small standing army and send it against the Prince of Orange. However, the king's lack of popularity was so great that his own troops abandoned him and passed over to the standard of his adversary, so that William was able, quite without difficulty, to enter into London. James was compelled to take refuge in France, first throwing the royal seal into the Thames.

Meeting in order to regularize in some way the political situation, the Parliament declared that the king, by fleeing and throwing the royal seal into the Thames, had in fact abdicated; that his son was supposititious; and that, therefore, the throne belonged to Mary and to William of Orange who together were proclaimed Queen and King of England. But in addition to these assertions, which do not conform to the truth and can only be explained as necessary to legalize a revolutionary act, the Parliament discussed and approved in the first days of the year 1689 a second Bill of Rights which was sanctioned by the new king. This act placed new limits on the action of the Crown and provided new guarantees to Parliament and additional individual liberties to all English citizens.

With this Bill, in addition to some provisions of minor importance that it contained, it was affirmed that the king could neither suspend the force and execution of the laws, nor exempt individuals from observing them without the approval of Parliament; that extraordinary tribunals were illegal and pernicious; that any Englishman possessed the right to present petitions to Parliament; that the constitution of an army without the permission of Parliament was illegal; that every Englishman of Protestant religion might carry arms for his personal defense; that Parliamentary elections had to be free and that Parliament had to be frequently convened; that in Parliament liberty of discussion could not be restricted and that the lists of jurymen had to be compiled in a way prescribed by law.

The first provisions precluded actions of the sovereign from being considered as superior to the law and with them the custom under which Parliament had achieved a necessary participation in the legislative power became irrevocable. With the rules concerning tribunals and jurors the citizens were protected against arbitrary persecutions by the executive power. Further, the right to bear arms and the liberty of petition were conferred on them. At the same time, the two houses of Parliament were guaranteed full liberty of discussion and of voting.

In addition, the executive was prohibited from seeking to exert influence on the will of the electors. But perhaps more than from the second Bill of Rights, the liberty of English elections was guaranteed by the fact that the functionaries of the local administrations were not career employees. These individuals, chosen from among the local notables, served without compensation and thus did not easily become blind instruments of the government. Finally, the prohibition upon a standing army without the permission of Parliament clearly showed how much distrust still remained of standing militias, which could become instruments of absolutism.

William, who was the third person with this name to reign in England, faithfully observed the second Bill of Rights, but exercised royal authority vigorously within the limits of the constitution. He died in the first months of 1702. But the previous year the Parliament, foreseeing that the immediate succession would go to Anne, Queen Mary's childless younger sister, and then would necessarily continue to a distant relative, a German prince from the House of Hanover, sought to limit further royal power with an act called the Act of Succession or the Act of Settlement. It contained the following provisions.

1. The sovereigns of England must be adherents of the Protestant religion.

2. No war could be declared by the king without the consent of Parliament.

3. No foreigner could be a member of the Privy Council.

4. Every act of the Crown in order to be enforced must be countersigned by a member of the Privy Council.

5. No public official could be a member of the House of Commons.

6. The appointment of judges was dependent on continued good behavior.

7. The king could not suspend the practice of impeachment.

8. No English sovereign could be absent from England without the permission of Parliament.

The first two provisions were evidently dictated by the particular necessity of excluding from the throne the male line of the Stuarts, who had converted to Catholicism, and from the necessity, no less impelling, of preventing English foreign policy from becoming influenced by that of such a small German state as Hanover.

But with the fourth provision a fundamental principle was affirmed that has formed the basis of all modern constitutions. It was established that if the individual person of the sovereign is superior to law, in such a way that he can never be called to answer for having violated it, nevertheless his political action must rest within the limits of the law, for no act of his can be valid unless the responsibility for it is assumed by a functionary who is not protected by royal inviolability.

The provision in paragraph seven aimed at rendering more certain this responsibility by the functionary who countersigned an illegal act of the king, by preventing the sovereign from rescuing him from accusation by the House of Commons and from the judgment of the Peers. By the fifth provision, which was soon thereafter modified, the incompatibility between the office of Member of Parliament and the exercise of a paid office dependent on the executive power was established. With the sixth provision the independence of the magistrates, who, once nominated, held office for life, was assured. The eighth paragraph was never effectively applied.

Therefore, with the second Bill of Rights and the Act of Settlement such limits were put on the royal authority as to cause the direction of English affairs no longer to depend exclusively on the sovereign and on those who had his confidence. In fact, through these fundamental laws, Parliament, retaining intact the prerogative inherited from the feudal age of voting taxes, acquired so many other prerogatives that it could be considered an important participant in sovereignty. It was not yet asserted, however, that this participation should become so complete as to permit the will of Parliament to prevail over that of the Crown, nor was it even intended that appointments by the Crown ought necessarily to be entrusted only to persons who enjoyed the confidence of the majority of the House of Commons. Thus, judging the regime in England as it was at the beginning of the eighteenth century, we can conclude that a constitutional, but not yet parliamentary, regime existed.

Parliamentary government was thus arrived at gradually and through customs that began to be established during the period from 1715 to 1760.

Parliamentary Government and Constitutional Reforms in Great Britain during the Eighteenth and Nineteenth Centuries

The King's Privy Council, mentioned in the Act of Settlement, was a consultative body that assisted the sovereign in the exercise of his political duties. In the seventeenth century it was composed of fifty or sixty members and included not only the high officials, but also a certain number of prominent personalities who, without official position, were called to serve because of the king's confidence in them. Naturally the Council was too large and it was unfit for the functions it exercised because of the difficulties of keeping discussions secret among so many people and of reaching rapidly well-thought-out decisions.

For this reason beginning with Charles II the sovereigns first used to discuss and reach agreement with four or five of the most influential members of the Privy Council, and then only formally to discuss the matter in plenary session. This limited group, which under Charles II and then James II, William III, and Queen Anne discussed and decided the most important affairs of state, was first called the Cabal and then the Cabinet.

Queen Anne, who reigned until 1714, at first acted cautiously by alternately choosing the members of her Cabinet from the Whigs and the Tories, the two parties that disputed supremacy in Parliament and in the country. Later she approached the most radical faction of the Tories and made an attempt, which failed, to leave the throne to her half-brother, the son of James II.[1]

The most important act in domestic politics during the reign of Queen Anne was the fusion in 1707 of the two kingdoms of England and Scotland into a single kingdom with one parliament.

After 1715 George I, the first king of the German House of Hanover, seeking to reign in England with as few problems as possible, had the idea of summoning to the Cabinet the most influential members of the House of Commons regardless of what party they belonged to. But Horace Walpole, who for about twenty years was Prime Minister to George I and George II, persuaded the two kings that for the sake of homogeneity it was better to appoint Cabinet members only from the party holding a majority in the elective chamber. At that time the Whigs held this majority. Since George I did not even know English the Cabinet got into the habit of meeting in his absence and then immediately submitting for his signature the decisions it had agreed upon. And since the plenary meetings of the Privy Council became more and more a formality, they conse-

---

[1] The names Whigs and Tories, which served to indicate in the eighteenth century the two parties into which the limited English ruling class of that time was divided, possessed in the beginning an offensive meaning. The Whigs were Scottish brigands and the Tories Irish brigands. As a political course the former aimed at enlarging the powers of Parliament to the detriment of the Crown, and the latter were supporters of royal prerogative. In the first half of the eighteenth century a part of the Tories did not recognize the Hanovers as legitimate kings and secretly favored the restoration of the Stuarts.

In the nineteenth century the Whigs took the name of Liberals and the Tories that of Conservatives, although many liberal laws had been proposed by the Conservatives.

quently became rarer, and the Cabinet, an organ legally unknown in the English constitution, became the body that in fact exercised the executive power.

George II, who followed the example of his father and was completely uninterested in English domestic politics, died in 1760. He was succeeded by George III, who, having been born in England, really wanted to be king of his country. Thus, the personal authority of the sovereign was felt again. After a series of more or less successful attempts to form governments that had his personal confidence, the king in 1783 succeeded in forming a government composed of men acceptable to him and presided over by the Younger Pitt. This Cabinet did not resign in spite of repeated negative votes by the House of Commons, and, after succeeding in winning approval of the budget by a majority of a single vote, dissolved the elective chamber and won favorable majority in the elections that followed. But this was the last event of that kind in the constitutional history of England. From that time on even if the king could keep out of the Cabinet individuals whom he disliked, and if he could effectively oppose some measure desired by his ministers, such as the emancipation of the Catholics, it was impossible for him to govern without the support of one of the two parties, the Tories or the Whigs, who contended for predominance in the House of Commons. Moreover, George III, earlier afflicted at intervals by mental illness, became blind in 1810; thus ended the period in which the interference of the Crown could still seriously modify the direction of English political life.

It was from this period that a truly parliamentary government was established in England; but if, from that time on, the political regime of Great Britain could be considered as completely altered so far as relations between the country and the king were concerned, the composition of the English ruling class remained very antiquated until 1832 and retained many traces of the medieval arrangements.

The right to vote was not only restricted to a small minority of the citizens, but it in fact was not granted on the basis of identical criteria of income and capabilities throughout the country. In the counties the Members of Parliament were elected on the basis of a single standard, but the electors were only those who possessed landed property. In the municipalities, on the other hand, the criteria that defined the electorate differed from one municipality to another. Furthermore, the number of representatives sent by each municipality to Parliament was not in proportion to the importance of the municipality itself. Some very small municipalities elected two representatives and some large ones did not even elect one. It is necessary to search for the causes of this anomaly in the history of English electoral law.

Originally, the king invited some municipalities to send their representatives to Parliament; but the invited ones, except for a few of great importance, were not always the same. Since the indemnity for the Members of Parliament was a burden to the represented municipalities, many of them, to avoid this expense, preferred to remain without representatives. Under the Stuarts the kings often avoided inviting those municipalities accustomed to sending representatives unfavorable to the Crown. Then, in order to put an end to such abuses, the Parliament, during one of its sessions during the reign of Charles II, approved a law providing that in the future only those municipalities would be invited that were represented in that particular legislature.

However, it happened that during the eighteenth century the socioeconomic conditions of England and the distribution of the population across the territory of the kingdom were greatly modified as Great Britain was changed from a primarily agricultural nation into an industrial nation. Many municipalities that had been small became important within a short time, while others, because of the decline of agricultural activity, saw their population diminish and become relatively small. As a result the paradoxical situation resulted by which a small borough of two hundred inhabitants sometimes sent two representatives to Parliament, although Manchester, with two hundred thousand inhabitants, did not send any.

Furthermore, in the counties only landholders could vote and the industrial and commercial middle classes which had acquired a great importance were excluded. In a few municipalities the electorate was rather large because it was easy to acquire the title member of the municipality, but in many others one was considered such only if he belonged to a certain family or a certain guild. Thus, the right to vote had become, after a fashion, a hereditary privilege.

In face of this state of affairs three different political currents manifested themselves in England. The conservative view maintained that England had become prosperous and powerful in the world with the constitution in effect at the time, which, if it did not correspond to rigorous principles of equality, still protected in a very efficient way the personal liberties of all Englishmen. A second viewpoint called for a moderate reform, such as removing the disparities and the greatest absurdities and allotting to personal property an influence equal to that of landed property. Finally, a third current, inspired by French democratic principles, advocated radical reform and universal suffrage. After desperate struggles, during which some blood was shed, the second view triumphed.

As early as 1829 Parliament approved and the king sanctioned a law emancipating Catholics. This law, the approval of which had been long delayed by the stubborn hostility of George III, permitted Catholics to enter Parliament and to be admitted to all civil and military public offices. Later, in 1832, the great electoral reform was approved. This removed the most strident disparities in the definition of the electoral colleges and conferred the franchise on all those who had moderate incomes, without distinguishing real estate from the interest on capital or professional gains. Thus, in summary, predominance in elections—which had at first with few exceptions belonged to an oligarchy of important families; i.e., a few thousand persons—became the patrimony of the English bourgeoisie.

Also in 1834 reforms in the local administrations were begun and a representative system gradually substituted for the old self-government by which offices were awarded by the king to the locally influential men. In consequence municipalities and counties are today administered by elective councils.

The democratic evolution paused between 1834 to 1867, years that perhaps represent the most splendid period in English history. But in 1867 another remarkable enlargement of the electorate took place and finally in 1884 and 1886 universal suffrage was nearly attained, as the right to vote was granted to all heads of households. In analogous fashion local electorates were constantly enlarged.

In 1911 a law greatly restricted the powers of the House of Lords by providing that within one month after a financial law was approved by the House of Commons, it became immediately effective. A similar procedure was established for other laws after the

House of Commons had approved them in three consecutive sessions. Furthermore, the Speaker of the House of Commons was given the power of deciding whether a law was of a financial nature or not.

In January, 1922, Ireland was granted substantial autonomy with a separate Parliament and government, but the northern part of the island, populated principally by Protestants of English origin, remained attached to England. Thus was cancelled the act which in 1800 had annulled the autonomy of Ireland and united it to the kingdom of Great Britain.

Finally a law in 1928 further enlarged the franchise by granting the vote to all women twenty-one years or older.

In conclusion, from what has been said above, it follows that parliamentary government with a democratic base is a relatively recent phenomenon in Great Britain. The predominance of the House of Commons originated in the eighteenth century and was affirmed decisively only in the first years of the nineteenth century, while it was only toward the end of the nineteenth century that the right to vote was granted to all Englishmen and only after the Great War also to women.

English Political Writers of the Seventeenth Century and Benedict Spinoza

We have seen that in England during the seventeenth century Parliament succeeded in gradually limiting the powers of the Crown after a bitter struggle of almost one hundred years. Naturally the struggle was fought with arms and the pen, so that in the same century we find a select group of English political writers who defend at one moment the cause of Parliament and in the next that of the Crown. We will speak only of the principal ones; that is, of those whose fame reached posterity and also spread beyond Great Britain.

It is often asserted that the English are an essentially practical people, and that they are not inclined to resolve political problems on the basis of general theories. But this affirmation, if it finds confirmation with some foundation in the political temperament of the English of the nineteenth century and of the present one, is erroneous if applied to the English political writers of the seventeenth century, among whom we find several great developers of doctrines. Their work precedes that of Montesquieu and Rousseau, who in France developed doctrines through which they acquired much fame. In the English writers of the seventeenth century we notice, on the one hand, an almost modern sense of reality, while, on the other, traces of the old medieval mentality.

It seems that the oldest English political writer after Saint Thomas Becket and John of Salisbury was John Fortescue, who was born around 1395 and died in 1476. Fortescue, having taken part in the War of the Roses, wrote around 1460 a treatise entitled *De laudibus legum Angliae,* which was published in 1537. Another of his works, which is less known, is entitled *Dominium regale et politicum.* According to its author, the *Dominium regale* was absolute monarchy and the *politicum* a monarchy tempered by assemblies of the nobility and representatives of the commoners. In the first as in the second work Fortescue appears to be an advocate of tempered monarchy, and thus the *De laudibus legum Angliae,* written in the fifteenth century, perhaps had greater popularity in the seventeenth during the conflict between Crown and Parliament. The political ideas of Fortescue approach those of the Monarchomachs of the end of the sixteenth century, of whom Fortescue could be described in a very moderate form as the precursor.

Among the English political writers of the seventeenth century, the first chronologically is Francis Bacon, Chancellor of James I, whose sentence for embezzlement of public funds we have mentioned. A man intellectually superior to his times and versed in almost all the sciences, he also wrote about politics and taught how to recognize the oncoming signs of revolutions, showing at times a quite uncommon psychological acumen.

On the other hand, a writer who shows greatly the effects of the medieval mentality is Filmer, who around 1650 wrote the work entitled *Patriarcha,* published in 1683. This work, today completely forgotten, was for many years sufficiently well known that Locke devoted a part of his work *Civil Government* to refuting it, and even Rousseau thought it opportune to fly some darts against the *Patriarcha* in his *Social Contract.*

Filmer was a partisan of absolutism which he believed legitimate because, according to him, kings descended by a line of primogeniture from Adam, father of all men. Such an idea was probably suggested to Filmer by the organization of the clans in northern Scotland. Each of these believed that it descended from a single ancestor, and that the head of the clan descended from the first-born.

A writer more worthy of fame was John Milton, the great poet of *Paradise Lost*, who lived through the period of the first English revolution and died during the restoration of the Stuarts. In one work of a political nature, declaring himself a Republican, he defended the English people and justified the execution of Charles I. In fact, for Milton the Republic was the form of government most in accordance with divine will. In the *Areopagitica*, another work of a political nature, he advocated liberty of the press, affirming that to kill an idea was more criminal than to murder a man.

But the most famous of the political writers of the seventeenth century was Thomas Hobbes. He was born in 1588, the year in which Philip II's "Invincible Armada" threatened England. He studied at the University of Oxford, but to little profit. Then, mastering the classical languages, he wrote an English translation of Thucydides, an author who, as we will see, had great influence on his thinking. Afterwards Hobbes traveled a great deal on the continent as a tutor to children of English noblemen, including the son of the Count of Devonshire. These trips put him in contact with the principal intellectual personalities of that time, among them Descartes. During the first years of the civil wars he was in France, where in 1642 he published in Latin the *De Cive*. Having returned to England, almost ten years later he published in English the *Leviathan*, a work in which he sets forth and defends principles analogous to those of the *De Cive*. Hobbes is the theorist of absolutism, justified however not in the manner of Filmer and later of Bossuet as a form of government conforming to divine will, but in a completely rational manner as that form most suitable to human nature.

In order to arrive at the justification for absolute government Hobbes starts with a description of the state of nature, which in that century was generally believed to have preceded the social state. In his description there is, without doubt, a recollection of the first book of Thucydides' *History* in which the author describes a remote age when men lived by robbery and violence and had as the only law the strongest fist. Such, according to Hobbes, were the customs of all primitive men. Neither people nor property was safe. Everyone had to defend himself from the violence of the others and each man was a wolf to all other men (*homo homini lupus*). Everywhere and at all times there was a struggle of everyone against all (*bellum omnium contra omnes*).

To escape this chaotic condition all individuals completely ceded their sovereign rights to the state, and each person put his efforts at its service so that the state could curb everyone's passions and remedy an unendurable situation. Individual property, according to Hobbes, had its origin in law and, therefore, in the will of the state. Thus the state could at its will limit property. Hobbes admitted the existence of God but the determination of the form of the religious cult was within the competence of the state. Although the state was all-powerful, it could not dispose of the life of the subjects, for this would be contrary to the end that individuals intended when they subjected themselves to its sovereignty. Consequently, the state could not oblige its subjects to enter military service.

The idea of the state of nature prior to that of a politically organized society was not new. The Monarchomachs had already formulated it and it was not completely unknown to writers of classical antiquity. But while the Monarchomachs, with the aim of limiting royal authority, starting from the state of nature maintained that men in the contractual pact from which the state arose had reserved part of their rights, Hobbes instead claimed that men, terrorized by the conditions in which they lived during the state of nature, had ceded virtually all their rights to the state.

Among all forms of government Hobbes preferred absolute monarchy as that which is farthest from the state of nature, because in absolute monarchy the will of the state is identified with that of a single individual. He added that those considered degenerations of the various forms of government—that is, oligarchy, mob rule, and, especially, tyranny—were inventions of people who wished to oppose the current regime.

To signify the omnipotence the Hobbesian state was to have, Hobbes compared it to the monstrous fish of which the Bible speaks, the Leviathan, which being the biggest of all the fish, could prevent the largest from swallowing up the smallest.

Hobbes had written the *De Cive* in defense of the absolutism that Charles I desired. The *Leviathan* [1] was published during the age of Cromwell's triumph, and it may be that Cromwell was able to take advantage of the theories of Hobbes. Hobbes, in exile on the continent, submitted to the dictatorship of Cromwell, Lord Protector, and was thus able to return to England. This act of submission caused him many troubles after the restoration of the Stuarts. He was accused of atheism and had to take up his pen again to defend himself against this accusation. Finally, having again adhered to the Stuarts, he was left in peace and died a nonagenarian.

In his old age he wrote *The History of the English Civil War.* With much insight he put among the intellectual origins of the civil war the classical education of youth, an education that, among other results, had the effect of diffusing the concept of political liberty.

John Locke, who was born in 1632 and died in 1704, personifies the liberal tendency as opposed to the absolutist one of Hobbes. His *Treatise of Civil Government* was published in 1690, less than two years after the second English revolution which occurred at the end of 1688. It was natural that a writer who was so close to this revolution and who was concerned with political affairs had either to justify it or condemn it. Locke justifies it. In his *Treatise of Civil Government* Locke, starting from the same hypothesis as Hobbes— that is, the conception of the state of nature and an ensuing social contract (a conception, as already noted, common to many writers of the seventeenth and eighteenth centuries)—arrives at conclusions opposed to those of Hobbes. Locke does not in fact acknowledge that fearful and terrible *bellum omnium contra omnes* described by his antagonist, but claims that man, even in the state of nature, maintains reason and is restricted by sentiments of natural justice. Normally this permits every individual to preserve his personal liberty while enjoying the fruits of his own work. The only thing lacking is authority that can guarantee these rights and thus individuals agree to concede some of their rights to the state, giving it the power to judge and to punish, as well as the responsibility for external defense. This delimitation of individual rights occurs through a contract, and the man who is invested with public authority cannot make use of

[1] In the Old Testament see what is said about the Prophet Jonah's changes of fortune.

it at his own will, because the authority has itself been entrusted to him for the protection of the rights of individuals. If therefore, he abuses it, he violates the contract and the people then reacquire their original sovereignty. In other words, this means that they may legitimately rebel.

For Locke private property finds its basis in a natural law that desires that every individual enjoy the fruits of his own work. Accordingly the state does not create private property but recognizes it and protects it. Land without man's work would produce only brushwood and wild fruits. It is human labor that permits it to produce fruits and corn, and it is proper that he who has sacrificed time and labor should have the absolute enjoyment of the products of his work. It may be noted, in passing, that Locke's theory, presented also by some economists in the nineteenth century, would be correct if tillable land was inexhaustible; that is, if every newcomer could occupy as much as he was capable of making fruitful with his own work. But since in civilized countries land is ordinarily limited, it is evident that the first occupants prevent others from exercising the right that they have themselves taken advantage of.

Locke wants the choice of religion to be free and not to depend on the state. However, he does not desire that atheists be tolerated for moral reasons nor Catholics because they would deny toleration to other religions. We owe to Locke the nearly complete elaboration of the theory of the three fundamental powers, which was later developed with some modifications by Montesquieu. According to Locke, these three powers are the legislative, the executive, and the federative. The last named would be that regulating relations with foreign nations. The executive and the federative powers are conferred on the king. Thus society keeps only the legislative power for itself and that is exercised by Parliament. Since private property is not a creation of the state, the taxes affecting it must be approved by Parliament, to which society gives the mandate of protecting its rights.

As can be seen, Locke's *Treatise of Civil Government* provides the theoretical justification for the English revolution of 1688. And it must finally be noted that Locke in this work appears to be opposed, although only incidentally, to universal suffrage.

Benedict Spinoza, who was born in Holland in 1632 and died

in 1677, is particularly known as a philosopher. Nevertheless he also wrote a *Treatise on Religious and Political Philosophy*, published in 1670, and a *Political Treatise* which he was not able to finish and which was published after his death.

In the *Political Treatise* the author observes that philosophers consider men not as they are, but as they should be, while politicians take into consideration human corruption and know that passions are an integral part of human nature. Thus in the state of nature right means power and in the state of nature everyone has a right to everything.

Up to this point it would seem that he follows Hobbes, but, at a particular point, he comes to different conclusions. In fact, according to Spinoza, man possesses reason which teaches him that society is useful, that peace is preferable to war, and love to hate. Thus, if men have ceded their rights to the state and have given it material force, they have done this because the state permits men to live in peace and according to justice. Acting differently, the state dissolves, for it fails to realize its ends and therefore, because of the need to be consistent with its own nature, the state must act in such a way that men are governed with wisdom and justice. Nor has the individual alienated his freedom of thought and thus his thought must remain free so long as it does not take the form of actual rebellion.

Turning to the examination of the differing forms of government, Spinoza observes that absolute monarchy is latent aristocracy and that the king only nominally has unlimited powers; in fact, his functionaries govern. The best monarchy would be one that is egalitarian and slightly socialist in the sense that the lands and houses should belong to the state which would rent them to private individuals. The power of the king should be limited by a council composed of members chosen by the king himself from lists presented by the heads of households. Later Spinoza speaks briefly of aristocracy and it seems that he judges democracy to be the most perfect form of government. However, at this point the work comes to an end because the author's death did not allow him to finish it.

9

Eighteenth-Century Political Thought

France in the Eighteenth Century. The First French Writers of That Century—Bossuet, Fénelon, Vauban, Saint-Pierre, D'Argenson, Boulainvilliers

In the seventeenth century the principal political writers were English. In the eighteenth century, however, primacy belonged to France. This was in turn a consequence of the intellectual pre-eminence that France at that time achieved in many branches of knowledge in comparison with other countries of Europe. One of the indications of this primacy was the predominance assumed by the French language. Actually, at first all scholars wrote in Latin or, if they also used their mother language, did not neglect to translate their works into Latin; but in the eighteenth century French became the universal language and French books penetrated all parts of the civilized world. Knowing how to speak and write French was at that time a necessity for all educated persons.

Between the seventeenth and the eighteenth century a great difference in the vision of the world is immediately to be noticed. This was, first of all, a result of the great progress in the natural sciences, which had its origin in the discoveries of Copernicus, and later in those of Tycho Brahe, Galileo, and Newton, who little by little aroused admiration in all thinkers and laid the foundations for astronomy and scientific physics. Also contributing to this intellectual renewal were the discoveries of new lands, which had occurred over the preceding centuries. Following these discoveries was diffused the belief, at least partly true, that nations until then deemed barbaric possessed civilizations older than the European and in some respects superior. China, in particular, was viewed in this manner.

But the inheritance of the Renaissance and the Reformation contributed more than anything else to the development of the critical spirit. The former, by multiplying contacts with classical thought, in a certain way totally emancipated minds from the principle of authority so prevalent in the Middle Ages, while the latter, by encouraging free discussion of the sacred texts, gradually undermined their prestige. In no other period did human reason show so much confidence in itself as it acquired in the eighteenth century because of the fundamentally antihistorical attitude of its culture. The eighteenth century felt the greatest contempt for those human institutions that were legacies of the recent past and that were deemed to be the fruit of ignorance and barbarism. Thus the conviction spread among the educated classes that human reason, emancipated from the blindness of superstition and ignorance, would be able in a brief time to reform the world, permitting many afflictions and all the absurdities and injustices to disappear.

Before beginning an examination of the political writers of the eighteenth century it must first be stated that when one says eighteenth century in a cultural and political sense, he does not mean to allude to the years between 1701 and 1800, but rather to those between 1715, the year of the death of Louis XIV, and 1789, the year when the great French Revolution broke out, or perhaps even 1815, which signaled the end of the Napoleonic wars. A historical period, as earlier noted, never corresponds exactly to the century understood in an arithmetical sense. Thus, for example, the nineteenth century, understood in the sense of a historical epoch, can be begun in 1815 and terminated in 1914.

With that said, we can note that toward the end of the seventeenth century Jacques Bénigne Bossuet, born in 1627 and died in 1704, possessed great fame. He was the theorist for the absolutism of Louis XIV and thus in complete contradiction with the immediate future. Bossuet, in his work entitled *Politique tirée des propres paroles de l'Écriture Sainte,* acknowledges the state of nature, but argues that the people in order to live in security organized themselves politically and conferred supreme power on a sovereign and his legitimate descendants. Then, once the people have alienated their rights, they must obey the prince even when he abuses his power. The prince must be responsible for his conduct only to God. As can be seen, Bossuet's theory of the divine right of kings reaches conclusions much more radical than those of the medieval writers or of the writers of the sixteenth and seventeenth centuries. It is sufficient to recall that Saint Thomas in the *Summa* justified rebellion in certain cases and acknowledged that the people could choose the form of political regime they judged most convenient. Thomas, in contrast to Bossuet, expressed his own preference for a mixed government in which the three forms of the traditional Aristotelian classification were fused and tempered.

Following Bossuet there were other writers in France who represent the dawn of the eighteenth century. Among these François de Salignac de La Mothe Fénelon can be recalled. He was born in 1651 and died in 1715. In his *Télémaque* Fénelon describes the ideal city of Salente in which the prince did not aim at enlarging the state, but rather at increasing, by means of peace, the happiness of the people.

Likewise Sébastien le Prestre, Marquis de Vauban, who was a great military engineer, wrote and published in 1707 a book entitled *Projet d'une dixme royale*, in which he suggested the replacement of all existing taxes with a single tax corresponding to 10 percent on all incomes. Thus, Vauban could be categorized among the writers on the science of finance. Neverthless, in this book there is an interesting description of the miseries of the working classes in France, which clearly evidences the new mentality then beginning to spread among the ruling classes of that country. This is confirmed by the fact that the publication of the *Dixme royale* caused its author to fall into disgrace with the king and the court.

Shortly thereafter Charles Irénée, the Abbé of Saint-Pierre, began publishing a project aimed at realizing universal peace. Another of his works of a strictly political character is that entitled *Discours sur la polysynodie*, in which he traces the plan for a radical reform of the French government. In this work the author attacks the despotism of the ministers, whom he would like to abolish, substituting for them councils or synods of five persons each referred to the choice of the king by the elders of the nation; that is, by the Academy of France, by the nobility, by the judiciary, and so on.

These ideas the Abbé of Saint-Pierre also disseminated orally in a type of political academy which, after the place where it met, was called *Entresol*. For some time the authorities left this academy undisturbed, but, as its members became more and more numerous and active, Cardinal Fleury, then Louis XV's Prime Minister, thought it opportune to close it by prohibiting its meetings.

Another writer who can be considered a precursor of new times was René-Louis de Voyer de Paulmy, the Marquis D'Argenson, who was born in 1694 and died in 1757. It seems that he was a part of the circle of intellectuals that met in the *Entresol* to discuss political subjects. Around 1730 he wrote a book entitled *Considérations sur le gouvernement de France*, which, however, was published only in 1765. In it he pleads for decentralization, criticizes the privileges of the nobility, and advocates the destruction of the remaining vestiges of the feudal regime.

In contrast Henri de Boulainvilliers (1658–1722) was explicitly opposed to the current of the new times. He wrote several works. The most important was his *Essai sur la noblesse*, published some years after his death. In it royal omnipotence is opposed on the grounds that monarchy had restricted the privileges of the nobility, which, composed of descendants of the Frank conquerors, could not be made equal to plebeians descended from the vanquished Gallican-Romans. Consistent with these principles, Boulainvilliers exalts the feudal regime and condemns those kings who presumed to confer the privileges of nobility on persons born plebeians. In a way he may be considered the precursor of De Gobineau and of the German writers. Toward the end of the nineteenth century and in the twentieth they sought to demonstrate that the different classes of society originated from differences of race and attributed the decline of political organisms to the exhaustion of the superior race.

It is necessary next to indicate the influence exercised by Voltaire, Diderot, D'Alembert, and all the Encyclopedists, in general. It cannot be denied that this influence has been very great but not always in a positive sense. It aimed at destroying the moral and intellectual base of the regimes and institutions of the time without

proposing equally effective substitutes. Thus, for example, in reject-
ing Christianity, the divine right that served to justify the absolute
authority of kings was attacked, albeit indirectly, while in demonstrating the absurdity of their privileges, the privileges of the nobles
and the clergy were undermined. Yet neither Voltaire, nor the
Encyclopedists generally, proposed any new system of government
to substitute for that in force at the time. Voltaire, who ridiculed
the Bible, was at the same time the friend and pensioner of several
sovereigns who were his contemporaries, and he accepted the absolute
regime provided that the sovereigns governed according to the advice
of those whom he called "the honest people"; that is, the philosophers
who had embraced the principles of the *Encyclopedia*.

Thus within eighteenth-century French political thought the
reconstructive function, that which created new theories to substitute for the old, was entrusted almost exclusively to two great personalities: Montesquieu and Jean Jacques Rousseau.

Montesquieu and Vico

Charles Secondat, baron de Montesquieu, was born in 1689 in
the castle called La Brède near Bordeaux of an old noble family by
tradition always associated with the judiciary. Although young Montesquieu was not inclined toward such a career he was required to
conform; this fact, together with the originality of his character,
certainly contributed to the development of a work in which he
harshly criticized the institutions and customs of the time, especially
for their ridiculous aspects.

The fruit of these opinions was the *Persian Letters*, published
in 1720. The author imagines that a Persian, having come to visit
France, writes to a friend in his own country and describes to him
French customs and institutions, providing an acute and biting satire
under an apparent ingenuousness. For example, when he says that
the king of France is accustomed to choosing his ministers from
among his servants, this is an evident allusion to the nobles who
helped the king when he got up from bed. Nor does he neglect to

attack the morality of the French ladies and he even ridicules the University of the Sorbonne which, although respectable for its age, was an expression of a culture largely superseded by the times.

And France laughed about it. The book had a great success, especially with the ruling class which was strongly ridiculed. This was a serious symptom of its decline, for a strong ruling class convinced of the legitimacy of its authority does not tolerate being caricatured.

If Montesquieu had been a man of mediocre intelligence, he would have continued on the literary course that had procured notoriety for him. But he possessed a strong and original intellect and knew how to change paths. His second work is entitled *Considérations sur les causes de la grandeur des romains et de leur décadence* (The Causes of the Grandeur and the Fall of the Romans). His subject this time was a very difficult one because if today, after so much progress in historical studies, the direct and indirect causes for the dissolution of ancient civilization are not yet completely explained, this was even less possible at the beginning of the eighteenth century. Nevertheless, Montesquieu was superior to his contemporaries in the development of the theme.

He worked about twenty years on his third work, published in 1748, which made his name famous with his contemporaries and with posterity. This book was entitled *Esprit des lois* (Spirit of the Laws) and it can be asserted that all of the political reforms that occurred in the nineteenth century carried the mark of the ideas enunciated in this work.

It begins with a definition that recalls the philosophy of Descartes by declaring that laws are the necessary relationships born from the nature of things. Afterwards more disparate subjects are examined. Thus, among other things, the author is concerned with slavery and divorce, but the political part has contributed most to the importance of the work and we will be concerned with this.

Until Montesquieu, the classification of the forms of government presented by Aristotle, which, we have seen, originated prior to the philosopher from Stagira, had reigned uncontested and it was always assumed that governments could be divided into monarchist, aristocratic, and democratic. Montesquieu believed that he could replace this classification with a more perfect one, conforming more to reality, and he divided governments into *despotic, monarchic,* and *republican,* subdividing the republics into aristocratic and democratic ones. It is worth noting that the word "republic" was used by the author in the modern sense of a form of government in which there is no hereditary sovereign. Furthermore, Montesquieu distinguishes monarchy from despotism because in the first the prince governs on the basis of laws that he himself has made or has accepted, while in the other his will is unlimited.

In order to explain why one of these forms prevails in a given country, the author establishes a relationship between the psychological conditions of each populace and the form of government adopted by it. According to him, therefore, a republic would exist where virtue prevails, and by virtue he means unselfishness and frugality of customs. Monarchy would prevail in the countries diffused with the sentiment of honor—that is, love of social distinctions, and in the high classes, the consciousness of duties toward the state. Finally, despotism would find its foundation in fear of punishment.

Developing a concept already mentioned by Bodin, Montesquieu examines the relationship between the form of government and the climate. Thus he finds that virtue and, consequently, the republic prevail in cold countries where passions are not very fiery, while despotism is found in warm countries where only the fear of punishment can restrain the violence of passions. Finally, monarchy would find a favorable atmosphere in temperate countries.

But undoubtedly the most interesting part of the *Esprit des lois* is that in which the author sets forth the theory of the separation of sovereign powers, a separation in which "power limiting power" would make liberty possible, that is, as government according to law. The powers, according to Montesquieu, would be three: the *legislative* which makes the laws, the *executive* which applies them to general cases, and the *judiciary* which applies them to particular cases. Each one of these three powers should be entrusted to an organ distinct and independent from the other two and only through this separation could a regime of liberty be realized.

In criticizing Montesquieu's doctrines, it can be pointed out first that his classification of the forms of government is not based, any more than that of Aristotle, on the essential characteristics of these forms. If Aristotle, in formulating the older classification, only had available the Hellenic city-states, Montesquieu also was limited to observing the European political systems of his times. Thus England, France, and Switzerland—with the possible addition of Turkey, which furnished him the example of the despotic state—were the models that principally inspired him. Nor is it accurate to say that monarchies form a type of government totally distinct from republics by reason of their essential characteristics. At times the political organization of a republic resembles more closely that of a given monarchy than that of another republic.

Perhaps even less justified is the distinction drawn between monarchy and despotism which, in the keen observation of Voltaire, are "brother and sister and at times they resemble each other so much that one can be mistaken for the other." And finally the correlation that Montesquieu found between virtue, understood in the meaning he attributed to the word, and the republican form of government cannot be accepted, nor even that between climate and the prevalence of republics, monarchies, or of despotism. In fact, precisely in the period in which Montesquieu wrote, Russia, a cold country, possessed an autocratic regime, while in classical antiquity Greece and Italy, countries with rather warm climates, had created and put into effect free forms of government.

The most durable part of Montesquieu's work was without a doubt that concerning the separation of powers, but even this can be considered as incomplete. Observing the political conditions of England in the eighteenth century, he formed the conviction that the liberty enjoyed by the English was the fruit of the separation of sovereign powers. But he neglected to point out that this separation did not correspond perfectly to his conception in which every power had to be concentrated in a particular organ; it was not accurate to state, for example, that the king in England did not participate in the legislative power and that the Parliament did not participate in the executive.

Furthermore, the point that escaped him was the political dimension of the separation that he noted, which was able to function well in England because behind every organ, whether directed by the king or the Parliament, was a special political force. Thus, behind the king was arrayed the prestige still enjoyed by the Crown as well as the entire bureaucracy. Behind the Parliament stood the entire wealthy English middle class, which held economic supremacy and which participated extensively in the administrative direction of the country through the forms of self-government. This omission on Montesquieu's part explains why in many countries where the representative regime has been introduced, and with it the separation of powers, this separation has remained entombed in constitutional documents, and has not functioned effectively because the multiplicity of directive forces, which in England allowed this separation to be very effective, has been lacking.

Of the Italian political writers at the beginning of the eighteenth century one very original one should be remembered: Gian Battista Vico, who during his lifetime never achieved a fame equal to that which he attained almost a century after his death.

Vico was a solitary thinker; his life slipped by in distress over financial and family worries. He spent nine years in Vatolla, a small village near Naples, as a tutor with a noble family. Later he returned to Naples where he had been born in 1668. There he obtained a position at the University as a teacher of rhetoric. The meagre stipend that he received compelled him to give private lessons in order to obtain the basic necessities of life. In 1734 he won a moderate pension from King Charles III, who named him historiographer of the court.

The principal work for which Vico is famous, *Principles of a New Science Concerning the Common Nature of Nations,* was published for the first time in 1725, enlarged in a second edition in 1730, and was rendered definitive in a posthumous edition of 1744.

A fundamental idea in Vico's system is that all human civilizations follow an upward movement. He distinguishes three phases in the life of a people. The divine period corresponds to the beginnings of civilization when society is governed by priests and the single bond uniting the society is a belief in a common divinity. During this period the first social institutions—marriage, courts, and the worship of the dead—are born. The second period is the heroic one, in which the strong dominate the weak, and power is in the hands of a few. During this phase material forces prevail. Finally, there is the humane period during which customs become refined and society tends continuously toward a more perfect organization. It could then occur that through successive degenerations in this last period, man might again fall into the violence of the heroic period and even into the primitive conditions of the divine period. As for forms of government, monarchy would prevail in the first period; aristocracy in the second; and democracy in the third.

With the formulation of this theory Vico certainly made important advances toward a true political science and he possessed genial instincts; but, at the same time, we must reluctantly admit that today his system needs to be completed and modified. This uniformity of forms that he believed he had identified in the political life of differing peoples did not always exist or, if it did, was within very broad limitations. In truth the causes which lead political organisms and civilizations to advance or decline are many and various, and their actions are not constant and uniform at all times and in all societies.

At any rate, Vico had the very great merit, given the times in which he lived, of asserting that the proper method for knowing the laws regulating the political and cultural life of societies consists in the study of their history, and that only through such study is it possible to arrive at truly scientific results. But, as already noted concerning Machiavelli, it is also necessary to remember with Vico that the historical material at his disposal was still scanty and imperfect. The critical study of history and its scientific explanation were in fact the work of the nineteenth century and thus we must excuse the Neapolitan thinker for these faults, which originated from the insufficiency of the materials at hand.

Jean Jacques Rousseau

Rousseau's influence on the history of political thought has been even greater and more profound than that of Montesquieu. Rousseau not only moulded the mentality of his contemporaries but the echoes of his doctrines were strongly felt in the following century: even today in the twentieth century, we live in an intellectual atmosphere more or less impregnated by the theories of Rousseau. Only in the last few decades have new currents of ideas been advanced.

The success of Rousseau's theories at the time they appeared is easily explained by the fact that they were precisely the ones anticipated by European society, and especially French society. In those days the diffusion of new ideas was above all the work of a secret association founded a little while before, called *Freemasonry*, which with the great optimism characteristic of the eighteenth century intended to realize a new social order that would make man, previously miserable and slavish, a free and happy being.

But if the period in which Rousseau lived contributed a great deal to the formation and the diffusion of his thought, it is also necessary to recognize that the thinker's great individuality contributed much to the creation of the intellectual atmosphere of his times and those immediately following. Accordingly it is appropriate to inquire into the circumstances and atmosphere that helped to mold Rousseau's intellect and character.

Rousseau was born in Geneva in 1712. The atmosphere of Geneva in those years was somewhat different from other European cities. Until 1537 Geneva had been an autonomous commune within which its bishop exercised predominant authority under the protectorate of the dukes of Savoy. But in 1537 when Calvin took up residence there the bishop was expelled and the commune, having become independent, allied with Berne and the other Protestant cantons in Switzerland. After this revolution the Genevans naturally enough were converted to Calvinism, and many French and Italian Protestants transferred their residences to that city. These exiles, who abandoned their own countries in order to keep their faith unimpaired, were quite unique in their rigidity of character. Since the great majority belonged to the educated classes they raised considerably the intellectual level of the city. But the atmosphere was restricted in such a way that it may be said that every individual was spied upon by every other. If someone wished to rebel against the thought and customs of the community his life became impossible. He was, as would be said today, boycotted and compelled to settle abroad.

After the city was freed from the protectorate of the dukes of Savoy it lived for many years in a continuous state of war, now latent, now open, with the dukes. Within the city sovereignty resided with the *General Assembly* of the citizens which, except in extraordinary cases, delegated its power to a *Grand Council* of two hundred members, and to a *Small Council* of twenty-five members which exercised the executive power.

In addition to the citizens who were descendants of the old inhabitants and the old immigrant families, there resided in Geneva others who had immigrated more recently and had not yet received citizenship; and finally, there were the subjects who lived on the outskirts of the city. In appearance the government was in the hands of the laymen, but in fact the *Synod of the Protestant Priests*, which enforced moral standards and exercised a censorship over worship, had a great deal of authority. If an individual was admonished by the Synod for some cause which in the view of the public was quite serious, he was disqualified and excluded from any public office.

In 1540 the Parisian bookseller Didier Rousseau immigrated to Geneva and obtained citizenship there. His descendants became watchmakers and accumulated a modest patrimony. David Rousseau, Jean Jacques' great-grandfather, left an estate of five hundred thousand gold francs, a considerable sum for those times. But this was divided among ten children. Jean Jacques' father, the grandson of David, a rebel against the Genevan atmosphere and an intemperate person, twice had to go into exile and used up almost all of his inheritance.

It is still a very common error to assert that Rousseau was a common man. From what has already been said it is easy to demonstrate that this does not conform to the truth. Rather, it is necessary to recall that watchmaking was at that time the prime industrial activity in Geneva and the large watch manufacturers constituted the aristocracy of the city. Thus Jean Jacques rather than a common man was a person who had fallen in rank, a misfit, what the French would call a *déclassé*.

His mother having died in childbirth and with his father in exile, young Rousseau was taken in by some aunts who provided him with an elementary education that conformed to the rigid Genevan morals.

Later the young boy was placed in a boarding house but he did not stay long because of his father's financial difficulties. Soon he was employed as an apprentice to an engraver. In those days it was the custom to place boys in the factories of qualified artisans so that they could learn the trade; the teacher, who was paid a small sum, took the apprentices into his home and exercised an almost paternal authority over them. This type of life was far from pleasing to Rousseau, who from this time on sensed the loss of the free air of the country and faced reluctantly the authority of a rigid and sometimes brutal master. Only on Sundays could he satisfy his desire for rural trips.

In that period the city of Geneva was a very short distance from the border of the lands of the former dukes of Savoy, now become kings of Sardinia, so that during the conflict between them and the Calvinist republic, it could be feared that the city would be occupied by the Savoyards with a sudden *coup de main*. Thus every evening as soon as the sun set the gates of the city were closed. Now it happened that one Sunday evening Rousseau was out late. He found the gates closed and could return to his teacher only on the next day; his teacher provided him with a strong corrective in the form of a flogging. A few weeks later the same thing happened again and he had no desire to face the anger of his teacher. Accordingly, he took flight from Geneva and crossed the Savoyard border.

The decision taken at this time by Jean Jacques, just sixteen years old, was certainly a very serious one and was to influence his entire future. A Genevan boy who abandoned his family and almost necessarily his religion, without means and without possessing a trade that could give him the means by which to live, almost certainly had to become a misfit. If the boy could not realize this, his father, having been warned in time, could very well understand it. He made a feeble effort to rejoin his son but then abandoned him to his destiny.

The first person whom the adolescent Rousseau met in Savoy was a Catholic curate who, seeing that the boy was a Genevan fugitive, gave him some food and directed him to the nearby city of Annecy where he would find a kind lady, Madame de Warens, who devoted herself to finding accommodations for Genevan refugees. Rousseau followed the advice of the curate. He went to Annecy and there easily found this lady. She made him welcome in her house for several days and then sent him to Turin to the hospice of the Catechumens where he received the preparations necessary for conversion to Catholicism.

Who was this kind Madame de Warens and what were her means of subsistence? She was a native of Valais. Originally a Calvinist, she was then converted to Catholicism. She was separated from the husband whose name she carried and lived on an annual pension of 1,600 Piedmontese lira which the king of Sardinia gave to her. Thus in a small city she could lead a rather comfortable life.

Inquiry has been made into the reason why two kings, as sparing with public money as were Vittorio Amedeo II and Carlo Emmanuele III, assigned a relatively sumptuous pension to Madame de Warens. From many indications found in the *Confessions* written by Rousseau, from a note in the State Archives in Turin ordering the payment of the pension to Madame de Warens with the usual formula adopted to pay spies, and from new documents found some years ago by Professor Luigi Foscolo Benedetto, proof has been obtained that the lady who extended hospitality to the young Rousseau was a secret agent of the Sardinian government. Her job was to keep watch over Geneva and, from time to time, to execute special missions entrusted to her.

Rousseau tells of remaining at the hospice of the Catechumens in Turin for about a month and of being sent away with the proceeds of a small collection taken up for him the day he was converted to Catholicism. In reality it appears that he remained in the hospice for about three months and that the shelter was not accustomed to abandoning converts. If Rousseau was abandoned it must have been his own fault.

After roaming the streets of Turin for some time he was employed as a servant. But low life with people of few scruples at a very young age ruined his character to the point that he committed a theft and charged a chambermaid with it. This period of his life was quite sad and obscure and not free from humiliations and shame, although by his own confession he found some masters who treated him humanely and one who gave him Italian lessons.

After nearly two years of residence in Turin he suddenly decided to return to Madame de Warens. This time she received him with enthusiasm and he became her lover. The relationship with Madame de Warens lasted for nine years although not without problems.

Those nine years of cohabitation with Madame de Warens, a woman of rare talents, were not without benefit to the intellectual development of Jean Jacques. Her home had a small library and was frequented by educated people. In this period Rousseau acquired much of the knowledge that makes a highly cultivated man. His intellect was really that of a self-taught man whose characteristic is a facility for learning and remembering ideas that are generally considered difficult and, in contrast, a difficulty in learning easy things. Thus, for example, Rousseau never managed to learn Latin well and the only foreign language he knew and spoke—and at that badly— was Italian, which he had learned in his youth first in Turin and later, as we will see, perfected in Venice.

Relations with Madame de Warens became always more difficult and at last Rousseau had to go away. First he settled in Lyons, where for some time he was a teacher of little success and then in Paris where he was more fortunate. He succeeded in securing presentation to the Academy of Sciences to whose judgment he submitted a new system of musical notation which, since it was more complicated than that in use at the time, was not adopted. Soon thereafter he was able to obtain the post of Secretary to Monsieur de Montaigu, who had shortly before been nominated the king of France's Minister Plenipotentiary to the Venetian Republic. Jean Jacques at this time performed his duties well enough, giving proof of zeal and ability. Approximately eighteen months later, around 1745, as a result of differences with de Montaigu he returned to Paris and formed a friendship with Diderot, Grimm, d'Holbach, and Madame d'Épinay. He was able to secure a post as treasurer to a banker and executed his job with competence and honesty.

In 1749 he read by chance in the *Mercure de France* that the Dijon Academy had announced an essay contest on the following theme: "Has progress in the arts and sciences made men better and happier?" This offered the outline, the polemic, in which Rousseau could develop and organize the concepts that had been maturing for a long time as the result of his studies and his experience.

Those who had selected the topic evidently expected an affirmative answer as did the educated public of that time. It was the general belief that progress in the arts and sciences had made the men of the eighteenth century better and happier than their forefathers. Rousseau instead upheld the negative thesis—that is, that civilization is corrupt and that the best and happiest people are those nearest to nature. In this work he enunciated for the first time that opinion, a synthesis of his thought, on which all his future works were based:

"Men are born good and society makes them bad." This is a highly revolutionary judgment which gave birth to all the subversive unrest of the eighteenth, nineteenth, and twentieth centuries because it was based on the premise that by changing social institutions, humanity would be able to reacquire its primitive goodness, and both egoism and wicked passions would vanish from the world.

Rousseau, imbued with the abstract, enlightening, and reforming mentality of the eighteenth century, did not take into account a very simple objection that today is within reach of all minds: if all men were born good it would be absurd that society is so badly organized as to make them wicked. Social organization necessarily must have a close connection with the average moral level of the individuals who are society's members.

Probably Rousseau's belief in the innate goodness of man and of his corruption by society were a consequence of the vicissitudes of his life. Born in Geneva, a city of rigid customs, and educated there in his early years in an atmosphere saturated with austere morality, he had faced at a very young age the morally negative influences of the troubled society in which he lived. Finally having abandoned Madame de Warens, seeing the possibility of becoming self-sufficient, it is natural that the germs of the puritan education he received in his infancy and early adolescence developed, inducing him to judge very severely his youthful mistakes.

In any event his work won the prize in the essay contest and had an extraordinary success—so much so that its author suddenly became famous. The reasons for his success can perhaps be found in the fact that Rousseau fought the general convictions of his century with arguments that his century appreciated highly, with the myth of the natural goodness of men, with a belief in the moral superiority of savages over civilized men, of peasants over townsmen, and of the ancient over the modern. The success obtained by his first work contributed a great deal to the modification of Rousseau's character. From that time on he felt predestined to grand things and assumed the mission of reforming human society according to the norms of reason and justice.

Four years after, in 1753, the Dijon Academy announced a new contest, with the theme "the origin of inequality among men." Again Rousseau entered the competition but with a much more developed work than the one he had written previously. In this second work the author manifests much progress in style over the preceding one, while as far as contents are concerned, this is perhaps the Genevan philosopher's most important work. Even if it did not have the immediate success of the *Social Contract* and some of his novels, it is certain that in the *Origin of Inequality among Men* are found the germs of the social doctrines to be so widely diffused in the nineteenth century.

In this work Rousseau begins by distinguishing two inequalities, a natural one based on differences of physical force, intellect, and energy, and an artificial one based on differences of social condition, and then asks whether the two inequalities coincide. After answering—of course—in the negative, he seeks to discover why everywhere the strong are subjected by the weak, the intelligent by the mediocre, the courageous by the pusillanimous; and assigning himself the task of resolving this important problem, with the emphasis very common to his times, he exclaims: "Oh man, whoever you may be, listen to your story which I have studied, not in historians' deceitful books but in the great book of nature which is the only truthful one."

And he continues by describing the conditions of men when they lived in what he calls the state of nature—that is, in isolation and solitude. At that time man was physically stronger, intellectually weaker, and morally better because, not being in society, there was no oppressive competition nor occasion for envy. Man, naturally good and merciful toward the sufferings of his fellow-men, remained thus because he lived alone and was free from wicked passions.

From where did the degeneration of humanity derive? Rousseau, unlike other followers of *jus naturae* who visualized the change from the state of nature to a politically organized society occurring suddenly, believed that this passage had been prepared slowly through a period of transition during which the human character degenerated by degrees. According to Rousseau, the first associations were born out of the necessities of hunting and fishing. The first families were thereby formed and within them occurred the first competitions and conflicts.

But the finishing stroke to human morality was given by the invention of metallurgy and especially that of agriculture. The passage from the *Origin of Inequality among Men* in which the Genevan philosopher notes the birth of private property as a consequence of the cultivation of the land has remained famous. "The first one," he writes, "who, having enclosed a piece of ground, dared to say 'this is mine,' was the real founder of civilized society. How many crimes, how much misery, how many horrors would have been spared the human race had the one who removed the stakes and filled up the ditches said to his fellow-men, 'Beware of this impostor. You are lost if you forget for a moment that the fruits belong to everyone and the land to no one.'"

Rousseau then continues to note how through private property what was then called capitalistic accumulation was made possible because the landowners, possessing plenty of goods, could easily buy the work of the have-nots. But, not having a police force to protect private property, a period of anarchy followed during which he who had more to lose was, naturally, the rich man. Then the man "alone against the many" conceived the clever idea of employing to his favor the forces of those who attacked him, of making his adversaries his defenders, of "affirming rules that were as favorable to him as natural law was contrary to him." This happened in such a way that men consented to organize themselves under a government and under laws that apparently guaranteed the life and property of all but that, in fact, were of use only to the powerful. Rousseau thus concludes: "This was, or must have been, the origin of society and of laws, which gave new chains to the weak and new forces to the rich, which destroyed natural liberty forever, and which established human inequality for good."

In the passages of Rousseau's work just cited the concept that the state is the instrument that defends the capitalist and the ruling classes against the proletariat is clear. Therefore, in these passages can be found the germs of all those theories and sentiments forming the basis of modern collectivism which, in order to prevent the exploitation of one class to the advantage of another, seeks to abolish private ownership of land and of all the instruments of production. Also in these passages are the germs of modern anarchism which, still more logically, seeks to abolish all political organization in order to take away from the rulers the means by which they exploit the governed with violence and swindling.

The work for which Rousseau has remained most famous is the *Social Contract,* published in 1762. One or two people have sought to point out some contradictions between the thought contained in the *Contract* and in the *Origin of the Inequality among Men.* It now seems that such a contradiction did not exist. In the two works the thought is not different. The theses that the author sets forth are diverse. In the *Origin of Inequality* he tries to search out the origins of social organization, while in the *Contract* the thesis is different. There, taking as a fact that the state exists and that it cannot be destroyed because it is not possible for men to go back to the life of the forest, by what conditions can it be transformed into a reality conforming to the laws of reason and justice?

And these conditions would be the following: since in the state of nature every individual exercised sovereign rights over himself, he should cede those rights to the social community only on the consideration that he participate in the formation of the *general will*—that is, of the state which in this way would be organized to protect the interests of the majority of the citizens. According to this reasoning, the only legitimate government would be a direct democracy; that is, a government in which the legislative power belongs to all the citizens, who are also responsible for designating the people to be entrusted with the execution of the laws.

And let us add that Rousseau would not permit the collectivity to delegate its powers to an elected assembly. Thus speaking of the English constitution, he asserts that the English, who were believed free, were actually free only once every seven years—that is, on the day that they selected their representatives.

Naturally then it was implicit in the system he devised that the will of the state would be that of the majority of the associated members and that to the minority would remain only the right to withdraw from the state by immigrating to distant countries. Thus in the *Social Contract* the rights that the individual maintains in the face of the sovereign powers are virtually unmentioned. In fact, concerning these rights it is asserted that the state can also impose a given religion on all those subject to its sovereignty. This imposition is justified by the fact that the moral principles of all religions are identical and the differences consist only in dogmas and the forms of worship.

It is of some interest that in the *Social Contract* there is one passage in perfect contradiction to the rest of the work: "to take the term in the strict sense of its meaning a true democracy has never existed and it will never exist because it is against the natural order of things that the large number rules and the small number is governed."

Dealing with the transfer of sovereignty, Rousseau, on the basis of the concepts of private law, judges that it is *inalienable, indivisible,* and *imprescriptible.* Thus are disproven directly or indirectly those writers who had claimed that people having ceded sovereign powers to a minority or to a dynasty could no longer legitimately recover them. After writing many other works, including some famous novels and pedagogical works, and also after writing his *Confessions,* which is his literary masterpiece even if it is not always completely reliable, Rousseau died in 1778 on the eve of that great revolution which he had contributed so much to prepare.

10

Pre-Marxian Socialism

Socialist Writers at the End of the Eighteenth Century. C. G. Babeuf and the "Conspiracy of the Equals." Writers Contrary to the French Revolution

Beginning at the end of the eighteenth century, but especially in the nineteenth, we find a great number of political writers who can be subdivided into four categories: (1) those who, connecting themselves with Montesquieu, formed the liberal current and thus, above all, aimed at fighting absolutism through the separation of the sovereign powers entrusted to the different organs; (2) those who formed the democratic current, which aimed especially at the realization of political equality through the adoption of universal suffrage; (3) those who formed a current, to become gradually larger in the nineteenth century, which was then called *Socialist* and considered political equality insufficient without economic equality. (4) Beginning with the first years of the last century, in those European countries that had not yet achieved national unity or else had completely or in part lost their independence, as was the case in Germany, Italy, and Poland, a fourth current was manifested that looked to achieve unity of the country and, where necessary, independence from a foreign power.

Naturally the four currents, which could easily be distinguished in the field of theories, often were mixed in actuality. Among the writers those who fought at the same time for liberalism and democracy, or for liberalism and unity and independence of a given nationality were common. And the example of someone like Ferdinand Lassalle, who was able to link the patriotic movement with the socialist movement, could also be cited.

Seeking to follow the usual chronological order we will speak first of certain French writers who, in the second half of the eighteenth century, launched the modern communist movement.

The first of these is Morelly, who remained obscure for a long time because his principal work was attributed to Diderot. In 1753, two years before the publication of Rousseau's *Origin of Inequality among Men*, Morelly published a kind of novel in verse, entitled *Basiliade*, in which the fundamental lines of a communist system are drawn. It seems that the author had taken his inspiration from Thomas More's *Utopia*. In 1755 Morelly published a treatise in prose on the same subject, titled *Code de la Nature*, in which, under the evident influence of the *Origin of Inequality* published almost contemporaneously, he confirmed and developed ideas noted in the *Basiliade*.

In his treatise Morelly asserts that for six thousand years humanity followed a false course. According to him, the origin of all evils is private property which makes equality impossible. It is therefore necessary to abolish it and to inaugurate the communist system, attributing to the state the lands and all the instruments of production. Everyone would have to work for the state and it would provide the needs of all the people. Until the age of twenty-five everyone would be employed in agricultural work, considered the most fatiguing. Only after twenty-five would one have the right to lighter employment.

Politically every nation would be divided into districts and the districts into cantons, with the eldest members alternating as head, thus constituting the central government. The family would exist but religion would be reduced to a pure deism. A cult would be bestowed on the Supreme Being. So far as public instruction was concerned, chairs of communism would be created through which it would be shown that the communist organization of society is the best and the most rational.

In the *Code de la Nature* some basic outlines of a communist system are already clearly traced. The book enjoyed little success, probably because of the defects in the author's style. It is difficult to understand how it could have been attributed to Diderot.

A writer much better known than Morelly, although often accused of plagiarizing from Rousseau, was Abbé Mably. His philosophy is contained in several works of which the best known is *Doutes proposés aux philosophes économistes,* published in 1768.

In his works the author, after criticizing the present organization of society, proposes what now would be called a minimum communist program. He would thus seek to begin with the abolition of inheritance among kinsmen, allotting legacies to the state in order to reach through successive reforms a complete system of communist organization.

Another writer with a certain degree of fame was Brissot de Warville, who, in his *Recherches philosophiques sur la propriété et sur le vol* published in 1780, is revealed more as an anarchist than as a socialist. Impressed by the excessively severe legislation against larceny in effect at that time, Brissot ends with a true defense of it. The right of ownership, he says, is a natural right, on the basis of which every man should be able legitimately to take possession of what is necessary to satisfy his primordial needs (food, clothes, a house, and a woman). In actual society can be found those who possess much more than they need, while others do not possess enough to be able to stay their hunger. Thus the true thief is the rich man and, with a phrase that will be later be repeated by Proudhon, he concludes: *la propriété esclusive c'est le vol* (property is theft).

Brissot de Warville was at the time a deputy to the National Convention and belonged to the relatively moderate Girondist party. When the Girondists fell from power, he lost his life at the guillotine.

The writers that we have recalled up to now published their works in the years immediately preceding the great French Revolution. The question is often discussed whether the Revolution moved in a socialist direction or not. To this question some have answered negatively and others affirmatively. In order to be accurate, it is necessary to distinguish the time of the National Assembly from that of the Legislature and especially from that of the Convention; within the period of the Convention it is necessary to distinguish the time before from the one subsequent to the fall of Robespierre, who sought to define ownership as "the right to enjoy that part of property which is assigned by the law." This is a vague and doubtful definition on which its author does not insist.

If the Revolution permitted private property, even while controlling it, nevertheless it waged a very effective war against the large proprietors of that time. It is known, of course, that the property of the clergy, of charitable institutions, and especially of the numerous émigrés was confiscated. This property was then bought at a low price by the bourgeoisie of the cities and by the peasants. Thus the number of middle-sized and small proprietors was augmented.

Although this transfer of property was quite extensive, it turned to the advantage of a limited number of persons, leaving the majority of citizens in the same conditions as in the years preceding the Revolution or perhaps even worse. Accordingly, there was great discontent among those who sought to realize a program of absolute equality.

An expression of this discontent was the newspaper, first a weekly, then a daily, called *Le Tribun du peuple*, founded and directed by Caius Gracchus Babeuf. In the age of Robespierre he was imprisoned and probably would have been sent to the guillotine if Robespierre had not fallen at the right moment. It seems that during his imprisonment he read Morelly's *Code de la Nature* and that this had much influence on his ideas.

In his newspaper Babeuf insisted that the republic must establish absolute equality and that political equality not coupled with economic equality was vain and derisive. From this originated the necessity for adopting communist arrangements. In the course of a polemic with the ex-Marquis Antonelle who, agreeing with the *Tribun du peuple* as to the end to be attained, dissented concerning the means and proposed a gradual realization of the communist regime, Babeuf responded that he saw no obstacle to the immediate and complete realization of communism. It would be as easy to abolish private property as it had been to abolish the monarchy, the privileges of the nobles, and other institutions of the ancien régime.

Around Babeuf and his newspaper was constituted in the meanwhile a communist group composed of, among others, Darthé, Bodson, the ex-Marquis Antonelle converted by Babeuf's arguments, and the Italian Filippo Buonarroti, the most educated of all and whose authority over his colleagues was very great. They organized themselves into the Society of the Pantheon, but aroused suspicions so that the Directory disbanded them with military force in 1795. In spite of this, the group remained intact, recruited new followers, and arranged a plot called the Conspiracy of the Equals. Of this plot two documents remain which Babeuf and his colleagues had prepared, that is, the *Acte d'insurrection* and the *Décrets*. The first document, describing a method that was to furnish the model for Lenin in 1917, established that the conspirators would have won power with violence and then would have constituted an insurrectional committee, which would have assumed the dictatorship and would have nominated the members of an assembly with sovereign powers. In the second document, an economic program was outlined that in the course of a generation would have realized an integral communism.[1]

The plot was revealed to the Directory by one of the conspirators and the Directory took energetic action to thwart it by arresting the principal people who had taken part. In the summer of 1796 the trial took place. The plotters defended themselves by affirming that they had had the good of the people in view, but Babeuf and one other were condemned to death, and the remainder to deportation. The latter afterwards were pardoned and some ended by supporting Bonaparte's dictatorship; one of them, the ex-Marquis Antonelle, became a subprefect. Only Buonarroti remained tenaciously attached to revolutionary ideas; and in the nineteenth century he was one of the leaders of the Carbonari and until his death in 1837 took part in almost all the conspiracies plotted. In 1829 he published in Brussels the *History of Babeuf's Conspiracy*, in which naturally he set forth communist ideas. Buonarroti thus can be con-

[1] We have used the term "communism" because this word was at that time commonly accepted. The word "socialism" was probably used for the first time by Pierre Leroux in an article published in the *Globe* in 1832.

Today in socialism there are many gradations and a distinction is made between socialism and communism. According to Lenin, integral socialism exists when all the instruments of production are in the hands of the state, and everybody works for the state which, however, pays the worker according to the quantity and the quality of production. Communism exists instead when the last traces of bourgeois immorality have disappeared and every worker is paid according to his needs.

sidered as providing the connecting link between the communism of the second half of the eighteenth century and that of the first half of the nineteenth.

The French Revolution could not help but inspire a political literature, whether favorable or contrary to the principles proclaimed by it. Edmund Burke, Irish by birth but a Protestant, was one of the most illustrious members of the House of Commons and became famous for having supported in 1785 in front of the House of Lords the charge against Warren Hastings, one of the conquerors of India. In 1790 he published the *Reflections on the French Revolution* in which he harshly criticized the doctrines adopted by the Constituent Assembly. According to Burke, the Declaration of the Rights of Man and all the legislative work of the Constituent Assembly were based on theoretical principles that could not be applied in practice. Furthermore, Burke demonstrated that all political reforms that were not the outcomes of political maturation and the social conditions of a given nation were doomed to failure. He concluded by affirming that the French revolutionary movement would lead unfailingly to a military dictatorship. His prophecy came true about nine years later. Burke's work was read widely and was translated into the major European languages.

Among the adversaries of the French Revolution a prominent place belongs to Joseph de Maistre, born in Savoy in 1757 and a faithful subject of the king of Sardinia. In his *Considérations sur la France* he sees in the crimes of the revolutionaries a necessary expiation of the sins of the French people, for whom, however, he has admiration. His thinking is shown at a more profound level when he judges that the political constitution of a nation can only be the necessary consequence of its history, and thus believes that constitutions based exclusively on theoretical preconceptions must prove transient. In his work entitled *Du pape*, adopting a medieval concept, he thinks that the head of the Catholic Church ought to have moral supremacy over all sovereigns.

Mallet du-Pan, a Swiss of French origin, who immigrated and died in Richmond near London in 1800, in a series of articles and pamphlets denounced the excesses of the revolutionaries while recognizing the justifiable sides of the great Revolution. His writings were widely circulated in the last years of the eighteenth century.

An Italian writer who can be cited as one of the ablest critics of the French Revolution, and especially of the Italian constitutions based on the French, was Vicenzo Cuoco. He was born in 1770 in Civitacampomarano in Molise and, having gone to Naples at a very young age, took part in the revolutionary movements of 1799, which, with the help of French arms, created the ephemeral Neapolitan Republic. There remains a part of Cuoco's *Letters* written to Vincenzo Russo, another Neapolitan patriot of ultra-democratic and communist tendencies. In these letters Cuoco criticizes the doctrinairism of the Neapolitan republics and shows how the constitution conceived by Mario Pagano and based in large part on the French one of 1795 was unsuitable for the Neapolitans in 1799. With a sense of reality much superior to that of his contemporaries, Cuoco in these letters affirms that political institutions could not be identical for different nations, that they are inevitably the consequence of the past of a people, and that they should be attached as much as possible to the past of the nation to which they are applied.

The man from Molise sets forth analogous ideas in his *Saggio storico sulla rivoluzione napoletana del 1799*, published in 1801, in which, however, he does not neglect to point out the heroic end of many of the Neapolitan republicans and the ferocious cruelty of their conquerors. The great sense of Italian sentiment that Cuoco shows in his writings is noteworthy, and his other works on pedagogical subjects are also valuable.

Charles Fourier, Robert Owen, Henri de Saint-Simon and Saint-Simonianism

We have already said that a perfect coincidence between the century as a strictly chronological period and the century as a cultural period does not always exist; we have cited the example of the eighteenth century in a cultural sense, which can be judged as terminating in 1789, and that of the nineteenth century, beginning in 1815 and ending in 1914. Sometimes between one intellectual period and the following there is almost a parenthesis, more or less long, during which it seems that thought is collected in silence while preparing those transformations which will come to light as soon as possible.

Such a period of stasis was evident in the years that passed from the consulate of Napoleon Bonaparte (the end of 1799) to the definitive fall of Napoleon the emperor (1815). During this period books dealing with political theories were rare, and rarer still were those in which could be discovered an original political thought; of this latter group very few were distributed much among the public. The world in that epoch was too agitated and preoccupied; only with difficulty could attention be given to theories and doctrines. Furthermore, it is known that Napoleon loved neither ideologies nor ideologists, and often imprisoned ideologues. The fact that some publications of a political nature did come to light during the Napoleonic period but acquired notoriety only after 1815 is noteworthy.[1]

One of the writers who began to publish during the Napoleonic period but became famous thereafter was Charles Fourier. He was born in Besançon in 1772 of a family of rather wealthy tradesmen. Employed in Lyons during the revolutionary period, he participated in the Girondist insurrection against the National Convention, which took place in that city in 1793. After the fall of Lyons, having been arrested and taken to Paris, he would probably have ended up on the guillotine if the fall of Robespierre had not occurred. Liberated from prison, he was enrolled in a cavalry regiment but after two years was dismissed from duty because a fall from a horse caused him very serious injuries.

Afterwards employed by a large dealer in Marseilles, he witnessed a scene that made a great impression on him. It was a time of famine and foodstuffs were very scarce and expensive; the dealer for whom he worked, in order to raise prices still higher, according to Fourier, threw almost four and half million pounds of rice into

[1] This temporary lack of thought and political propaganda during the Napoleonic period was very well pointed out by Manzoni when he wrote in "Cinque Maggio":

> . . . due secoli
> l'un contro l'altro armato,
> sommessi a lui si volsero
> come aspettando il fato.
> Ei fe' silenzio ed arbitro
> si assise in mezzo a lor.

the sea. This fact, the credibility of which could be doubted, induced Fourier to study the laws of social organization and the most opportune means to remedy the evils of society. The fruits of these studies were *Théorie des Quatre Mouvements, Traité de l'association domestique et agricole*, and *Le nouveau monde industriel*, published in 1808, 1822, and 1823, respectively.

In these works, especially the last, Fourier sets forth a complete cosmic and sociological system. He begins with the principle that the disorganization of work produces a large dispersion of energies, which results in less production than that obtained through work in larger dimensions and wisely organized; he cites kitchens as an example, which if they were concentrated in such a manner that one hundred families could be served by the same kitchen, the same result could be obtained with less expense. Accordingly he planned the institution of communities, each one to be composed of ten thousand people, which he called *phalansteries*.* In these communities the distribution of the various duties would be made according to what he called "passional attraction." In his opinion, by nature the allotment of vocations among individuals is perfectly proportional to the needs of humanity for each type of work. Although these last ideas border on lunacy, Fourier cannot be denied a degree of respect because his analysis of the differing human passions is acute and not lacking in originality.

Still stranger are certain consequences that, according to our author, the institution of the phalansteries would have. The land would be rejuvenated by a new creation, there would be a continuous spring, and the more severe climates would become tempered, human life would be prolonged to one hundred and seventy-five years and man would domesticate certain strange monsters called *anti-lions* and *anti-whales*. Thanks to the first, wagons would be hauled with such velocity that breakfast could be eaten in Paris and supper in Marseilles, and with the second ships would move at

---

* Perhaps Mosca meant to refer to *phalanx* not *phalanstery*. According to Fourier, a phalanx is a cooperative community of approximately 400 families of four members each. The phalanstery is the common building or central part of the palace. In Fourier's words, it is "the edifice of the experimental phalanx." Fourier speaks of each community in terms of 1500 to 1600 individuals; therefore Mosca's figure of 10,000 seems quite high.—Trans.

extraordinary velocities. The admirers of Fourier have claimed that with this he prophesied railroads and steamboats. It could be answered that when Fourier wrote steamboats had already been invented and that railroads were introduced a few years after, without being preceded by the phalansteries, and it can certainly be affirmed that their institution would not have had as a consequence the realization of other prophecies of the sociologist from Besançon.

Given the ingenuousness of the times, in which many believed possible an immediate and radical reform of society, a small number of persons could be found who became followers of Fourier. But Fourier did not succeed in finding the necessary finances to organize the first phalanstery. He died in 1837 and some decades later Besançon dedicated a monument to him.

A practical experiment of communism was attempted in the first decades of the nineteenth century by the English philanthropist Robert Owen. He founded in Canada some villages, in which work, production, and distribution of commodities were regulated according to communist principles.* As might be expected, these villages either did not prosper or, because of the nature of events, were forced to adopt normal systems of economic organization.

A writer of much more importance was Count Claude Henri de Saint-Simon. He was born in 1760 and was of the same family as the Duke de Saint-Simon, who became famous for his *Mémoires* of the age of Louis XIV. His father was Count de Saint-Simon and his mother, of whom very little is known, was also a Saint-Simon. The writer thus came from the old aristocracy of the ancien régime, but he was not very rich, because his father, who was a younger son, had been disinherited and the fortune of his mother had been confiscated during the Revolution.

Henri de Saint-Simon very early manifested the originality of his character and his disdain for common prejudices. At the age of thirteen he refused to make his first communion. Another time, bitten by a dog with rabies, he burned the wound himself with a hot coal and provided himself with a pistol to commit suicide as soon as he recognized the first symptoms of rabies.

Another characteristic of his mentality was the conviction

---

* Owen's most famous community was, of course, the one in New Harmony, Indiana.—Trans.

that he was from his early years destined to realize an extraordinary and almost divine mission. At fifteen he ordered his butler to repeat to him every morning when he woke him up: "My lord, wake up because you have great things to do." Much later in a letter to Louis XVIII he began in this manner: "Prince, listen to the voice of God who speaks through my mouth." This Messianic vocation contributed toward giving a certain coherence to his disordered material and intellectual life.

Having entered the army with the rank of an officer, like all the nobles of that time, he was part of the contingent sent by the French Government to aid the rebellious Americans against England. Although he fought valiantly, he had little interest in the events of the war, but studied rather the social conditions of the American colonists and wrote to his father that he intended to publish a book in which, studying and setting forth the path of the human spirit, he would show the paths to follow in order to accomplish the improvement of society.

Having left the army after the peace, he devoted himself to constructing more or less bizarre designs and projects, like the one he proposed to the Spanish government. He suggested that a canal be dug from Madrid to the sea.

When the revolutionary fire burst out in France, Saint-Simon was at first attracted, but afterwards withdrew. His objective temperament and his pronounced tendency toward impartial observation of facts and social phenomena prohibited him from following blindly in some determinate direction of ideas, from meeting with more and more doctrinaire and violent revolutionaries, or with more and more blindly reactionary emigrés. But his withdrawal from active politics did not save him from the revolutionary whirlwind. He was a noble and this caused the serious presumption that he was of anti-revolutionary tendencies. Thus he was arrested and probably would have lost his head on the guillotine if with the fall of Robespierre he had not been liberated.

As soon as he was liberated he resumed the program to which he was dedicated from his youth: to determine the laws regulating the life of human societies, laws that, once established, would point out the way to make the progress of different nations more rapid, continuous, and secure. But he understood that in order to actuate this program it was necessary, first of all, to become more cultured and that in order to devote himself completely to his studies without being disturbed by preoccupations of a material nature, he had first of all to secure a sufficient patrimony to assure his complete independence. Thus he formed a partnership with a Prussian banker and speculated, buying and reselling with profit the property of the emigrés and the Church which had been confiscated in the Revolution. When he liquidated the partnership with the banker, he kept as his share about a million francs.

Believing this would be enough to guard him from poverty he dedicated himself to his studies. First he lived at the Polytechnic School and then at the Medical School. He went to classes conducted by the most famous professors and his house became one of the intellectual centers in Paris. Renowned mathematicians, physicists, philosophers, economists, and historians assembled there. Conversing with them he became acquainted with the different levels of scientific development that every branch of knowledge had achieved and he formed a relatively clear idea of the most important problems that each science proposed to resolve. But his culture, which was quite extensive, was never profound, since, having been acquired through conversations with competent persons rather than with methodical studies it always resembled that of a genial dilettante.

Unfortunately, the capital that Saint-Simon had thought sufficient in order to dedicate himself to his studies was used up before he had completed them. This was in part the consequence of the expensive life he led and perhaps more important, in part, the consequence of his irregular administration. He then suffered from poverty and in order to live had to accept a small job at a pawnshop, which kept him occupied twelve hours a day and did not leave him the time to dedicate himself to study. This period of difficulties was interrupted for two years when Diard, his old manager, met him by chance and took him home. Providing for his needs, Diard allowed him to continue his studies. But after two years, Diard died and Saint-Simon returned to his life of misery. In 1814 he obtained a small pension from his relatives, but soon after used it to pay the expenses of publishing his works.

In 1824 desperation induced him to shoot himself in the head with a pistol: he lost an eye but survived. Aided and comforted by a small group of disciples which finally was formed around him, he died in 1825.

The scientific production of Saint-Simon began in 1802 with his *Lettres d'un habitant de Genève,* in which the basic lines of his system can be perceived. He became more productive after 1815, when within a few years he published *L'industrie, Du système industriel, Catéchisme des industriels,* and finally in 1825 *Nouveau christianisme.* It is very difficult to condense into a few pages his principal ideas, whether because of the breadth of the themes dealt with or because it is necessary to bear in mind that several of his works remained unfinished, especially for lack of funds.

According to Saint-Simon, in every organized unity there are two powers: one that gives moral and intellectual direction and the other, material direction. These two powers are exercised by two organized minorities which, united, form the governing class, or that which now would be called the ruling class. In the Middle Ages the moral and intellectual direction of society was entrusted to the priesthood and the material direction to the warlike nobility; but with time, because of the infiltration of the Arab culture and the rise of the communes, a change took place which in the course of the centuries gradually diminished the spiritual and material conditions for the supremacy of the clergy and the warriors. In the nineteenth century, when faith in the supernatural had become very lukewarm and wars more and more exceptional, intellectual and moral direction had to be entrusted to scientists and material direction to the heads of industry. From this it can be seen that Saint-Simon ascertained the necessary relation between the intellectual, moral, and material conditions of a society and the formation of its ruling class, which by its nature has to respond to the necessities of the times.

But our author was not able to forget that between the Middle Ages, when society was organized for war and directed by religion, and the nineteenth century, there had been an eighteenth century in which Montesquieu built the foundations of the liberal system and Rousseau carefully formulated and then popularized the fundamental principles of the democratic system. Saint-Simon, however, believed that the eighteenth century had been an intermediate period, dominated by *legists* and *metaphysicians* whose work had been useful in overthrowing the last manifestations of medieval organization, but was powerless to reconstruct new social orders. Thus, according to Saint-Simon, both the divine right of kings and popular sovereignty, understood as the expression of the will of the majority of the citizens, were now out-of-date.

Although he did not accept the dogmas of liberalism, when he sought to propose the type of constitution that responded to his ideas he ended by suggesting the creation of three chambers, which were to be nominated by artists, scientists, and industrialists.

In his last work, *Nouveau christianisme*, Saint-Simon was very much concerned with the future of the lower classes and expressed confidence that their lot would be improved by a government of the scientists and the great industrialists. In this work he insisted on demonstrating the necessity for a moral direction to society. In his first works he had believed that the Christian religion could be replaced by the cult of Newton. Later he expressed his confidence in the utilitarianism of Bentham, and then he finished by accepting as a moral guide the Christian religion, rid, however, of its dogmatic side, and with views analogous to those of the modernists.

In almost all his works a mixture of original views and profound intuitions into the conditions of European society at the beginning of the nineteenth century alongside more or less absurd, sometimes almost infantile, conceptions can be noted. The keenness of his thought too often lacked that equilibrium and temperance that are necessary if the part of the truth which is partially seen is not to degenerate into paradox. He has been defined as a blacksmith of ideas, and the definition is just, for many of his ideas were then adopted by later writers who developed them and framed them in their systems without remembering the man who had enunciated them in the first place. Among these can be included men of great fame such as Auguste Comte, Herbert Spencer, and Karl Marx. It is worth noting that among his ideas the one that had less immediate success and left fewer marks among the writers of the two generations in the first seventy years of the nineteenth century was the one concerned with the necessary existence of the ruling class and the qualities it ought to possess. Most probably the long silence greeting this idea is explained by the fact that it was in advance of the times.

Saint-Simon during his life had few followers and his works were little read partly because he lacked the talents of a writer. His only moment of notoriety came when a trial was started against him in 1822 as a subverter of institutions and for having offended the royal family. At that time the opposition press naturally took the side of Saint-Simon, but after his acquittal the newspapers again ignored him and he returned to obscurity.[2] In the last two years of his life a small nucleus of disciples formed around him which remained intact after his death. Soon after, the nucleus became more numerous. But the Saint-Simonian doctrine acquired great notoriety only after 1830, when the July Revolution fed all the intellectual currents aimed at achieving fundamental reforms in society.

After 1829 Saint-Amand Bazard, one of Saint-Simon's disciples, in a series of conferences had tried to coordinate the teacher's ideas in a complete system; but Bazard and the other disciples did not always remain completely faithful to the teachings of the founder of their school. They accepted as fact the ideas of Saint-Simon concerning the political necessities of the Middle Ages and the modern age; they acknowledged that the seventeenth century had known how to destroy but had been incapable of reconstructing; they recognized the necessity for a social hierarchy constituted of those who had the capacity to command. But, at the same time, they thought a program of absolute justice could be realized on the basis that there should be an exact correspondence between the service that the individual renders to society and the reward that he receives for it, and especially, the rank that he occupies in the social hierarchy. Their motto was: "to each according to his own capacity, to each capacity according to his work." In order that an organization might be constructed on such a basis, Bazard and the other Saint-Simonians, while conserving private property, wanted

---

[2] The action was brought against Saint-Simon for having published his famous parable which momentarily gave him a degree of fame. In this fable the writer asserted that if there were fifty fewer chief courtiers, among them the relatives of the king, fifty fewer of the richest proprietors who lived on income, and fifty fewer of the highest functionaries, France would suffer no harm, for the dead would immediately be replaced by others who were worth as much; but if fifty of the most illustrious scientists, fifty of the most important organizers of industry, and fifty of the greatest artists were to die, the potentiality of France would be notably diminished.

private inheritance to be abolished, reserving inheritances due to death to the state only. According to these writers, for the exploitation of man by man it was necessary to substitute the exploitation of nature by organized humanity. And since with progressive steps slavery had been replaced by serfdom and then by the hired laborer, they thought that soon a system of production would be adopted in which the worker would enjoy all the fruits of his work.

Thus Saint-Simonianism, organized and developed by Bazard, and later by Enfantin, had its highest development between 1830 and 1832. Many Frenchmen, who subsequently became famous and distinguished themselves as scientists, financiers, and industrialists, adhered in that period to the Saint-Simonian movement. Among them was Ferdinand Marie Lesseps, who conceived the project for cutting through the Isthmus of Suez. In those two years hundreds of thousands of printed pages spread the ideas of the school.

If, however, the establishment and diffusion of the school was rapid, its decline, begun by a disagreement between Bazard and Enfantin—the most authoritative members of the group—concerning relations between the two sexes, was as rapid. Specifically, Bazard wanted to maintain the family, while Enfantin' was a supporter of a form of free love. In addition to this dissension a criminal action brought against the heads of the Saint-Simonian organization toward the end of 1832, and the spread of new schools of more socialistic emphasis, contributed to the decline of the Saint-Simonian organization. However, these schools utilized more or less Saint-Simonian doctrines. They left a great imprint on thought, and especially, on the opinions of many Frenchmen, and also on some illustrious foreigners, who, during their youth, had witnessed the rapid and temporary bloom of Saint-Simonianism.

French Socialist Writers in the First Half of the Nineteenth Century and the First Anarchist Writers

Already in 1829 Buonarroti had published in Brussels his *History of Babeuf's Conspiracy* setting out in detail the communist organization of society intended by the conspirators. This book undoubtedly contributed to the spread of communist ideas among French intellectuals and workers. This diffusion was further facilitated by the impressive organizations of manual workers that were a consequence of the growth of large industry in France after the first decades of the century.

Proceeding in chronological order, the first among the French socialist writers during the period from 1830 to 1848 was Pierre Leroux.

He was born in 1797. Because of the poverty of his family, he had to abandon at an early age his studies and practice the trade of a typographer. For obvious reasons, of all workers the typographers have better opportunities to improve their knowledge. After 1830 Leroux was a follower of Saint-Simonianism. In fact, he put at Bazard's service the newspaper *Le Globe* which he had founded. In 1832 the split between Bazard and Enfantin occurred and Leroux abandoned Saint-Simonianism while continuing to write on social themes.

He was a very prolific writer and contributed also to the *Revue des deux mondes*, founded in those years. His system is at the same time theosophic, social, and political. His thought, very often contorted and obscure, was set forth principally in two books: *De l'Egalité*, published in 1838, and *De l'Humanité*, published in 1840.

According to Leroux, humanity has its high destiny marked out by God. God has created humanity and is manifested in it. The human spirit is inclined by its nature to make progress continuously, and on the death of every individual the spirit passes, purer, to vivify the body of another individual. The continual progress of humanity is proven historically by examples (Leroux gives the customary ones among these writers) of the slave who becomes a farmer, of the farmer who becomes a wage-earner, and who in the immediate future will be emancipated completely from the tyranny of capital. Another proof of the progress of humanity is given by religion, which begins with fetishism, passes on to polytheism which, in turn, is supplanted by Christian monotheism. The last, having completed its mission, will soon be replaced by a higher religion, which will be affirmed during the nineteenth century. This period, according to Leroux, would indicate the end of the era of inequality and the bargaining of that of equality.

We have already pointed out that Leroux in 1832 was most probably the first writer to use the term "socialism," which was to be widely circulated.

He was often engaged in controversy with contemporary economists, some of whom claimed, as Locke did, that private property had as its sole origin the work of the individual. Leroux shrewdly observed that the production of wealth is due in part to the efforts of the individual and in part to the social organization which allows the single individual to work profitably. He therefore proposed that the distribution of wealth be controlled by the state in accord with three criteria: the quantity of each individual's work, the quality of his work, and the needs of the worker.

In summary, Leroux was capable of incorporating a comprehensive program of social reform, albeit in good part utopian, into a systematic philosophy of history, and, although he had been preceded by Saint-Simon and the Saint-Simonians in this method, it cannot be denied that in 1840 his works had considerable impact.

Another famous French socialist, almost contemporary to Leroux, was Louis Blanc. He was born in Madrid in 1811 into a wealthy French family. At the age of nineteen he found himself obliged to work to live, because his father had been ruined by the July Revolution. With the help of an uncle he was able to complete his studies and finally found a modest means of support giving mathematics lessons. Before long he began to write articles in political journals and in 1839 founded the *Revue du progrès,* intended to unite the most advanced democratic groups.

In 1840 he published the famous treatise, *De l'organisation du travail,* in which he set forth his program for social and political reform. The book begins with a description, as gloomy as ever, of the conditions of the proletariat at that time. The causes for this state of affairs were pointed out in two institutions: the private ownership of capital and competition. The capitalist was in fact forced to produce at the lowest possible cost and thus was compelled to pay the workers as little as possible; this was easy for him to do since with the constant presence of a large number of unemployed, the offer to work was always greater than the demand.

Blanc thought he had discovered a remedy for this state of affairs in the creation of *social workshops.* The state would contract a loan of some hundred million francs in order to furnish to workers' cooperatives the means necessary to work independently of private capitalists. And since the loans made to the workers would not be encumbered by interest, the cooperatives would be able to compete vigorously with the private capitalist enterprises, "killing competition with competition," to use Blanc's phrase.

But, besides reforming society, Blanc wanted to change its political organization. He argued that the government of the state should be formed of the representatives of the workers' cooperatives; he also wished to abolish inheritance, retaining it between fathers and sons, and annexing all estates to the state when there were no children. He had no modifications concerning the family and religion.

The popularity which Louis Blanc came to enjoy within a short time brought him, after the revolution of February, 1848, a post in the provisional government. Together with others, he rashly promised the workers that the Republic, within three months, would notably better their conditions. In order to realize such an end national workshops were instituted. But they were limited to the function of employment agencies which paid the workers a small allowance, and they never succeeded in offering enough jobs or sufficient compensation for work. The experiment failed. Naturally the situation worsened rapidly and the national workshops were soon abolished. This provoked the sanguinary days of June, 1848, in which about six thousand workers perished in addition to losses among the police.

Louis Blanc then left France for London. A bold opponent of Napoleon III, he did not return to France even when he was granted an amnesty. In his old age his revolutionary ideas mellowed and in 1871 he did not take part in the Paris Commune.

Besides *De l'organisation du travail*, he wrote a *Histoire de dix ans (1830–1840)*, in which he severely attacked the bourgeoisie then in power and King Louis Philippe, and a *Histoire de la révolution française*, in which he exalted the most burning revolutionaries.

A writer of decided communist tendencies was Étienne Cabet. He was born in Dijon in 1788 and became a lawyer. He went to Paris at the age of thirty, but did not win fame for himself. After the revolution of 1830 he was nominated Attorney for the Crown in Corsica by the Minister of Justice. In his installation speech he expressed opinions contrary to the regime in power and was compelled to resign. Later he was a candidate in the constituency of Dijon and was elected in 1831. In the Chamber of Deputies he was among the most violent members of the opposition and continued his attacks even in the extremist newspapers with which he actively collaborated. He was found guilty of insulting the king in the press and, rather than undergo the punishment, preferred to go for five years to England. There, having read More's *Utopia* and Morelly's works, he became a convert to communism and he published in 1842 a novel entitled *Voyage en Icarie*. In this novel Cabet imagined that a great English lord went to a faraway country called *Icarie*, which was organized along communist lines. In this country everyone worked on behalf of the state and the state provided for the needs of all without worrying about the quality and quantity of work each individual provided. According to the morality prevailing in Icarie, individual capacities were a gift of nature and there was no merit in one being more intelligent, willing, or active.

The political organization of that country naturally was democratic. A large assembly existed, elected by universal suffrage, to which was delegated every type of deliberation over all economic and political questions. This assembly was composed of two thousand people and was divided into several committees, each entrusted with a specific function. The executive power was assigned to an executive of fifteen members, elected by universal suffrage from among forty-five people nominated by the assembly.

The official religion in Icarie was an orthodox deism. The family was retained and there were no adulterers because, the dowry being abolished, all unions were inspired by love and had very happy consequences. Freedom of the press did not exist because, while useful in a bourgeois regime in permitting the dissemination of communist ideas, in a communist regime it turned out to be injurious. This social and political organization was arrived at through a revolution which occurred in 1782. It was a violent and bloody revolution, which the author described in detail.

The *Voyage en Icarie* had a remarkable but temporary success. It was soon forgotten and about forty years later was plagiarized by Bellamy in another novel entitled *Looking Backward*, which was translated into several languages and enjoyed a brief vogue. Almost no one was at the time aware of the plagiarism.

As previously pointed out, the diffusion of socialist ideas in France from 1830 to 1848 was much facilitated by industrial development, which caused large concentrations of workers to form in the large cities. In 1840 the first socialist congress, a forerunner of the future International of Karl Marx, was held in London. Even then attempts were made to reconcile socialism with Christianity and, especially, with Catholicism. This attempt was made by Buchez who in 1839 published a book entitled *Essai d'un traité complet de philosophie au point de vue de catholicisme et du progrès*, and continued to uphold the same system of ideas in the newspaper *L'Atelier*.

Besides the Christian-socialist movement of Buchez it is appropriate to recall the Christian-democratic movement championed by two priests, Lamennais and Lacordaire, plus the Comte de Montalembert. In the newspaper *L'Avenir* they upheld the absolute separation of church and state, universal suffrage, and freedom of teaching. Opposed by the French bishops, they appealed to the pope who ended by condemning their doctrines. Lacordaire and Montalembert yielded to the judgment of the pope, but not Lamennais. Because of his work entitled *Paroles d'un croyant*, in which he disputed the legitimacy of his condemnations, Lamennais ended by being excommunicated summarily.

It may be useful to remember that after Buchez the attempt to reconcile Christianity, and especially Catholicism, with socialism was taken up again in the Rhenish provinces in Germany and also in Italy, but with very mediocre results, since the two intellectual and moral currents to be reconciled are in reality irreconcilable. In truth Christianity is based on faith in the infinite, while socialism has its foundations in the materialistic conceptions of the eighteenth and nineteenth centuries. The one resolves the problem of social inequality with an invitation to the compassion of the rich; the other proposes equality as a right which the disinherited should realize even by the use of force. It is easily seen how substantial and profound are the differences between the two visions of the world and the two methods for the practical realization of the respective programs. It is not by chance, therefore, that communism, where already in power as in Russia, makes every effort to destroy religious sentiment.

A writer contemporary to those mentioned, but who might be classified among the anarchists rather than among the socialists, was Joseph Proudhon. Born in Besançon in 1809 of poor parents, he was allowed to attend classes in a school in his native city without tuition, but soon had to interrupt his studies and take up a trade in order to help his father. He became a typographer and this skill permitted him to extend his knowledge of culture and events. He commenced with biblical and theological studies but became excited over the study of political economy which he learned primarily from the books of Pellegrino Rossi. In his youth he suffered very much from a poverty that, as he himself confessed, lowers and debases character.

The work that gave him notoriety was his pamphlet *Qu'est-ce que la propriété?* (What Is Property?) published in 1840. In this Proudhon, repeating a phrase written about sixty years before by Brissot de Warville, replies that *property is theft;* but fundamentally he is opposed to communism and limits himself to substituting for property a type of temporary possession. Further, he was convinced that economic reforms had to precede political reforms.

Up to 1848 he continued to develop his ideas in two other works: *De la création de l'ordre dans l'humanité* and *Système des contradictions économiques ou Philosophie de la misère.* But although his motto was *destruam et aedificabo,** he was in reality violent and skillful in criticism, but uncertain, obscure, and confused in reconstruction. He attacked simultaneously all political and social institutions and opposed all religion. In *Philosophie de la*

* "I will destroy and I will build up"—Trans.

misère he sought to display his knowledge of Hegelian philosophy, the echo of which had already reached Paris, even while having only a superficial notion of it. Thus it was easy for his old friend Karl Marx to point out Proudhon's omissions and errors in a work published in Brussels entitled *La misère de la philosophie.*

After 1848 Proudhon went as an exile to Brussels and there published in 1861 a work entitled *La guerre et la paix,* in which he condemned Napoleon for favoring the accomplishment of Italian unity which he deemed contrary to the interests of France.

An anarchist still more radical than Proudhon and who followed him was the Russian Mikhail Bakunin. Of a noble family, he began as an artillery officer in the Russian army. Then he went to Paris where he had contacts with Proudhon and the French socialists. Recalled to his own country, he did not wish to return to Russia and his property was seized.

Bakunin advocated universal revolution, atheism, and the abolition of any authority. According to him, all means, even the most inhuman and ferocious, were lawful in order to achieve the desired end. In 1849 he participated in a communist insurrection in Dresden. Condemned to death simultaneously in Austria, Prussia, and Russia, he obtained commutation of the sentence to life imprisonment and was confined in a Russian fortress. He succeeded in escaping in 1857 and took refuge first in London and then in Switzerland. Then he went to Italy where he had several followers among them Carlo Cafiero. In the final stage of his life he clashed sharply with Marx and, above all, with Mazzini.

As can be seen in this chapter, the earliest representatives of all the revolutionary schools met, in part unintentionally, in Paris from 1830 to 1848, and then spread their doctrines throughout Europe, and successively, even to America. In Paris for the first time the French revolutionaries came into contact with their foreign disciples, especially Germans and Russians. Diverse as the programs of the reformers were, all were based on the faith that a complete reform of social institutions, which would accomplish the reign of absolute justice and complete equality, was near and achievable. This faith in progress evidently originated from the optimistic vision of human nature that the eighteenth century had elaborated and the nineteenth had inherited.

11

Nineteenth-Century Political Thought

The Italian Patriotic Writers

Turning to the Italian political writers who contributed toward creating that intellectual and moral movement that was the best preparation for the conquest of independence and the unity of Italy, we must begin by saying a few words about Gian Domenico Romagnosi. His name and works, if they are not completely forgotten, are not appreciated by the younger generation as they should be.

Romagnosi, who was born in 1781 and died in 1835, was a highly cultured man. His works deal with many and varied arguments, linking to historical, juridical, and political studies those of the physical sciences. His principal work with a direct connection to politics is the *Scienza delle costituzioni*. It was written about 1815 and published after his death in 1848. This work is clearly influenced by the thought of the age in which it was written. This is hardly avoidable in a book concerned with political science; however, the work is rich with profound and very original views.

The author tends to cherish a tempered monarchy based on a just equilibrium of the ruling forces prevailing in society. Some of these forces are of a material nature and others of a moral and intellectual nature. Wealth and military force would be among the first, and public opinion and religion among the second. The assembly, which would limit the royal power, must represent the moral and material forces prevalent in that age and society. Romagnosi believed that the legislator could not create at will any of these forces, but could certainly take advantage of action and direct their course.

Among these political forces, religion, property, and standing armies would be favorable to the principle of authority. Public opinion, personal property and civic militias would be favorable to the principle of liberty.[1]

From what has been said, it seems that Romagnosi knew intuitively what was the weak side of Montesquieu's theory of the separation of powers, for the Italian thinker, carrying it to its logical conclusion, argued that every organ that participated in sovereignty must have its base in some ruling force of the society. It is regrettable that the *Scienza delle costituzioni* was not published earlier and studied more carefully after its publication because, following its outline, Italian political science would have been able to cover much ground during the nineteenth century.

The writings of Vicenzo Gioberti, Cesare Balbo, and, above all, Giuseppe Mazzini undoubtedly exercised more effective influence over the Italians in the period of the national *Risorgimento* than that of Romagnosi.

Vicenzo Gioberti, born in Turin in 1801, began his philosophical studies at a very young age. Fulfilling his mother's wish he was ordained and nominated Chaplain to the Court of the King of Sardinia. However, the young priest had already been won over to liberal ideas and it seems that he even collaborated with Mazzini's *Giovane Italia*. When the Court received word of this he was released from his appointment. Leaving Italy, he went to France for quite a while and then for several years to Brussels where he taught philosophy and in 1843 published his famous book, *Primato morale e civile degli italiani*. In 1845 he published *Prolegomeni al Primato* and in 1847 *Gesuita moderno*. In the last two publications he replied rather harshly to critics of the work published in 1843 and especially to the Jesuits.

---

[1] In order clearly to understand this last thought of Romagnosi it is necessary to remember that from 1815 to 1848, and also some decades after, the civic militia, otherwise called the *national guard*, was deemed the guardian of the safety of the liberal constitutions, and precisely for this purpose, its institution was decreed in almost all statutes and fundamental laws of that period.

After Carlo Alberto promulgated the *statuto*,* Gioberti, returning triumphantly to his country, was first elected to and then elected president of the Subalpine Chamber of Deputies. Toward the end of the year 1848 and after the armistice of Salasco he received from Carlo Alberto the appointment to preside over the ministry formed at that time, but he resigned in February, 1849, deeming dangerous the revival of hostilities against Austria, which in fact led afterwards to the defeat of Novara. Having resumed the painful road of exile, he returned to France where he died in 1852, soon after publishing *Il rinnovamento civile d'Italia*, which can be considered his political testament.

In the *Primato* Gioberti, after exalting the past glories of Italy, prophesied the rise of Italian national unity in the form of a federation of the then existing Italian states presided over by the pontiff. To Italy, which had been the intellectual and moral guide of the civilized world during the period of pagan civilization and during that of Christian civilization, Gioberti assigned a new mission: revived and governed by a liberal regime, Italy would once again become the intellectual and moral center of humanity. A new civilization would rise from its bosom.

The pages of the *Primato*, written in passionate style and trembling with patriotism, were avidly read at the time by the educated Italian classes. In the years immediately preceding 1848 no other book was so warmly received as that by the Piedmontese priest. Such a success is explained by the spread of liberal ideas and by national sentiment, which, however, was then still combined in many minds with religious sentiment and a still lively enough attachment to the small states into which Italy was divided. Thus the philosophy of Gioberti, who sought the realization of constitutional reforms through a spontaneous grant by the princes rather than by violent revolution, and who also wanted Italian unity re-established while retaining respect for the church and without eliminating virtually any of the small states, was appreciated by all those—and they were many—who wanted Italian independence and the beginning of a liberal regime.

* Carlo Alberto was the King of Piedmont-Sardinia; when Italy was unified in 1861 the fundamental law or constitution of the new state was the *statuto* given by Carlo Alberto to his subjects in 1848.—Trans.

The weak point of the *Primato* was its failure to mention any way to free Italy from Austria, which occupied Lombardy and Venetia.

Pius IX, who was elected in 1846, at first appeared to be a liberal pontiff and invoked from God a benediction over Italy. The ideas of Gioberti seemed prophetic and the popularity of their author became very great. Then came the defeats of the Piedmontese army, and, with the exception of the Sardinian states, elsewhere in Italy the constitutional regimes were suppressed. The behavior of Pius IX soon showed the incompatibility of Gioberti's neo-Guelph program with the liberal and national one. Naturally the critics and the disillusioned did not spare attacks on the author of the *Primato*, who, exiled in Paris, answered by publishing a book, the *Rinnovamento civile d'Italia*, in which he disclosed how all the parties shared responsibility for the failures of the Italian cause in 1848 and 1849. But, at the same time, he recognized the necessity for joining all the diverse Italian states into one and thus of abolishing the temporal power of the pope. According to Gioberti, a religious renewal would be the necessary consequence of this abolition.

Another writer who exerted a certain influence on the thought of Italians in the period of the *Risorgimento* was Cesare Balbo.

Piedmontese like Gioberti, he was born in 1789 and died in 1853. In 1821 he was in Spain as a military attaché with the Sardinian legation. At that time he wrote a history of the war the Spanish had conducted from 1808 to 1814 against Napoleon. Later he published other historical works and a history of Italy. In 1844 appeared *Le Speranze d'Italia*, a book read by many, in which the author accepted the federal program of Gioberti. However, with more practical sense than Gioberti, he saw that the major obstacle to the independence of Italy was Austria and that it was necessary to drive her back beyond the Alps; thus he proposed that the presidency of the Italian confederation be entrusted to Piedmont, which among all the Italian states showed the best military organization.

In the last years of his life Balbo, elected a member of the Subalpine Parliament, sided with conservative positions and often opposed the politics of Cavour, especially when he sought to abolish the privileges of the ecclesiastics.

Giuseppe Mazzini obtained greater and longer lasting fame, whether as a writer or as a man of action, than Balbo or even Gioberti. He was born in Genoa on June 22, 1805. It seems that his first impulse to reflect on political and social problems came in 1821 when the Piedmontese refugees passed through Genoa, returning from the unsuccessful attempt to establish representative government in Piedmont. His first writings were of a literary type, but soon he entered the secret society of the Carbonari and faced his first police persecutions. After spending six months in jail, in 1830 he was forced into exile to Marseilles, where he undoubtedly had some contacts with the Saint-Simonians, who were then propagating their doctrine throughout all of France. In fact, it can be asserted that the influence of Saint-Simonian thought, and especially that of Pierre Leroux and Jean Reynaud, who for a time adhered to Saint-Simonianism, had a great impact on Mazzini's development.

However, it is necessary not to forget that from the first years of his political activity Mazzini allied to his program of political and social reforms one for the redemption of divided and oppressed nationalities, which included at that time Italy. Proof is found in a letter he sent to Carlo Alberto in 1831, in which with noble words he exhorted the King of Sardinia to expel the foreigners beyond the Alps.

It is difficult to summarize Mazzinian thought briefly since it includes a complete set of ideas concerning religion, as well as views on political and social and even international relations. Furthermore, his ideas are never presented as an organic whole, but must be traced back and coordinated in his numerous writings and, above all, in the very rich collection of letters.

According to Mazzini, there are two possible means by which man can arrive at knowledge of the truth: the first is the intuition of the human spirit when it is rid of greediness and common passions, and the second is universal consensus on fundamental concepts. These two methods lead the writer to acknowledge the existence of God, Father, Intellect, Love, Creator, and Educator of Humanity. To try to deny God's existence is folly, to try to prove it is blasphemy. God is revealed and expressed in humanity, in whose development he has written and writes in every epoch a line of his law.

The continual progress of mankind is the law given by God to life. This progress is achieved through a series of successive revelations; from belief to belief humanity acquires a clearer vision of its own mission. When a religion has exhausted its possibilities for development a new period begins with the revelation of new dogmas. These are foreseen first by precursors, but they conquer the spirit of the multitudes when they become incarnate in the life of one or several individuals privileged because of love and virtue. The new revelation is preceded by a period of crisis, during which the old religion decays, but the kind of truth that it contains remains indelible.

The various religious phases through which humanity has passed are represented by fetishism, polytheism, and Christianity. The nineteenth century is one of those periods of crisis that precedes a new religious revelation that will raise the moral level of the world. This revelation will occur in a nation that will be a teacher to all the others and will be promulgated by a group of precursors and apostles.

The new religion will acknowledge the immortality of the soul but without an eternity of punishment, and by means of successive reincarnations every individual will continually raise his moral level. It will be above all the religion of duty, and by practicing it every individual will contribute to the moral progress of humanity.

In the new epoch being prepared, the instinct of association will be more and more developed. There will not be communism, but wealth will be proportioned to the work of each individual and capital will no longer exploit work but will be associated with it. It is worth noting that as he grew older Mazzini continually pointed out his divergences from Marxist socialism and the revolutionary anarchism of Bakunin.

In politics Mazzini was a democratic republican, because he claimed that equitable association could not exist except among individuals perfectly equal in rights and in duties. God would be the true sovereign and the nation the true interpreter of divine law: universal suffrage would be the custom according to which the people, good and infallible because of God's inspiration, would entrust the direction of the nation to the best in terms of judgment and virtue.

Mazzini, in fact, replaced the divine right of kings with the divine right of the people. He has even been accused of mysticism and utopianism because he believed in the regeneration of economic and political relationships after an approaching moral elevation of humanity. Although the accuracy of his assertions and his previsions can be legitimately doubted, at the same time it cannot be denied that they are less absurd than those of the people who put their trust in communist institutions or in anarchy, considering them sure ways of attaining the moral elevation of humanity.

According to Mazzini, nations would constitute the various organs of humanity: to each God would entrust part of the regenerating program. In Europe he found thirteen or fourteen nationalities that would correspond to as many states. Austria and Turkey must disappear, because they were not based on national homogeneity but were created by material force and diplomacy.

Among all the nations Italy would have the highest mission, that of beginning the new epoch and providing the intellectual and moral guide to Europe and thus to the world.

Mazzini's thought, in addition to being one of the principal factors in the Italian national reawakening to the period of the *Risorgimento,* aroused much sympathy for the Italian cause in other European countries, especially in England and even in the United States of America. The great apostle died on March 10, 1872. Before dying, he censured with burning sentences the leaders and events of the Paris Commune.

Tocqueville, Comte, and Herbert Spencer

Not all the French political writers who in the first half of the nineteenth century and the years immediately following exercised great influence on the minds of their contemporaries belonged to the various socialist schools. Among those occupying other positions it is necessary to remember Alexis de Tocqueville and August Comte for the fame, in part merited, that they acquired.

Tocqueville, who was born in 1805 and died in 1859, became

famous with a work published partly in 1835 and partly in 1840, entitled *Democracy in America*. In 1831 he had gone to the United States to study the penitentiary system and during his stay was at leisure to study the institutions and public and private customs of that country in which democratic ideas more and more prevailed. The French thinker decided to observe objectively the consequences of this political course. He pointed out the advantages and the dangers of democracy and, at the same time, appeared to be convinced that the move toward universal suffrage as the only base for public power, in America and perhaps even in France, was fatal and inevitable.

While recognizing in Tocqueville the quality of impartial observer generally attributed to him by his contemporaries, one cannot deny that his *Democracy in America* is outdated today. Indeed when Tocqueville was in the great republic of North America—that is, in 1831 and 1832—universal suffrage had either not been generally adopted or had been in effect too short a time for the consequences of its systematic application to be manifest. In fact, in the New England states and in almost all the oldest colonies it was instituted in the decade from 1830 to 1840, and in those places further west and of more recent formation it had been in effect for hardly a generation.

Tocqueville noted that in America the distance separating wealth from poverty was much less than in Europe, yet he did not foresee that within a few decades this was to change until it surpassed that of Europe. He did not attribute proper importance to the fact that America at that time still possessed much unoccupied, fertile land where any man of bold and enterprising character could easily find his way and improve his own position. Finally, so far as political equality was concerned, the author of *Democracy in America* could not help noticing that even in the states of the north, where Negro slavery had been abolished, and where Negroes, at least theoretically, were admitted to the electorate, a Negro could go to vote only at the risk of losing his life.[1]

Tocqueville entered politics in 1849 and became Minister of Foreign Affairs in one of the governments of Louis Napoleon Bona-

[1] See *Democracy in America*, Part II, Chapter 10.

parte, then President of the French Republic.* While he held this position, the French expedition against the Roman Republic took place. Withdrawing from active politics after the *coup d'état* of December 2, 1851, he published in 1857 his work, *L'ancien régime et la révolution*, in which he showed an originality of view and maturity of judgment much superior to that appearing in his youthful work. His was the first truly scientific study of the French Revolution, and it can be said that with it Tocqueville pointed the way to Taine, who adopted, developed, and improved the method of his predecessor in his volumes entitled *Les origines de la France contemporaine*.

Another French writer who attained such fame in the middle of the nineteenth century and the decades immediately following as to be deemed the founder of sociology and the positivist method was August Comte. He was born in Montpellier in 1798 and died in 1857. Having moved at a very young age to Paris, he was admitted to the polytechnic school from which he was then expelled for his ultrademocratic ideas. In 1817 he became acquainted with Saint-Simon, who exerted a great deal of influence on his intellectual formation, and had continuous contact with him until 1824, when he was brusquely separated from the teacher.

In 1822, while still collaborating with Saint-Simon, Comte had published a short work titled *System of Positive Polity*, in which are already presented the ideas that he was to develop when he reached his scientific maturity. But his principal work was beyond a doubt the *Positive Philosophy*, which he published in six volumes from 1839 to 1842.

In this work the author sought to reconstruct the scientific history of humanity and to identify the stage of maturity that the various branches of human knowledge had reached at the time. According to Comte, the intellectual studies are three: the theological, the metaphysical, and the positive. The theological stage exists when man explains natural phenomena and social events, such as pestilences, famines, victories, or defeats, as resulting from the intervention of divine or superhuman beings. The metaphysical phase exists when these events are explained by attributing them to primary

---

* This sentence, omitted in the edition translated, has been restored from an earlier edition.—Trans.

causes, which are either the fruits of the imagination or of superficial and unconnected observation as, for example, when it is believed that the destinies of individuals and nations depend on the conjunction of the planets or that the health of the human body on the combination of humors. Finally, the positive period is reached when, abandoning, if necessary, recognition of the primary causes of these facts, the laws that govern them are carefully studied and placed at the service of humanity.

According to Comte, there are six branches of human knowledge: mathematics, astronomy, physics, chemistry, biology, and sociology. The first are simpler sciences, the others by degrees more complicated, and the last two, especially sociology, had not yet reached the positive period.

It cannot be denied that the three intellectual stages noted by Comte correspond to reality but it can be observed that the stages, rather than being neatly distributed in differing historical periods as our author suggests, may coexist in the very same period and nation. In fact, even today in the most civilized countries we may easily find people who believe in miracles and who are thus in the theological period, and others who believe that the wealth of a nation consists exclusively of the quantity of metals it possesses and thus place themselves in the metaphysical period. The one as much as the others is regulated in other matters according to scientific norms even if it ignores, as often happens, how such norms have been established. On the other hand, even the most ignorant savage who believes that the sorcerer of the tribe can produce rain and remove illnesses cannot remain alive without some positive knowledge through which to orient himself in deserts or forests and by which he succeeds in capturing the animals on which he feeds. Thus, no more can be asserted on the subject except that, with the development of culture, scientific interpretations of natural and social deeds will gradually, but perhaps never completely, substitute for theological and metaphysical ones.

Nor can it be denied that Comte's assertion concerning the immaturity of sociology, in contrast to the natural sciences, is correct. It can also be admitted that this is due in part to the greater complexity of this branch of knowledge, although even the French philosopher would have had to recognize that the most difficult observations for man to make are those in which he must observe himself. And he should also have pointed out that while in the natural sciences the observer can avail himself of the experiment—that is, the artificial reproduction in a scientific study of a phenomenon—in the social sciences he can make use only of the experience. Thus he must limit himself to studying the event, where, when, and how it spontaneously happens. No one, for example, will claim that a regime like that now existing in Russia is desired or that it could be produced artificially with the intention of observing the practical effects of a collectivist state.

The last important work by Comte is entitled like the first *System of Positive Polity*, or *Treatise on Sociology*. It was published from 1851 to 1854 in four volumes and contains a comprehensive plan for the religious and political reorganization of society. According to Comte, the intellectual and moral direction of civilized nations ought to belong to a priesthood of scientists, assisted on the material side by the directors of industries, who were to be recruited by co-option since Comte was opposed to democracy and believed that the delegation of sovereign powers through popular suffrage was a revolutionary act to be avoided at all costs. Furthermore, returning in this work to the law of the three intellectual stages, he attributed to classical antiquity the theological state with its contemporary prevalence of polytheism and aggressive militarism, to the Middle Ages the metaphysical phase with a prevalence of monotheism and feudalism, which, according to Comte, could be considered as defensive militarism. Finally, the modern epoch would enter in the positive period and would replace militarism, whether aggressive or defensive, with industrialism.

Even a shallow knowledge of world history is sufficient to demonstrate the groundlessness of these claims. For example, it cannot be admitted that classical antiquity, especially in its greater periods, was more affected by the theological method than the Middle Ages, and the link between aggressive militarism and polytheism and between defensive militarism and monotheism can be deemed absurd. He neglected, among many other things, the significant part that Islamic monotheism, in early times eminently aggressive, played in the history of the world.

Several writers have accused Comte of plagiarizing from

Saint-Simon. From the summary we have made of his thought it is evident that some fundamental concepts of the philosopher from Montpellier show a close relationship to those of the man who was for seven years his teacher. But it is also necessary to recognize that, in the vastness of his culture, his method, and his style, the student was much superior to the master and gave his ideas a development and a coordination that Saint-Simon would not have known how to achieve. And in considerable part the diffusion of Comte's ideas in the second half of the last century among many of the educated people of western Europe were due to these merits of the writer.

An author who sought to develop Comte's ideas on positivism and on the contrast between the military and the industrial state was the Englishman Herbert Spencer, who was born in 1824 and who died in 1904. He showed strongly the influence of Darwinism which, in that period, had won the allegiance of a large proportion of the promoters of the natural sciences. It is important to realize that in the period from 1870 to 1895 no writer in the social sciences had greater fame than Spencer, especially in Italy, and that perhaps today no one is more forgotten.

In his first work pertaining to sociology, or what could more properly be called political science, Spencer set forth the obstacles that must be conquered by the promoters of this discipline. According to the author, these were in part objective and in part subjective. The former were caused by the complexity of the material to be treated, the latter by the state of mind of the scholar who deals with it. Because if he is to be able to interpret social facts correctly, he must first of all rid himself of all *a priori* ideas, all opinions, and all the passions implanted in him by the atmosphere in which he has lived and lives. He should show no preference for a particular religion, political party, social class, or nation. And perhaps it might have been opportune to add that he should have no interest in upholding some given thesis or opposing another if this can aid or impair the success of the book and especially its author.

According to Spencer, in addition to this negative preparation the sociologist should prepare himself positively through the study of biology and psychology; the former in order to comprehend the close relationships between the organism of the human individual and the social organism, the latter in order to be able through an education to speed the effects of the evolution that slowly but surely guides humanity toward superior political arrangements.

Most important are the *Principles of Sociology*, published in several volumes during the full maturity of the writer but left unfinished. In this work Spencer begins with the principle that the evolution of human societies is a continuation of the evolution that has acted and acts in the extrahuman world and that this evolution occurs through the slow and progressive differentiation of the vital organs. These are internal and external. The first serve for defense and attack, the others for the feeding of the social body. Through the prevalence of one or the other, there would exist societies of a military type founded on compulsion, or those of an industrial type based on contract. The struggle for survival among the various societies, attributing victory to those better organized, would produce first the military type and then the industrial.

It is difficult to provide an exhaustive criticism of these concepts in a few pages. We will only say that the characteristics that, according to Spencer, distinguish the industrial type from the military are very unclear. For example, when he asserts that organization of the military type is coercive and that of the industrial type spontaneous, he forgets that any political organization is at one and the same spontaneous, because it is a consequence of the sociable nature of man, and coercive, because man is not able to live without belonging to some, even primitive, political organization. Furthermore, Spencer ignores almost completely or neglects the history of the great political organisms that great civilizations have created or developed, and rests almost all his assertions on reports of travelers describing the customs and institutions of barbarians and savages; he forgets that it is not in simple and primitive organisms that the laws regulating the life of complex and developed organisms can be found. Lastly, it would not be risky to assert that the least questionable of Spencer's ideas are those bearing a close relationship to the ideas of Comte, who in turn had drawn heavily upon the intellectual inheritance of Saint-Simon.

12

Socialism
and Karl Marx

The First German Socialist Writers and
Ferdinand Lassalle

There was no lack of socialist writers in Germany in the nineteenth century. The most famous of these were Karl Marx and
Ferdinand Lassalle.

Before beginning a discussion of these writers it is useful to
remember that the most notable advocates of socialism in that
country were Jews, and this is because the moral situation of the
Jews there was still quite difficult. They were excluded from the
most important public offices and, at the same time, scorned and
feared by the Prussian nobility because of their financial power. All
this pushed them instinctively toward rebellion. Secondly, it is necessary to bear in mind that the democratic-socialist current in the past
century experienced its major development in the Rhenish countries
which were in close contact with France.

A philosopher who was only occasionally concerned with
politics was Johann Gottlieb Fichte, born in 1762 and who died in
1814. In 1793 he published a work entitled *Beiträge zur Berichtigung
der Urtheile des Publicums über die französische Revolution*, in
which he raised the question of the legitimacy of revolution in
general. In this book he argued that it is impossible to have any
absolutely unvarying constitution, for every constitution is a product
of the time and of the needs of the moment, and he derived the right

to insurrection from the pre-existence of a social contract. The idea of a contract is, according to him, contained in the idea of the state. It alone gives rights and imposes duties.

In 1797 he published *Grundlage des Naturrechts* in which, among other things, he says that he who has nothing has the right to take something. In conclusion, Fichte shows himself in this work to be a supporter of representative government, but then makes the form of government depend on the degree of respect for legality to which a nation has arrived and he deems admissible every constitution that offers no hindrance to general progress and the development of the faculties of every citizen.

The complete defeat of the Prussian army at Jena in 1806 by Napoleon caused the birth or reawakening in Fichte of patriotic feelings, so that he published in 1806 his *Reden an die deutsche Nation*, exhorting his fellow-countrymen to have confidence in the future intellectual and political greatness of Germany. He died in 1814 from typhus contracted in a military hospital where his wife had gone to care for wounded Prussians.

After Fichte it is necessary to recall Weitling, a worker, who from 1838 to 1847 published several works of a socialist nature in which the influence of the French Socialists and especially of Fourier, Buonarroti, and Cabet is evident.

Karl Marlo was the pseudonym under which Winkelblech published in the same period a book of sentimental tone which contained an interesting description of the miseries of the worker. The author tries to demonstrate that in the distribution of the goods produced by his work the manual laborer is victimized by the capitalist, and declares himself a supporter of a revision of the system of distribution between workers and capitalists.

Among the socialist writers or sympathizers, we may also recall Rodbertus, a Prussian nobleman who was also a minister in Prussia in 1848. While he did not write any systematic works, his political and social ideas are spread in the letters, pamphlets, and newspaper articles that he published at various times. Rodbertus notes the disadvantageous position that the worker finds himself in before the capitalist. The capitalist can employ his capital at the most opportune moment and can also for some time keep it inactive without suffering notable loss, but the worker has only his working effort to make wealth, which in the days when he is not employed remains unproductive.

This argument by Rodbertus corresponds to the truth to a degree. However, it can also happen that the capitalist has urgent and pressing need of the laborer's work, as occurs, for example, in the cultivation of rice, in which, if the crop is not harvested on the days when the plant has reached maturity, all the enormous capital investment is lost. Lastly, Rodbertus, in whose writings a desire for peace and social harmony appears, invoked the intervention of the state in order to eliminate the conflict between capital and labor.

Ferdinand Lassalle was the son of a Jewish banker from Breslau. From his early years he showed a rebellious character, so much so that he was thrown out of the commercial school that he attended. He possessed a truly extraordinary facility for learning, so that he was quickly able to obtain his degree in philosophy at the University of Berlin. It is worth noting that Marx as well as Lassalle took his degree in philosophy and that in the German universities the faculty of philosophy includes political economy among its disciplines.

After writing some pamphlets of little importance, Lassalle went at a very young age to Paris where he made contact with the revolutionary elements, not only French but also Russian and German, who then had their center in the French capital. Returning to Germany in 1846 at the age of twenty-one he had a love affair with a Countess von Hatzfeldt, who initiated a lawsuit for separation from her husband. It happened that some important documents in the hands of the husband were stolen by people who, it was discovered, were friends of Lassalle. He was therefore suspected of having instigated the crime and was brought to trial, but in the end was acquitted. However, this acquittal was not repeated in his other trials, which were based upon his publications in the press and which brought him a sentence of six months in jail.

Meanwhile the separation trial between Countess von Hatzfeldt and her husband continued; Lassalle was the Countess' attorney and his pleadings had great success. Finally in 1854 the case was won by the Countess. As an honorarium to her lawyer, she gave Lassalle a sum sufficient to provide him with an annual income of fifteen thousand lire in gold.

Afterwards he published a work on the philosophy of Heraclitus. Of the works of this philosopher only a few fragments—famed for their obscurity—have remained. His contemporaries called him Heraclitus the Obscure. This work, however, gave Lassalle occasion to demonstrate a profound philological and philosophical erudition which made his name known among the German intellectual class.

In 1859, Lassalle participated in the political reawakening of Germany with a historical drama entitled *Franz von Sickingen*. In this play, in which the action occurs at the beginnings of German Protestantism, the author advocates the creation of a unitary and Protestant German empire. This program corresponded to the one that Prussia, under the leadership of Bismarck, was to realize a few years later.

Another work written by Lassalle in this period was *Das system der erworbenen Rechte*. In this book he claimed that right had its own life which is developed under the empire of well-defined laws. Furthermore, he asserted that the right to property has to be disciplined and limited according to the particular exigencies of society.

As is evident, these ideas of Lassalle were scarcely original, since as far as the life and evolution of law are concerned, the phenomenon had already been clearly ascertained by Savigny, and, as for the limitation of the rights of property in the name of the state, it can be noted that it had almost always occurred, especially after the application of the Napoleonic code.

Lassalle, after the revival of his political activity, belonged at first to the Progressive Party which was a supporter of the parliamentary regime and was opposed to Bismarck, who defended the pure constitutional regime. Thus the progressives did not want the action of Parliament to be limited only to approval of the budget and laws, but sought to extend the parliamentary power to all aspects of political life. Bismarck, on the other hand, energetically denied any such power to Parliament and refused to recognize as politically effective a vote of no confidence by the elected chamber in the government. This struggle developed in acute form from 1860 to 1866, until, after the war against Austria and the victory of Sadowa, the elected chamber acknowledged its defeat and approved in a single sitting the budgets for six fiscal years. From that time until 1918, first in Prussia and then in all of Germany, the constitutional regime prevailed over the parliamentary one.

Lassalle took an active part in the struggle described above and his policy, which was very radical, gave occasion to trials at his expense. His apologia, which was printed and spread throughout all of Germany, increased his popularity. A time came when the violent measures that he proposed—for example, the refusal to pay taxes—placed him in conflict with his party colleagues. He then decided to abandon the Progressive Party and conceived and publicized his *Working Man's Program*.

In this program Lassalle proposed universal suffrage as a means of achieving sociopolitical reforms. These reforms were to consist of the organization of the workers in producers' cooperatives which would be subsidized by the state through a loan of three hundred million marks. For these ideas Lassalle was opposed to Schulze-Delitzsch, head of the German Liberal Party, who rejected state intervention in economic relations between capital and labor. And from this very controversy with Schulze-Delitzsch emerged Lassalle's work *Herr Bastiat Schulze-Delitzsch, oder Kapital und Arbeit.*

In the dispute between Lassalle and Schulze-Delitzsch, the latter had argued that the workers should organize themselves in producers' cooperatives without the help of the state, forming the capital of the cooperatives with their savings. Responding to these theses Lassalle formulated the so-called *iron law of wages*, which from that point became one of the main points of socialist doctrines.

Bearing in mind Malthus' theory, Lassalle affirmed that the population tended to increase in greater proportion than did capital; from this he deduced that the workers, because of the competition of the unemployed, must content themselves with a minimum salary, hardly sufficient to live on or to raise a family. In these conditions saving was impossible and state intervention became necessary.

Although in the struggle over the emergence of the parliamentary regime in Prussia Lassalle had been an adversary of Bismarck, in the last years of his life he moved near to the "Iron Chancellor." If on many things the two men were far apart, on others they had points of view in common.

Bismarck was not opposed to universal suffrage, which he

adopted in the German constitution of 1871, nor to the intervention of the state in relations between capital and labor. Some laws that he sought—for example, limitations on the work day and on female and child labor, workers' old-age insurance—bear witness to his inclinations. Furthermore, Bismarck worked for the unity of Germany. Lassalle was an ardent exponent of such unity and had advocated it in his drama *Franz von Sickingen.* Both people shared many points in common: both deemed force a necessary means to realize political reforms, and both were men of action. And if Lassalle now and then proposed violent action, Bismarck did not refrain from affirming before a commission of the Prussian Parliament that German unity would be realized with iron and fire. It is certain that toward the end of 1863 and in the first months of 1864 Lassalle had several long meetings with Bismarck, as the latter acknowledged in 1878 during a sitting of the Reichstag.

In 1862, in his discourse on the constitution, Lassalle argued that constitutions should not be interpreted literally, but according to their spirit, because behind every political organ a political force must exist that supports it. Thus in a representative regime the influence of the king and of the elective chamber is proportionate to the strength of the political forces standing behind the king or the chamber. If, instead, behind the constitutional organs corresponding political forces do not exist, their power, notwithstanding the norms written into the constitutional document, will in fact amount to almost nothing. This is a very profound idea which reveals in Lassalle a lucid, acute, and essentially realistic mind.

In 1863 Lassalle founded the Universal German Working Men's Union, which sought to obtain in Germany universal suffrage and the intervention of the state on behalf of manual workers. Almost contemporaneously Marx had founded the First International, which proposed to unite proletarian forces throughout the world. This divergence of views necessarily sharpened the dissension latent up to that time between the two great agitators. This discord was also owed to the jealousy Marx felt for Lassalle.[1]

---

[1] While Lassalle, until the moment of breaking off their relations, was a sincere friend of Marx, praised his works publicly, entertained him in his home when Marx came to Berlin, and at times even helped him financially, Marx on the other hand praised Lassalle's works and behavior when he wrote to

In the year 1864 Lassalle's life was tragically ended in its prime. After his relationship with Countess von Hatzfeldt, which had been or had become a platonic friendship, he sought to marry a young Russian intellectual, who, however, rejected him. In 1864 he fell madly in love with the daughter of a Bavarian diplomat, Helene Dönniges, who at first returned his love but later, since her parents were opposed to a marriage with a Jewish revolutionary, tried to cut off all contact with him and became engaged to a Rumanian aristocrat, a certain Yanco Racowitza. Lassalle then wrote a violent and insulting letter to Helene's father, who gave it to his daughter's fiancé, who challenged Lassalle to a duel. In the duel Lassalle was wounded and two days later he died.

With the death of Lassalle control of the German working-class movement gravitated to Marx. It is probable that if his rival had lived, German socialism would have retained a more national and less cosmopolitan character.

Karl Marx, the Capital, and Historical Materialism

Karl Marx, who was born in Trier in the Rhineland on May 5, 1818, belonged to a well-to-do Jewish family. When he was barely five years old his father, with the entire family, was converted to Protestantism, changing the old surname of Mordechai to Marx.

Achille Loria, who has written an excellent biography of Marx, has observed on this subject that the wealthy German Jews, out of a love for justice, often advocated socialist doctrines. As we have already noted, the love of justice was joined to the reaction against humiliations at the hands of the German nobility, especially Prussian, and the unjustified exclusions of which the Jews were victims. Thus, they could not become army officers, nor could they be admitted to the magistracy or a diplomatic career. And not always was a recent conversion to Christianity enough to forget the origin of the converts.

---

him and at the same time judged him severely in letters sent to others. Not even after Lassalle's death did he completely cease denouncing him.

Young Marx followed a regular course of studies and took his degree in philosophy, writing a thesis on the philosophy of Epicurus. He then wrote some articles on social subjects in the *Rheinische Zeitung* and in 1844, already married to the daughter of a Prussian noble, Baron Westphalen, went to Paris. Here he had occasion to meet Proudhon, who introduced him to that cosmopolitan circle of French, Italians, Germans, and Russians who in the capital of France professed more or less revolutionary and socialist ideas. The influence of these people was soon felt by the young Marx, already by nature predisposed to rebellion, and the Parisian socialists soon numbered him among their comrades.

Subsequently the Prussian ambassador, informed of Marx's revolutionary activity, secured his expulsion from France. He then went to Brussels where he published a work on the poverty of philosophy. It contained a harsh criticism of Proudhon's work *Philosophie de la misère*, in which Proudhon had unsuccessfully tried to demonstrate his profound knowledge of the doctrines of Hegel.

The revolution of 1848 broke out and Marx returned to Paris. In the same year, together with Engels, he compiled his famous *Communist Manifesto*. In it were introduced the seeds of two fundamental ideas, which later, as subsequently developed, were to become two main points of the Marxist system. The first referred to the relations between capital and labor, which it said were not arbitrary, but the inevitable products of the instruments and methods used in production. The second idea maintained that the entire social, judicial, religious, and political framework of society was a consequence of the economic factor and thus of the technique of production.

In the same year revolutionary agitations broke out in the Rhenish provinces. Marx returned to his country and founded the *Neue Rheinische Zeitung* in which he presented his ideas, but the revolutionary ferment ceased and he suffered persecutions by the police. To escape these he was compelled to return to France. The Prussian government requested his extradition. The French government limited itself to requiring Marx either to live in Brittany, a Catholic region, thus hostile to socialist theories, or to leave French territory. Marx preferred to abandon France and went to London.

In London he did not experience police persecutions but he often suffered from misery, and perhaps the claim of some of his biographers attributing the harshness of character of the author of the *Capital* to these economic difficulties is in part true. For a time he was compelled to write articles for newspapers and magazines, but the earnings realized from these essays would have been insufficient without the generous help of admirers and friends, among them Engels and Lassalle.

In 1859 Marx began the publication of a volume that had as a theme the *Critique of Political Economy*. Of this book only the introduction appeared in which he developed and explained the two concepts already identified in the *Communist Manifesto:* that is, the dependence of the relations between employers and workers upon the technique of economic production, and the other principle according to which the entire political, juridical, and religious framework of a society is seen in a given age as a consequence of the type of economic organization realized by that society. This doctrine then assumed the name of *historical materialism.*

Following through the logic of this conception, the author tries to demonstrate in the same book that systems of economic production have gone through four phases: the Asiatic, that of classical antiquity, the medieval, and the present one—that is, the bourgeois phase. In each phase economic transformation was followed by a change in the civilization. Further, beginning with the first, he notes that in each of these four historical periods were born the seeds that, developing, have produced after violent struggles and social crises the successive era. According to this law, the end of the bourgeois phase would be its transformation into a communist regime, which would close what Marx called the prehistory of human society.

But the work that gave Marx world fame was the first volume of the *Capital,* written in England and published in 1867. To summarize it in a few pages is difficult, because the ideas contained in it are not systematically and separately set forth, but are interwoven in almost all parts of the book. Some of the theses upheld in the *Capital* are strictly of an economic nature, while others are of a sociological nature and are the exposition of a complete system for interpretation of universal history.

In the economic section Marx begins by inquiring into the origin of capital, which, according to some economists who were his contemporaries, was the result of savings by those who possessed capital or of savings by their ancestors. Marx claims that the first capitalistic accumulations had their origin in the beginning of the sixteenth century, especially in England, a country the author of the *Capital* considered typical for the study of the phenomenon. In England in that period vast areas formerly used for cultivation of grain were made into pasture for the breeding of sheep, whose wool was actively sought and paid for at high prices by the manufacturers of woolen cloths in Flanders. And, since pasture land requires far fewer workers than are needed for growing grain, a considerable number of workers were at once left unemployed and compelled to settle in the cities where they offered their labor for very low wages.

Evidently the description of English economic conditions at the beginning of the sixteenth century was based upon Thomas More's account in the *Utopia*.

After seeking to demonstrate the immoral origins of the original capital, Marx attempted to prove that capital increased continuously because the capitalist takes away from the worker a part of the recompense owed him for his labor. This argument is based on a theory of the economist David Ricardo, that the value of an object is equal to its cost of production; i.e., to the cost of the raw material contained in it plus the cost of the quantity of work put into making it. Thus, for example, the price of a hat would be the sum of the cost of the raw material plus the interest on the capital employed in the factory, plus the work of the wool-comber, plus that of the dyer, and so on. Now, according to Marx, if the contractor, after paying for the raw material and after deducting the interest on the invested capital, derived any profit, this profit could only be a part of the reward due to the laborer for his work and was taken from him. This theory, which seeks to demonstrate that the profit of the capitalist corresponds to an equivalent of work not paid for, was called the theory of *Mehrwert*, or *surplus value*.

In the sociological section, Marx, developing the ideas already contained in the *Communist Manifesto* and the *Critique of Political Economy*, tried to demonstrate their truth with historical examples. According to Marx, the changes in the relations between workers and employers during the four epochs—Asiatic, Greek, feudal, and bourgeois—were and are determined by the technique of production, and furthermore, every social and political revolution had as its cause an economic change.

Lastly, in every epoch Marx sees the seeds of the economic and social system that must then triumph in the following epoch. In the present era, which, as we have seen in his *Critique of Political Economy* he called the *bourgeois* era, he sees the germs of another age that will bring about communism. It is in fact inevitable that in the bourgeois society, because of the competition among the contractors themselves, a concentration of capital in the hands of an always diminishing number of individuals will occur and there will be, therefore, a steady increase in the number of proletarians. Continuing this process, it is inevitable that a day will come in which in front of a minimum number of capitalists will be found the immense crowd of proletarians. It will be easy for them then to destroy the capitalist regime and cause the state to become the only possessor of capital and the instruments of production. The establishment of the communist regime will therefore be inevitable.

What we have said is in schematic lines the contents of the *Capital*. We will now examine one after the other the various assertions made by Marx, pointing out within the limits of our ability the truth and error they contain.

So far as the origin of capital is concerned it is necessary, first of all, to observe that the first capitalistic accumulations did not take place only in England in the sixteenth century, but that all civilizations, even the oldest, had some capital, now more, now less. Thus they spent their savings in the creation of instruments of production. And it is unquestionably true that without saving there could not be capital. What can be admitted is that under certain conditions it is easy to save, while under others—that it, when we are poor—it is very difficult. It can also be admitted that capital does not always remain in the hands of those who have formed it by saving and that it slips out of the hands of those who do not know how to utilize it.

Is it true then that the profit realized by the contractor when business goes well—that is, the *surplus value*—is a theft which he executes to the damage of the worker? In the large majority of cases it is not true, and Marx, in order to arrive at this conclusion, found it necessary to disregard observation of many facts.

A first observation easily seen is the relationship between the number of workers and the quantity of capital invested. There are industries that employ many machines and very few workers and there are many others that employ many workers and very few machines. Now, if the profit of the capitalist contractor corresponded to the total of salaries not paid to the workers, it is evident that where the workers are more numerous the profits ought to be greater. Ordinarily this is not the case; more often the contrary occurs.

We have seen that Marx leans on the theory of the economist Ricardo, who had claimed that the value in exchange of an object is proportionate to the quantity of work employed to produce it; but the author of the *Capital* has forgotten to add that Ricardo took into consideration the quality as well as the quantity of work and admitted that this also was one of the elements entering into the determination of value.[1] In fact, the examples that could be cited to demonstrate that the quality of work can influence the determination of the value of a service or of a commodity are infinite. A mediocre surgeon, or one with that reputation, often works more than a famous colleague, yet still his professional earnings are noticeably less. And the same can be said of two painters and even of two tailors or two shoemakers, of whom one is in more demand than the other.

Further, notwithstanding that the quantity and quality of the work may be the same, the cost of production of a commodity can vary a great deal. If a field is devastated by hail that has halved the harvest, the cultivator must sell his grain at the same price, even though it cost him more, as that of his neighbor who did not suffer any damage. Equally obvious is the influence that the price of grain in an exporting country exerts over the price to the importer, independently of the cost of national production of grain.

The truth is, therefore, that the value of a commodity or of a service is the result of a combination of elements, all of which more or less influence the determination of relative abundance or relative scarcity, or, in other words, the equilibrium between demand and supply.

In order to affirm then that the profit of the capitalist contrac-

---

[1] It can be seen that in the second edition of his treatise Ricardo admits that "work of a different quality is paid for in a different way."

tor is made up of a part of the salary taken from the worker, it is necessary to close our eyes to recognition of a very important co-efficient of industrial production, and, in many cases, of agricultural production; that is, the great advantages of what the economists have called *division of labor*, and what would perhaps be better called *organization of labor*. The classical example of the pin factory is often cited. A dozen workers, each of whom attends to one of the various tasks necessary to the manufacture of a pin, obtain a result one hundred times better than that obtained if each one of the workers by himself makes the entire pin. Now this is only one of many examples of the results which can be achieved through the organization of labor. One hundred organized workers can obtain, not only in quantity but also in quality, a result immensely superior to that reached if each one of the hundred workers works in isolation and on his own account. Given this result, it is natural that a part of the profit goes to benefit the organizer, especially as managing capacity is a rare quality, and on it depends, in large part, the success of an industrial and even an agricultural enterprise.

Next we come to *historical materialism*. This is based upon two assertions: on the basis of the first that relations between employees and employers depend on the technique of production; through the second, the conclusion that the entire political, religious, and juridical organization of a society is a consequence of the prevailing type of economic organization.

In the first assertion there is only partial truth, for the relations between employers and employees are not always exclusively or even principally determined by the technique of production, but show the influence of other moral and material elements. Thus, for example, it cannot be denied that Christianity [2] has contributed a great deal to the disappearance of slavery, even if slowly, in central and western Europe, and that the humanitarianism of the nineteenth century contributed much to its disappearance in the colonies. And it is important not to forget that toward the middle of the fourteenth century, without any change in the technique of production, there was almost a doubling of salaries in consequence of the scarcity of labor caused by the destruction of the black plague.

---

[2] It is known that in the Middle Ages instances were not rare in which the testator on his death bed liberated his slaves and emancipated his serfs.

Still more numerous are the examples that could be cited against the second assertion since very frequently very important changes in human societies have occurred without corresponding mutations in the relations between the possessors of the instruments of production and the manual laborers.

The Roman Republic, for example, was transformed into the empire of Augustus and his successors, and therefore, the classical city-state became an organism with a bureaucratic basis, without the systems of production being modified and without the laws regulating property and the distribution of wealth being altered. The only change that occurred, and that not generally, was within the group who were owners, because especially after the second civil war much private property was confiscated and distributed to the soldiers of the triumvirs.

It is difficult to cite an instance of the dissolution of an entire society comparable in importance to the fall of the Roman Empire in the west and to the almost contemporaneous triumph of Christianity; nonetheless, we see that the system of economic production remained identical before and after the emperors received baptism and before and after the invasions of the barbarians, for it is well known that the servitude of the serf did not originate from the barbarian invasions but was already general during the decline of the Roman Empire.

And if from antiquity we move to less remote times, we see in Italy during the fourteenth century that the communes were very frequently transformed into signorie without any noticeable modification in the system of production and in relations between the possessors of capital and the workers. Similarly in France during the seventeenth century the formation of the absolute bureaucratic state took root without any modifications occurring at the same time in the system of production and the economic relations derived from it.

Nor should it be believed that there is a perfect synchronization between the development of large industry and the adoption of a system of representative government with the consequent diffusion of liberal, democratic, and even socialist ideas.

In fact in England the beginnings of large industry occurred in the eighteenth century, when parliamentary government had functioned already for half a century, but the ruling class still retained its old aristocratic bases. In France, Germany, the United States of America, and in all of western Europe the development of large industry and the great centralization of capital and labor consequent upon it, took place generally after 1830; because only then did the application of steam to ships and to land transport become widespread, and pit coal acquired capital importance as a factor of production. What can be conceded on this subject is that the large factory, making necessary a large aggregation of workers, contributed powerfully to the development and diffusion of communist ideas, which had already been enunciated long before Marx and which, in fact, are in large part the corollaries of those formulated by Rousseau.

But this is not meant to deny that the prevailing system of economic production, with its particular relations between those directing production and possessing the instruments of production and their assistants, is one of the facts that tend to modify the political arrangements of a society, and that the prevailing system has its necessary reaction also in the conceptions that provide a moral basis to these arrangements. The error of historical materialism is in the assertion that the economic factor has to be considered as a single cause and that all other factors ought to be considered as its effects, when every branch of human social activity feels the influence of all the others and at the same time influences them. Thus every factor contributes to the determination of modifications taking place in the others and at the same time feels the effect of their changes.

Nor can we forget the influence that changes in arms, tactics, and systems for recruiting armies have had on political arrangements. In fact, the transformation in a democratic sense of the Greek "polis," which occurred in the sixth century B.C., was greatly influenced by the military predominance secured by the heavy infantry of the hoplites, recruited from the middle class, over the ancient war chariots of the Homeric epoch and over the cavalry which had been a speciality of the aristocratic classes. We have already pointed out the political effects of the innovations introduced in ancient Rome by Caius Gracchus and Caius Marius on the recruiting of the legions, and it is known that toward the end of the Middle Ages the predominance of the monarchy over the feudal regime was due, in part, to the introduction and subsequent improvement of firearms. And when the history of the nineteenth and twentieth centuries can be studied with a serene mind the political effects of obligatory military service extended to all citizens, introduced by the French Revolution and then adopted and improved first by Prussia and then by the other states of the European continent, will easily be brought to light.

And we will also say that it seems absurd to include among simple effects, without ever giving them the dignity of causes, those political or religious doctrines that furnish the moral basis of the state organism, and that, penetrating deeply into the conscience of the ruling classes and of the popular masses, legitimize and discipline authority, justify obedience, and create that special intellectual and moral atmosphere that contributes so much to directing the course of human events.

It is useless to try to determine whether moral forces predominate over material ones, or material ones over moral ones, since every moral force tries, as soon as it can, to consolidate itself by creating to its own advantage a base of personal interests—that is, of material forces—trying therefore to place at its disposition economic and military power. On the other hand, every material force endeavors to justify itself by leaning upon some conception of intellectual and moral order.[3]

Therefore, the truth is that the factors of human history are so complex and interwoven among themselves that any oversimplified doctrine seeking to determine which among these factors is the principal one, which is never moved but always moves the others, leads inevitably to erroneous conclusions and applications. This is especially true when this oversimplified doctrine is intended to explain, following its own method and particularly observing all events from only its own single point of view, all the past and present of humanity. And still worse results occur when, following the same system, an attempt is made to predict the future.

Finally, the assertion of Marx that every historical period contains the seeds that, developing, will give birth to the next, can

[3] Engels was a student and friend of Marx, and also his most faithful collaborator. After the death of Marx, in letters dated from 1890 to 1895, Engels recognized that moral factors, or political, philosophical, and religious doctrines, if they are influenced by economic factors, react in turn and modify the results of them.

be accepted as accurate. However, this affirmation is not new. On the contrary, it cannot be overlooked that this law was already known to all important historians. But the conclusions the author of the *Capital* then draws from this assertion are certainly not correct. Thus he affirms that the present bourgeois period inevitably prepares communism because capital, as a result of competition, becomes always more concentrated in fewer hands, with the result that at a certain point it becomes easy for the many proletarians to expropriate the very few capitalists and to make the state proprietor of all the instruments of production. Now statistics have already shown that the number of average capitalists and average proprietors tends, in general, to increase rather than diminish and if large industrial enterprises often incline toward larger concentrations of capital, small industry does not show signs of disappearing, and the ownership of capital tends to subdivide through the widely accepted use of stock companies.

Totally incorrect is the conclusion that is then drawn from Marxist doctrine; that is, that once collectivism is realized, an era of equality and universal justice will be introduced during which the state will no longer be an instrument for class domination and there will no longer be either exploited or exploiters. In a communist regime the governors, besides having at their disposal the sovereign powers and the armed police, are the administrators of the great and single state economic concern and are able to prescribe for each individual the quantity and quality of work, the place where it should be carried out, and the recompense to which he has a right.

Perhaps never as in that time would the tyranny of the organized minority, which always or almost always constitutes the state, display within a civilized country more efficient instruments for the oppression of the majority of the citizens, who, in this case, should be called subjects. If communism were adopted the modern European state would become a political organism worse than that which functioned in East Asia under the most odious tyrants.

And it is a childish hope to believe that the abuses inevitable in a communist state could be tempered through a democratic system of governance; i.e., the selection of the governors by the governed. In a regime that has at its disposal every type of favor and every type of punishment, that has at its disposition whatever means of propaganda and whatever instrument of deception, that permits no organization outside of its own and prohibits any discussion of its methods of government, popular suffrage would always necessarily give favorable responses to the governors. Only one thing could weaken it; that is, if there were serious dissensions among the governors and, above all, if these dissensions were manifested through civil wars, *coup d'états* by armed supporters and political assassins.

After this discussion it is desirable to point out the reasons for the undeniable success of the *Capital*. The influence this book has exerted on the minds and sentiments of millions of individuals, and thus on political events, if not comparable to that exerted by the Gospels, by the Koran, or by the doctrines of Confucius, has contributed powerfully, and probably will continue to contribute to the creation of those psychological conditions in which we must trace the origins of important historical events that have already occurred and are yet to occur in the twentieth century in Europe, America, and Asia.

Nothing can be born out of nothing and the thought and way of feeling human, like the nature of which fundamentally they are a part, are not radically changed. Every doctrine, every religion that succeeds in conquering a large part of the world, has been almost invariably preceded by analogous doctrines and religions which have prepared minds and hearts to accept them. Apparently the *Capital* would not have found propitious ground if there had not first been Rousseau and then the French Revolution to proclaim the advent of liberty together with equality and, in inseparable company, fraternity. Not much intelligence was needed to perceive, as Babeuf, Buonarroti, and many others had already seen, that political equality is insufficient if unaccompanied by economic equality, and economic equality cannot be achieved if the private ownership of land and of the instruments of production are retained. Nor is the influence of that optimistic conception of human nature to be forgotten which, born in the eighteenth century, has not yet terminated, but is perhaps near to finishing its historical cycle. On the basis of this conception man is seen as born good and society, or more accurately social institutions, must be responsible for making him wicked, so that by changing social institutions, humanity would be permitted to develop its natural goodness just as if it had been liberated from a prison.

Thus the *Capital* was only the conclusion of an intellectual and sentimental movement that had been maturing for more than a century. In a period during which the infallibility of science had taken the place of faith the *Capital* constructed an entire pseudo-scientific system with which it claimed to show that the realization of communism was the inevitable result of the historical evolution of human society. And it is well known that no argument can more convincingly be cited in support of a doctrine than that which predicts its triumph as inevitable.

Secondary reasons for the importance acquired by Marxism are the adaptability of the text to diverse interpretations, so that the *Capital* can serve evolutionary socialists as well as the revolutionary ones, and the frequent obscurity that is often mistaken for profundity. Furthermore, it is necessary not to forget that the communist doctrines find sustenance in several tendencies of human nature, good and bad but all certainly very common, which include an aspiration toward absolute justice, plus the envy and hatred felt by all those who have been born or have fallen into the lower classes of society toward those more elevated.

Whoever has dispassionately read the *Capital*, or better still brief extracts from it that make intelligible to everyone the essential parts of the doctrines of the teacher, must agree that in these the last two sentiments are clearly and strongly incited. The capitalist (the man who has money) is considered and depicted as a man of another race, of another blood, whom the poor should not consider as an equal, but as a dangerous being, a tyrant, degraded and degrading, whose elimination only can render possible the liberation of the proletariat.

And since the capitalists are defined as *bourgeois*, a term commonly understood not only to include the large industrialists, the bankers, and the large landowners, but also those who belong to the numerous middle class, which with a moderate wealth combines the scientific preparation needed for the liberal professions and the state bureaucracy, so in practice the destruction or removal of the bourgeoisie would signify the substitution of the old ruling class with a new one. In this new class an inadequacy of training would be equalled, or rather surpassed, by the immense breadth of its powers or by the lack of scruples in adopting them.[4]

Henry George and George Sorel

In 1870 the North American Henry George published a book that enjoyed a great success and wide circulation since it was translated into almost all the European languages. The book was entitled *Progress and Poverty* and in it the author appeared to be a moderate socialist, inasmuch as he did not seek the socialization of industry or of personal property, but only of land.

George was struck by the enormous increases in the value of land which occurred at that time following upon increases in population and improvements in the means of communication in the United States, particularly in the large area between the Allegheny Mountains and the Pacific Ocean. A site which when far away from the inhabited districts could be bought for a dollar an acre acquired the value of fifty dollars an acre, if a railroad line were located nearby and if the population became dense in its vicinity. Such increased value was almost always due entirely to the economic development of the country and the proprietor of the land had contributed nothing to it at all. Therefore, it was not just that an individual enjoyed an advantage that was not the consequence of his work or of the employment of his capital, but that originated solely in social progress.

Thus George wanted the so-called *Ricardian income*—that is, the value acquired by a site as a consequence of its position or its greater fertility, not through improvements introduced by the proprietor—to be transferred to the state. In exchange, the state would abolish all the taxes afflicting the poor and would provide allowances

---

[4] See G. Mosca, *Elementi di scienza politica* (Bari: Laterza, 1953), Part I, Chapter 10, in which the inevitable consequences of a collectivist regime are set forth. These pages were written and published toward the end of 1895. The English translation of this work is known as *The Ruling Class*.

to the poorest when they were without work or were no longer able to work.

George believed that avarice and greed in men are caused by fears that they may come to lack for necessities in a more or less near future. He was convinced that if this fear could be dispelled from the spirit of men, the difficult search for wealth, which was the tragic origin of so many evils, would be ended. In support of his thesis he cited the example of the round tables that in his time were used in hotels. At them, he said, the table companions did not grab at the dishes, seeking to serve themselves the best morsels and in the largest quantity, because they were sure there would be excellent and sufficient food for everyone. Likewise, if in society all were certain they would never be reduced to the painful condition of the poor, men would no longer be forced to accumulate more and more riches. The comparison, however, while ingenious is not appropriate. First of all, not at all hotel round tables did things proceed so properly as George describes. This was so much the case that they were abandoned. In the second place, the greed for food is necessarily limited, for no man can fill his stomach beyond its capacity, but avidity for wealth is unlimited for it serves not only to satisfy the material appetites, but is a very potent instrument for power. The rich man, besides finding himself in the enviable position of complete independence, possesses the possibility with his wealth of imposing his own will on others and of dominating them completely, and all of us know how great in man is the desire to impose himself on his fellow men and to subdue them to his will.

In the last chapter of his book George deals with the laws that regulate the progress of human societies. In this chapter the author sets forth some original and at times profound views. He claims that human progress is not indefinite and continuous, and shows how some civilizations have decayed and some have disappeared, attributing their decline to the slackening of those moral forces that serve as cement among individuals of the same nation; in other words, to the disappearance of the religious or political ideals that held individual selfishness in check.

Lastly, it is right and proper to note that in George's book the pungent and violent hatred for the upper classes found in almost every page of Marx's *Capital* does not appear. Instead in *Progress and Poverty* can be found a true and sincere compassion for the sufferings of the humblest classes of society.

In ancient times as soon as Christianity was widely diffused, discussions began of the interpretation to be placed on the sacred texts. Similarly for half a century the large Marxist movement generated disagreements over the most faithful manner of interpreting the *Capital*. Major differences arose over the ways of achieving collectivism and over the period in which it will be possible. There have been and are those who believe easier and, above all, preferable the gradual and peaceful realization of Marxist doctrines, while others seek rapid action and believe violence to be indispensable. George Sorel is among the latter.[1]

Sorel, who was born in 1847 and died in 1922, was, like Spencer, an engineer and began to write on social problems around 1888. Unlike the parliamentary socialists, he showed at times sympathies for the men of the extreme right. In 1907 he published his principal work, entitled *Reflections on Violence,* and in 1910 published in *Devenir Sociale* a series of articles, which were then published in a book entitled *The General Strike and Violence.* Perhaps Italy is the country where the doctrines of this syndicalist writer found most sympathy, and they collected a larger number of followers.

Sorel does not believe in historical destiny (in direct contrast with his teacher Marx), but instead believes that violent rebellion is necessary for the realization of collectivism. Thus he often violently attacks the Reformist Socialists, who appeal to the proletarians to secure their votes. Once elected to Parliament, they believe they are fulfilling the mandate of their electors when they obtain some small social reform that serves to calm the popular classes and to appease the struggle against the bourgeoisie, thus prolonging its power. Therefore, he does not want representatives of socialism in the legislative chambers. Instead he wants the proletariat to organize

[1] On this argument a lively polemic occurred at the end of 1917 and in the following year between the German Marxist Kautsky, an advocate of the evolutionary method, and Lenin, who naturally preferred the so-called immediate dictatorship of the proletariat and violent revolution.

itself in class-based syndicates, and through strikes, first partial, then general, move to the assault upon the bourgeoisie which holds power. Having destroyed the bourgeois regime, Sorel seeks the establishment of a regime, both collectivist and syndicalist, but the particulars of this new regime are not clearly set forth by the author. As far as religion is concerned, Sorel speaks of Christianity with respect but believes that it is already outdated and that Christian morality thus is no longer suited to the needs of modern society. Therefore, it must be replaced by a new morality which will be the worker's morality.

Let us set aside the violent attacks of the author against the reformists. These are the customary attacks of the younger and more militant socialists against the recognized and older leaders of the party. Instead let us focus our attention on the syndicalist doctrines that Sorel advocated.

These doctrines are founded in reality since in many economic relationships in the last century an evolution has been confirmed that has replaced the old individual and free relations between the consumers of a commodity or service and their producers with a coercive relation between individual consumers and a management that alone can provide the commodity or service.

The most obvious examples of this fact are furnished by electric lighting and by the gas used as fuel in kitchens. Half a century ago houses were lighted by kerosene and candles, which everyone could buy from any grocer, while now electric light is generally furnished by a single enterprise, public or private, which enjoys a monopoly. The same is true of gas, which has replaced coal in kitchens. And the same has happened in transport, since railroads depend on one or very few private or state concerns.

Now, every enterprise devoted to one of these services must employ the appropriate category of skilled workers. If these were organized in syndicates, it would be sufficient if one or, better still, several struck since such a strike would seriously disturb the regular functioning of human activity in a large city and even at times within an entire nation. Modern life can be compared to a watch which unfailingly will stop if only one of its many springs fails to function.

From this inevitable state of affairs the danger is created that one day one or several syndicates may impose themselves on the entire society if the state, which is the natural protector of collective interests in the face of minorities, is not strong enough to keep rein on them and to prevent the orders of the leaders of the syndicates from being obeyed by their followers to the disregard of the orders of those who hold the public powers.

13

The Doctrine of
the Superman
and Racial Theories

A course in the history of political institutions and theories would not be complete if some recent theories that have had an impact on the mentality of contemporary generations were not taken into consideration. One such would be Nietzsche's doctrine that aims at exaggerating the influence that certain individuals, privileged through their intelligence, will, and thirst for authority, have exercised or should have exercised, on the history of nations. The other doctrine, much more widespread, which today is called racist theory, asserts that humanity is divided into superior and inferior races, that the first are the authors of all progress and have a right to authority, while the others must undergo servitude.

Friedrich Nietzsche, born in Röcken in Germany in 1844, taught comparative philology at the University of Basel until 1879, the year in which he abandoned his position in order to dedicate himself completely to philosophical and social studies. Having become mentally ill in Turin in 1889, he was put in a sanatorium where he died in 1900. As a writer he began his career with a book on the Greek philosophers prior to Socrates, dwelling especially on the obscure Heraclitus, after which, according to the author, began the decline of Hellenic thought. In 1885 he published in a limited edition of forty copies a book of which a much larger edition was issued in 1892. This work was entitled *Thus Spoke Zarathustra*.

In it the author develops the theory of the superman, already mentioned by Carlyle, and it advocates the worship of force. Furthermore, he denounces Christianity as a source of moral decline and criticizes those laws that limit the development and power of supermen and that are based on the premise of a fictitious equality contrary to human nature. The style of his prose is original and is formed of brief sentences attributed to Zarathustra or Zoroaster, who would have been the author of the *Zend-Avesta*, the religious, moral, and political code of the ancient Persians, and who it seems lived about five or six centuries before Christ. Nietzsche also published some other works, among them *Beyond Good and Evil* in which he argued that the hero—that is, superman—ought to be free from every moral restraint.

Nietzsche's ideas show a very great similarity to those of Carlyle, as well as to those which Plato in one of his dialogues put into the mouth of the Sophist Callicles; [1] but as enunciated by the mysterious Zarathustra, they exerted a considerable influence on the mentality and sentiments of educated European and American youth in the last years of the last century and during the present one.

The racist doctrine has distant origins. It is known that in the old eastern civilizations every people had its national god to whom was attributed, as against the gods of other nations, a pre-eminence that naturally was united to the pre-eminence of the people he protected. Such were Marduk or Shamash in Babylonia, Asshur in Nineveh, Ammon in Egypt, and such was probably in the beginning the character of Jehovah, with whom the descendants of Abraham, Isaac, and Jacob had concluded a special pact of alliance.

If from the old east we pass to Greece we readily observe how completely the Greeks believed themselves superior to the barbarians —that is, to all those people outside their own civilization—and the Romans of the period of Augustus displayed the same attitude when Virgil in his immortal verses sang:

> tu regere imperio populos, Romane, memento,
> haec tibi erunt artes pacique imponere morem,
> parcere subiectis et debellare superbos.

To the great honor of the three great world religions, Buddhism, Christianity, and Mohammedanism, all three extended the bond of human brotherhood to every people embracing their faith.

[1] See p. 25.

With this, Christianity completed the work of Rome, which, as has already been noted, had also created a moral and cultural unity of the ancient civilized world during the centuries of the empire.[2]

Thanks to Christianity it can be asserted above all that the notion of the organic superiority of a given people over all others remained unknown in the Middle Ages. But it reappeared briefly and in a puzzling way at the beginning of the seventeenth century when Campanella, in his *Monarchia ispanica*, affirmed that in every period there has existed a people superior to all the others and, as illustrations, recalled the Assyrians, the Greeks, and the Romans; from this he deduced that in his own period hegemony belonged to Spain. As is known, in the later *Monarchia delle nazioni*, by the same author, superiority in the civilized and Christian world was attributed to France.[3]

But it belonged to the nineteenth century and to the present one to witness the revival and energetic affirmation of the idea of the organic inequality of the different human races and thus of different people. This, in part, was a consequence of the power that national sentiment acquired in these centuries. In part, it is due to the simultaneous diffusion of philosophical systems that claimed to have found some single law regulating the destiny of all human societies; and, finally, it is due in part to the influence acquired by new branches of knowledge, anthropology and comparative philology, during the most recent generations in the intellectual world and to the application of their results to political science.

We will recall briefly the names and works of the principal advocates of racist doctrines.

The first suggestions of a special mission for a given people— more precisely, for the German people—were visible at the beginning of the nineteenth century in the *Reden an die deutsche Nation* (Addresses to the German People) by Fichte. In this work published in 1808, he sought to restore the faith of his compatriots in their own power. They had been overwhelmed by the defeat at Jena and the

[2] See p. 45.

[3] However, it seems that the idea of the supremacy of Spain over all other states was not advocated only by Campanella at the beginning of the seventeenth century, for in 1612 a book was published in Spain by Juan De La Puente that had as a title *Defensa de la precedencia de los reyes catolicos de España a todos los reyes del mundo*.

military annihilation of Prussia, which occurred at the end of 1806 and in the first months of 1807 through the action of Napoleon I. Then in 1837 *Die Philosophie der Geschichte* (The Philosophy of History) by Hegel was published. This work, printed after the death of the author, assigned to the Germanic people the mission of guiding the political world to its third phase, that in which liberty would be no longer the privilege of only a single person or of a narrow class, but would be granted to all the elements of society.

In Italy in the first half of the nineteenth century Gioberti's *Il Primato* was published. In this work he attributed to his nation a *moral* and *civil* primacy; similar views were expressed in the same period by Mazzini. In the second half of the same century in Germany the notion was asserted that not only a cultural but also a political and military hegemony belonged to the German people. This idea, enunciated on several occasions by Bismarck, is very apparent in the volumes of history by Heinrich Treitschke and also in his lectures on scientific politics, published by his former students in 1897, four years after his death.

Perhaps greater than Trietschke's success was that around 1890 of a book by a young man until then unknown, Julius Langbehn, a true prototype of those learned Germans in whom erudition and love of country, united with a large dose of mysticism, attenuate much good sense, if not eradicating it completely. The book, whose author was anonymous because he signed it only "a German," was entitled *Rembrandt als Erzieher* or *Rembrandt as an Educator,* and received a very remarkable reception. Thirty-five editions were eventually published. It was even believed that the book was an echo of the thought of William II, who had just ascended the throne only a short time before and was still young. The great success of the book provided its true author, when he was known, the honor of personal acquaintance with Bismarck, who had fallen from the Chancellorship shortly before but was at that time more popular than ever in Germany. In this book Langbehn started from the concept that the genius of a race is revealed simultaneously in its art and its politics and he cited the Dutchman Rembrandt as representative of the race who lived in Lower Germany, especially in the great plain extending between the Rhine and the Elbe.

As naturally in art as in politics the Low German represented

intelligence because his was the branch of the Aryan race least defiled by mixture. The author thus considered the Low Germans—
inhabitants of the left bank of the Elbe—superior to the Prussians,
but he praised the work of the Hohenzollerns and deemed as suitable
the constitution of the German empire, because the Prussians had
conceived this notion of the state and the West Germans that of the
fatherland. However, he opposed the spiritual hegemony of Berlin.

After some time the work of Langbehn was rather forgotten,
but came back into vogue after the war, and it appears that from
1918 to 1925 fifteen new editions were prepared. The psychological
condition of the German people after the great war provide sufficient explanation why *Rembrandt als Erzieher* returned to favor.

Furthermore, the racist theory is not limited to asserting the
superiority of some chosen people over all others but, approaching
the doctrine of the ruling class, claims that the minority which in
every nation directs political, military, and cultural activity belongs
to a race different from that of the governed majority; in other
words, difference of social class depends principally on difference of
race.

The first to set forth this thesis was the Frenchman Count de
Boulainvilliers whom we have already discussed.[4] In his *Essai sur la
noblesse*, published in 1732, ten years after the death of the author,
he claimed that the French nobility was descended from the Frankish
conquerors and the plebeians were descended from the defeated
Gallo-Romans. Thus the author disapproved of those French monarchs who sometimes granted to commoners titles of nobility and
justified the privileges of the nobility upon differences of race.[5]

But Boulainvilliers was almost forgotten when another Frenchman, Count Joseph Arthur de Gobineau, who was born in 1816 and
died in Turin in 1882, published between 1853 and 1855 four volumes
of a work entitled *Essai sur l'inégalité des races humaines*. In it the
author tried to explain all the historical events of humanity as a
consequence of the superiority or inferiority of a given race and of

---

[4] See p. 155.

[5] On this subject it can be recalled that Sieyès in his famous pamphlet on the
Third Estate admitted that the French nobility was descended from the
Frankish conquerors, but drew the conclusion that their descendants should
return to the forests of Franconia.

cross-fertilization between the superior race and the inferior one. Because of its intelligence, energy, and courage the white race was superior, but it had not always known how to avoid mixture with the yellow race and with the black. The purest branch of the white race was the Aryan and among the peoples of Indo-European origin the least polluted was the Germanic branch, in which the purity of blood was revealed by the frequency of tall, blond individuals with blue eyes.

According to de Gobineau, there were ten human civilizations, seven of which were located on the Eurasian continent: the Indian, Egyptian, Assyrian, Chinese, Greek, Roman, and Germanic. All seven had been created by or at least fertilized by some branch of the Indo-European race; the first six decayed, or stopped in their development, because the Aryan nucleus fused with the mass of the inferior classes formed by Semitic elements, or yellow and black ones.[6] In the New World the author of the *Inégalité des races humaines* enumerated three other civilizations—the Alleghenian, the Mexican, and the Peruvian—but wisely refrained from searching out which branch of the Aryan race had created them.

According to de Gobineau, in every civilized society of the nineteenth century there were three ethnic types: the nobility, descending more or less in pure form from the Aryan group that had founded or given new strength to the political, military, and administrative organization of the given people; the bourgeoisie, composed of half-breeds in whom the proportion of the blood of the dominating race was still strong; and finally, the multitude, enslaved or at least oppressed because it belonged to an inferior species; that is, Semitic or Negro in the southern countries, yellow in the northern.

---

[6] The two most important branches of the white race were the Indo-European and the Semitic. The Indo-European or Aryan branch included the northern Indians (mixed a good deal with a dark race), and Persians, Greeks, Latins, Slavs, Lithuanians, Celts, and Germans. Recently in the interior of Asia another branch, now extinct, of the Aryan race has been discovered, the Tocharian.

The so-called Semites included the Arabs, Syrians, residents of Mesopotamia, Jews, the ancient Phoenicians, and the Abyssinians (the last much intermixed with the Negroes). It would seem that Semitic populations once inhabited a part of Asia Minor. These would be a Semitic sub-branch, or would have an affinity with the Semites, the old Egyptians, and the Berbers of Northern Africa. The Aryans were distinguished from the Semites principally by the nature of their languages.

When the blending of blood reached the point that the superior classes lost their original virtues, then the society disintegrated and the varied social conditions approached more and more closely a common level of equality, reached by lowering what was high and elevating what was low.

In sum, in the conclusion of his work de Gobineau offers some consolation to the reader by proffering the hope that the always increasing dilution of Aryan blood will reach its end when the superior race has finished its mission of creating a single type of civilization extending throughout the world.[7]

In 1881 the Polish Jew Ludwig Gumplowicz published a work entitled *Der Rassenkampf*, which had some success. In it the author affirmed that in every political organism there are two ruling classes formed by two different races, both placed over a third class which was formed of commoners. The first ruling class enjoyed military and political supremacy and possessed the land; the second, pre-eminence in industry, commerce, and banking. In explaining the origin of the concepts of this writer it is necessary to remember that he wrote in Hungary, where the Magyar nobility, often of a race different from that of the Slav and Rumanian peasants, virtually monopolized the military and political direction of the country and had at its disposal almost all the property, while the Jews possessed almost all the working capital and were dedicated to industry and commerce.

It is not surprising that the *Essai sur l'inégalité des races humaines* had more success in Germany, where an association was founded for the diffusion of the ideas of de Gobineau, than in the writer's native land. Perhaps even more successful in Germany was the work of a writer of English birth, Houston Stewart Chamberlain, who in 1899 published *Die Grundlagen des neunzehnten Jahrhunderts*, completing the theories of his French predecessor while keeping in mind the progress made in comparative anthropology.

---

[7] Before dropping the subject, it is appropriate to note that de Gobineau's assertion—that when the Europeans arrived an Alleghenian civilization existed or had existed in America—had no foundation. The Allegheny are a relatively low chain of mountains which divide New England from the great plain extending to the Rocky Mountains; in this mountain chain the Indians had established no civilizaton that could remotely be compared to the Mexican or the Peruvian.

According to Chamberlain, it was less a question of physical characteristics than of intellectual and moral ones that distinguished the true Germans from other races. Naturally the moral Nordic type, which was the superior one, abounded especially in Germany but, because of the blending of races, individuals belonging to the same type could be found in England and, more occasionally, in France and northern Italy. Thus, for example, Dante, Marco Polo, Saint Francis of Assisi, Giotto, and Michelangelo were all Germanic, and the Serbs, although speaking a Slavonic language, were also Germans because they have a folk-poetry worthy of Nordic folklore. This greater breadth of interpretation permitted the author to arrive at less pessimistic conclusions, because he believed that through careful selection and appropriate crossbreeding the Nordic types could be conserved where they were prevalent and cultivated where more rare.

But the success of Stewart Chamberlain was more recently surpassed by that of Oswald Spengler, a German writer who was born in 1880 and died in 1937. In 1917 and 1920 he published two powerful volumes entitled *Der Untergang der Abendlandes*, or *The Decline of the West*, which were followed in 1922 by a pamphlet entitled *Preussentum und Sozialismus*, or *Prussianism and Socialism*. In these works the author first of all sought to establish that the history of all peoples who have created civilizations obeys inevitable and constant laws; naturally Spengler seeks to search these out.

According to Spengler, who was inspired by de Gobineau but who further modified his classification, there were eight original cultures: about three thousand years before the Christian era the Babylonian and Egyptian cultures flowered; one thousand five hundred years later the Indian culture, the Chinese, and the primitive Hellenic—centered at Crete—asserted themselves; toward three hundred B.C. the Arabic or magic culture existed; two hundred years later the Mexican; and finally, toward the tenth century A.D. in the great plain found in northern Germany, the Western or Faustian culture was born.

The author assigns to each one of these cultures a life of about a thousand years, and the millennium was divided into two phases, an ascending one, which would end five centuries after its beginning and a descending one, in which the culture would become a civilization with a life very nearly equal to the first. With much display of historical erudition (although very often the facts are distorted to support the thesis of the author) he establishes a further parallelism between the different cultures and civilizations, trying to show that all have passed through analogous phases. And the parallels are extended also to the individuals who have had an influence on the different moments of the various cultures. For example, Philip of Macedon and his son Alexander the Great in the Hellenic culture would correspond to Napoleon I in the Faustian culture.

The principal cause for the decline of every culture was the extinction or degeneration of the old nobility, which occurred when the rural and warlike aristocracy which based its power on force and courage was replaced by the wealthy bourgeoisie of the cities, who in assuming the direction of a state apparently based upon egalitarian democracy, surely prepared an absolute regime.

The Faustian or Germanic culture should likewise obey the law of progressive degeneration and disappear after the inevitable thousand years. But the culture would be able to endure to the twenty-second century, which permitted Spengler still to assign to the German people an important part in the history of the world. Meanwhile in the twenty-first century a new culture would perhaps begin to form in the very extensive eastern plain of Europe, where now the Russia of the Bolsheviks exists but, with unusual prudence, the author refrains from making any precise prophecies on the subject.

Finally, in his publications *Der nordische Gedanke der Deutschen* and *Die Rassenkunde des deutschen Volkes* Hans Günther supports theses analogous to those of de Gobineau. To be precise, in these works the author recognizes that the German people are the result of the fusion of diverse races. Thus he argues that in Scandinavia and in northwestern Germany the Nordic type prevails, whose physical characteristics are a tall stature, a dolichocephalic cranium, blond hair, and blue eyes. This human type is also to be distinguished by superiority of intellectual and moral qualities.

Then he admits that, to the east of the Elbe River, the Prussians have been defiled to some extent by crossbreeding with Slav blood and that the Bavarians, and, in general, the Germans of the south, are in large majority non-Nordic. He also acknowledges that some Nordics can be found sporadically in northern France, northern

Italy, and particularly in the eastern parts of England. As Chamberlain had already done, he deplored the fact that the number of Nordics tends to diminish, because, being more enterprising and courageous, they emigrate more easily and suffer greater losses in war. Furthermore, they are less resistant to the unhygienic conditions of the large cities and contract tuberculosis more easily. Thus, according to the author, the legislator should act in a way that does not diminish the Nordic element, which among the races that populate Europe is indisputably the best.

An entire volume would be necessary to examine exhaustively how much truth and how much error there is in the more or less unfounded affirmations of the writers with whom we are concerned. Therefore we will limit ourselves to noting the principal objections that can be cited against them.[8]

First of all, it is to be deplored that none of these writers, convinced of the importance of the racial factor in the destiny of peoples, worried about stating precisely the significance of the word *race*. In fact, one commonly speaks and writes of the white race, of the black race, and of the yellow race, and one may mention also the Semitic race and the Aryan, also the Latin race, the Germanic, and the Slav. In the first instance the question is one of easily perceptible somatic differences, so that a white cannot be mistaken for a Negro or for a yellow person; while in the second, and, above all, in the third case, the differences are relatively minimal and are revealed only in the averages of somatic measurings, but are not so marked as to preclude a Semite being mistaken for an Aryan, or still more to the point, a Frenchman or an Italian—that is, a Latin—for a German.

Certainly when the differences of race are very marked, as for example, between a European and a Negro from the center of Africa, it can be asserted that innate racial superiority has been one of the factors—perhaps the principal factor—for different attitudes toward civilization. But a similar assertion would be at minimum imprudent if it were a question of whites or of yellow people, since it cannot be denied that the Chinese have been able to create a

---

[8] Many other arguments against the excessive importance attributed to race as a factor in the history of peoples can be found in G. Mosca, *Elementi di scienza politica* (Bari: Laterza, 1953), Part I, Chapters 10, 11, and 12.

civilization that had its moments of splendor, and that the Japanese have demonstrated a very great ability to assimilate first the Chinese civilization and then the European. And the testimonies that the very ancient civilizations of Mesopotamia and Egypt have left us show how important it is to reject the allegations of the intellectual and moral inferiority of the so-called Semitic race and its sub-branch of the same; it is enough by itself to cast a quick glance over the history of Europe in order to be convinced that none of the peoples who live there have shown continuously unquestionable superiority over all the others.

It is opportune to recall that perhaps nowhere today is there a people who can boast of belonging to some single one of the sub-races or descents that comparative anthropology has clearly identified. From the beginnings of history it can be observed that the oldest civilizations of southwest Asia and Egypt were the product of peoples in whose veins ran blood mixed by several races or sub-races in a mixture always growing more accentuated; and the same occurred in Europe, where in almost every nation the three principal subraces that have populated and populate this part of the world were found fused.[9]

Nor can the doctrine of Boulainvilliers, de Gobineau, and Gumplowicz be accepted on the basis that the difference between

[9] It is now generally accepted that the three noted subraces are the Mediterranean or Euro-African, of medium stature, predominantly brown hair and eyes, and a dolichocephalic cranium (relatively narrow and long); the Euro-Asiatic or Alpine, of average stature, more or less clear chestnut hair, and a brachycephalic cranium (that is, relatively more wide than long); and the Reihengräber, tall in stature, blond, and dolichocephalic. The first is found, for the most part, in the three southern peninsulas—that is, the Balkan, the Italic, and the Iberian—and in Southern France, and also has a certain number of representatives in the rest of France, in Southern Russia, and in England; the second prevails in a large part of Russia, in central and southern Germany, in Switzerland, in central France, in northern Italy, and in part of the British Isles; and the third forms the majority of the Scandinavian population and has a certain number of representatives in northern Germany, in the north of France, in England, and also in northern Italy. However, in all the European countries where one of the noted subraces prevails, some representatives of the others are found. In central Italy, for example, the representatives of the Euro-African subrace would be in number very nearly equal to the Euro-Asiatic. The first anthropologist to adopt the measurement of craniums as a fundamental criterion for ethnic classifications was the Swede Retzius in 1845.

social classes would be due to a difference of race; for if this has occurred at times, in the large majority of cases in normal times it is from within the ruled classes themselves that the rulers have emerged. In central and western Europe the superimposition of a foreign population on the native one occurred in the first centuries of the Middle Ages, when the German barbarians invaded the Roman Empire. The examples of the Iberian peninsula and of Sicily could also be cited, which were conquered by the Arab-Berbers at the beginnings of the eighth and ninth centuries, or that of England conquered by the large company of mercenaries led by William the Conqueror in the eleventh century. But in all these cases, when differences of religion did not prevent the fusion, within a few generations the conquering population amalgamated with the conquered, and if Boulainvilliers and de Gobineau had been better acquainted with the histories of France and Spain they would have known that, a little more than a century after the Franks conquered Gaul and the Visigoths Spain, numerous Gallo-Romans had become members of the Frankish aristocracy and numerous Spanish-Romans of the Visigoth. It is likewise necessary to remember that in the Iberian peninsula as well as in Sicily many among the conquered were converted to the religion of the victors and divided their fortunes, and to realize that everywhere unions of the victors with the women of the vanquished were frequent.

De Gobineau's list of human civilizations has little foundation, for some might be added to it and others deleted. Spengler's has even fewer. In addition he tried to assign to every civilization an inevitable duration of about a thousand years and an equally inevitable course through which each would pass in identical phases of progress and decline. On the subject it is enough to recall that the Chinese civilization lasted almost four thousand years without notable interruptions; that the Egyptian retained its essential characteristics for two and a half millennia—that is, as many years as passed from Menes to the conquest of Egypt by Cambyses; and that the duration of the Babylonian civilization was almost identical for the span was almost equal that separates the time of Lugalzaggisi and Sargon the Elder from that of Nebuchadnezzar. And it could also be argued that it is far from clear why Germany is identified as the country within which the contemporary western or Faustian civilization was born when the revival of European culture after the dark centuries of the oldest Middle Ages came about at least contemporaneously in Italy, France, and Germany; indeed if any one country preceded the others, it was Italy.

Then when one speaks of the culture, or of the civilization of a people, one should presumably allude to that part of human activity that is revealed in religion, politics, art, science, administrative and military organization, and economic production, which is due to the collective work of that nation and to its original elaboration. However, serious errors will be committed if it is not kept in mind that, for four or five millennia until today, there have been no perfectly original civilizations, save perhaps the Chinese and those of the indigenous Americans, since it has now been proven that the civilization of India was influenced by the Hellenic civilization which it had contact with in the period of Alexander the Great. In fact, the different civilizations are not and have not been, as was visible to de Gobineau and to Spengler, organisms perfectly isolated one from the other, but have been, and are today more than ever, communicating vessels each one of which has up to a degree profited from the results obtained by the others, and each one of those following has been able to capture completely or in part the heritage of its predecessors.

Without presumption it can certainly be affirmed that there has been no previous civilization superior to the one that flourished in Europe and America during the nineteenth century. But it is necessary to remember that the Aryan branch of the white race, which has generated the conception of a white race, inherited from its distant Greek and Roman ancestors many of the ideas and judgments that immensely facilitated its task, and that first the Greeks and then the Greeks and the Romans, in their turn, learned much from the old eastern civilizations. From these civilizations originated many plants and domesticated animals; these civilizations created the first capital and the first machines for man to use, also the earliest alphabets, which made possible the transmission of the entire thought and knowledge of preceding generations to the subsequent. Lastly, from these civilizations Christianity originated, the religion that has contributed so much to elevating the moral condition of the peoples who have adopted it.

In conclusion, it can be said of racist theory what was said of historical materialism; that is, that both contain a part of the truth. They are very far from containing all the truth. Undoubtedly the particular and hereditary attitudes of a people are one of the elements that contribute to elevating or lowering the intellectual and moral level and that therefore influence the political institutions. But these attitudes are a consequence more of a history that has unfolded as the result of the action of many other factors, rather than of the exclusive influence of race. And it must not be forgotten that the contribution race has made to the psychological formation of a people may be large when racial differences are, as has already been mentioned, significant, yet minimal when they are so small that only averages of cranial measurements can reveal them.

As the study of political economy has provided some elements to the constitution of Marxist theory and Darwinism has furnished others to the so-called positivism of Spencer, so anthropology and comparative philology, history, and archaeological discoveries have contributed to the formation of racial theories. In general, of course, it is not reprehensible that political science should profit from the results obtained by other disciplines, provided that the method borrowed is applied with maximum prudence, without allowing it to mislead with apparent analogies, and without distorting and misrepresenting historical facts and the observations of anthropology and of philology to support the prejudices of the writer.

And among these prejudices the most dangerous of all is that which so many illustrious thinkers have demonstrated when they have tried to find some single law on which the progress or the decline of political organisms must inevitably depend. To mention no others, Plato, Polybius, Campanella, Vico, Leroux, de Gobineau, Marx, and today Spengler, searching for this law, have tried to read out of the past a sure prediction of the political future of different peoples. Without temerity it can be affirmed today that none of these outstanding men has succeeded in his intent, principally because success is impossible. Indeed all their systems operate facilely in a manner open to criticism and any analogous system will operate similarly. It is impossible to succeed in tracing the sole cause for the progress or political decline of people, which depend on multiple causes, some internal and some originating instead from foreign political units with which a given people finds itself in contact.

As there is no sole cause to which is owed all the illnesses that afflict the human body, so it is vain to search for the sole and certain origin of changes in a social organism, which is no less complicated than that of the human individual.[10]

---

[10] Professor Günther has recently published a series of works on the races that the European peoples belong to, on their influence, on their history, and on their political institutions.

According to Professor Günther, there are at least six races populating Europe today: first of all, the Mediterranean, the Alpine, and the Reihengräber (which Günther calls Nordic), which have already been mentioned. Furthermore, there are the Dinaric race, which prevails in the Balkan peninsula, and the Baltic race scattered principally through eastern Prussia, Poland, Silesia, and northwest Russia.

In the Canary Islands and in the northwest of Europe the residues of a sixth race can be found that populated Europe in the Palaeolithic age. Further, Professor Günther supposes the existence of a seventh race whose characteristics cannot yet be specified exactly. Lastly, the Jews are said to belong to an extra-European race originating in Syria.

According to Günther, physical, moral, and intellectual primacy belongs to the peoples in whom the Nordic race predominates, such as the Scandinavians and the inhabitants of northwest Germany; Nordic man can be distinguished by his self-control, energy, and love for justice and truth. In fact most of the eminent men of Europe and America have the temperament of the Nordic race.

Obviously, the conclusions that Professor Günther arrives at present substantial analogies to the theories of de Gobineau, Chamberlain, and Langbehn, and the method adopted by Günther is likewise analogous to that of his predecessors. It consists in establishing a constant and a priori correspondence between the racial characteristics of a people (stature, form of cranium, color of hair and eyes) and its psychology as revealed in the events of its history.

This method might be effective if applied with maximum objectivity, if the historical facts examined were interpreted exactly, and if facts contrary to the thesis supported by the writer were also born in mind. It does not seem that Professor Günther and his predecessors have always taken these precautions.

Let us conclude by repeating once more that the predominance of a given ethnic element may be one of the causes that contributes to the creation of the type of civilization adopted by a people; but when the ethnic differences are not very noticeable, as is true of those who can be ascertained among the European peoples, the ethnic factor is almost never the principal cause for the psychological differences that can be distinguished between one nation and the other, and still less can they be considered the sole cause of these differences.

14

The Theory of
the Ruling Class

The two traditional classifications of the forms of government are those formulated by Aristotle and by Montesquieu. The former divided governments into monarchies, aristocracies, and democracies according to whether sovereign powers were concentrated in a single person, in a limited class, or in the totality of the citizens. Montesquieu defined as despotic those regimes in which the will of the single sovereign was not restrained by custom, by local and class privileges, and by the law which the sovereign himself dictated. He labeled as monarchic those regimes in which such restraints functioned alongside the monarch; finally he defined republics as those political organizations in which there was no hereditary head of state and in which sovereignty resided either with a part of the populace, as occurred in aristocratic republics, or with all citizens, as was true in the democratic ones.

These classifications first of all had the common defect of being conceived on the basis of observation of a single moment in the history of political organisms. Aristotle's was in fact based on conditions of the Hellenic city-state in the fifth and fourth centuries B.C., and Montesquieu's took into account only the organization of contemporary European states. At that time there was no hereditary head of state in Venice, Genoa, or Switzerland, and France possessed a monarchy limited to a degree by custom, by the relative independence of the magistracy, and by privileges of class and corporations. In Turkey there was a single despot who, apparently, ruled according to his own will. However, one could read between the lines of the *Esprit des lois* that its author found the perfect type of tempered monarchy in the regime then in force in England.

But the major defect of these classifications lies in the superficiality of the criteria on which they were formulated, for they take into account apparent characteristics rather than the substantial ones that differentiate the various political organisms. Thus if we refer to the classification of Montesquieu we can easily note that there may be greater differences between the political structures of two republics than between a particular republic and monarchy. To cite an example, there is today a greater difference between the republic of the United States of America and the French republic than between the latter and the Belgian monarchy; nor is it necessary to recall the great difference between a modern republic and those found in antiquity or in the Middle Ages. And, on the other hand, if we refer to the Aristotelian classification we must recognize that it is impossible for a single monarch to govern millions of subjects without the aid of a hierarchy of officials, or of a ruling class, and that it is likewise impossible for a democracy to function if the action of the popular masses is not coordinated and directed by some organized minority; that is, by another ruling class.

Today a new method of studying politics tends to concentrate the attention of researchers especially on the formation and the organization of the ruling class now in Italy generally called the *political class*.[1] In truth, this method is not entirely new, since isolated institutions of the importance and necessity of a ruling class can be found even in classical antiquity as well as in the writings of Machiavelli, Guicciardini, and Rousseau. And they are found even more in some nineteenth-century authors, among whom a prominent place must be given to Saint-Simon.[2] But it was only toward the end of the last century and during the present one that the new vision of the political world has become more widespread.

One of the first results of the new method was the formation of the concept that, since 1883, has been labeled the *political for-*

---

[1] The expression has also begun to be used by foreign writers along with the term *elite* employed by Pareto.

[2] See G. Mosca, *Elementi di scienza politica* (Bari: Laterza, 1953), Part II, Chapter 1.

mula; [3] that is, the observation that in all countries to have achieved even a limited level of culture the political class justifies its power by leaning on some better belief or sentiment generally accepted in that epoch and in that nation. These beliefs could be, according to the situation, the presumed will of the people or of God, a consciousness of forming a distinct nationality or chosen people, traditional fidelity to a dynasty, or trust in an individual endowed with exceptional qualities.

Naturally every political formula must be in harmony with the degree of intellectual and moral maturity of the people and the period in which it is adopted. Thus it must closely correspond to the particular conception of the world that a people has at a given moment, and it should constitute the moral cement among all the individuals who are part of that society.

Therefore, when a political formula is, let us say, outdated, when faith in the principles on which it is based has weakened and the sentiments that have created it have cooled, it is a sign that profound transformations in the ruling class are imminent. The French Revolution occurred when the great majority of the French people no longer believed in the divine right of kings and the Russian Revolution broke out when almost all intellectuals, and perhaps even the majority of the workers and the Russian peasants, no longer believed that the Czar had received from God the mission to govern Holy Russia autocratically.

The converse is also true; when a political formula is in harmony with the mentality of a given period and with the most widespread sentiments of the people, its utility is unquestionable, because very often it serves both to impose limits on the action of those who command and in a kind of way ennobles obedience, which is no longer seen as the result exclusively of physical coercion.

Given the fact that in every political organism the existence and functioning of a ruling class is necessary, it is evident that the efforts of those who seek to study political phenomena must concentrate on the examination of the different types of organization and formation of the ruling class.

So far as organization is concerned it can be asserted that until

[3] G. Mosca, *Sulla teorica dei governi e sul governo parlamentare* (Turin, Loescher, 1884).

now there have been three different types: the feudal, the bureaucratic, and a third type that is less common, but that cannot be neglected, given the intellectual inheritance it has left and the importance it has acquired in a particular period. We are here alluding to the Hellenic and Italic city-state.

The system that for historical recollections we have called feudal is the most simple and primitive but at the same time the least perfect because it accomplishes only with difficulty the coordination of all the efforts of a people toward some single civil or military end. The principal characteristic of the feudal system consists in the division of the territory of the state into many parts, in each one of which the representative of the overlord joins in his own hands all sovereign powers. This is what thus occurred in Europe in the Middle Ages, when the baron was at the same time military chief and judge and could also impose fines and taxes within the boundaries of his fief.

This allowed every part of the state to maintain an almost independent position vis-a-vis the central organ, and also, with relative ease, to become separated from it. Therefore, in feudal regimes the unity of the state and cohesion among the diverse parts can be preserved intact only when the central organ is directed by a superior man who possesses so much prestige and so much energy that he can impose himself on the local leaders; or else when the national sentiment is so strong as to hinder greatly the subdivision of the state, as happened in Japan before the Tokugawa shogunate.[4]

The bureaucratic system is characterized by the fact that governmental activities are not distributed geographically but functionally. Thus military direction is separated from the judicial and the judicial in turn from the financial, and each branch of the separate manifestations of sovereignty is entrusted to as many special hierarchies of officials, each one receiving its direction from the central organ of the state. With the various activities of government entrusted to different persons, the action of the small group at the head of the state organization becomes more efficacious and surer, and

[4] The Tokugawa shogunate was established in the first years of the seventeenth century; from then until the nineteenth century the central power in Japan was sufficiently strong, for the Daimios, or the large feudatories, were closely supervised and a considerable part of the country, especially its strategic points, depended directly on the shogun.

only with great difficulty can a part of the territory separate itself from the rest and lead an independent life.

The ancient eastern empires and the Mohammedan states almost always retained the characteristics of the feudal state, but in ancient Egypt we find at times traces of an evolution toward the bureaucratic state. An initial bureaucratization can also be discovered in China, during the greatest epochs of Chinese civilization in spite of the great breadth of powers conceded to local governors. Still greater was the independence of the satraps, or local governors, in the ancient Persian empire and it is known that this excessive independence was one of the principal causes for the relatively rapid dissolution of the Caliphate of Baghdad and the empire of the Great Mogul.

The passage from feudal organization to bureaucratic usually occurs very slowly; a characteristic example of the duration of this transformation is France, where the struggle between the centralized monarchy and the feudal regime lasted, with various phases, almost seven centuries, from Hugh Capet to Louis XVI. Bureaucratic states also can pass through disaggregations and dissolutions, although with more difficulty, as happened in the Roman Empire of the west in the fifth century A.D.; the dissolution was then more complete and lasting than usually taking place in periods of decline of feudal states. At such times the breakdown of the political organism is accompanied by a transformation of the moral forces and by a decline in the economic forces originally directing the society.

We have already noted the original characteristics that distinguished the ancient city-state of Greece and Italy from other types of political organization, characteristics that can also be found in part in the medieval commune that arose in western Europe after the eleventh century.[5] In both situations the ruling class was apparently very large, because given the brief tenure of public offices and their rotation, it included a good part of the population of the hegemonic city.[6] In fact, however, especially in Rome, the most

---

[5] For ancient Greece and Rome, see pp. 17–49; for the medieval commune, see pp. 61–63.

[6] It is a well-known fact that in Greece slaves, resident foreigners, and at times even those who were not children of citizens were always excluded from citizenship. Likewise it is known that Aristotle, who certainly was not an aristocrat, did not want to admit small businessmen and small industrialists to the public office.

important offices were almost always filled by members of a certain number of eminent families, and in Greece when the democratic current prevailed so as to impose an absolute equality among all citizens, this occurred after civil wars and plunderings of the rich which prepared in turn for the formation of a more limited oligarchy around the tyrant.

Likewise in the medieval communes the most important offices were ordinarily reserved for the heads of the *Arti Maggiori*, or as happened in Venice, for a certain number of high ranking families, and where this concentration of power in a limited class did not take place the commune was almost always replaced by a signoria analogous to the ancient tyranny.

We know that in the ancient city-state as in the medieval commune it was almost impossible to enlarge the state without changing the order on which it was based. Only the political wisdom of Rome could in part overcome this difficulty. But even Rome had to transform itself into a bureaucratic state when its rule was extended to the entire Mediterranean coast. However, observation of the power and the resistance to disasters that this type of political organization —in proportion to its size—could show on some occasions can arouse astonishment. Thus it is known that Athens sent about forty thousand men to Sicily when it undertook its unfortunate expedition against Syracuse and that, in spite of the fact that very few returned to their country, it could still resist the Peloponnesian League for almost a decade. Also it is known that Rome in spite of enormous losses could win the first and second Punic Wars, and that Pisa, which in the thirteenth century did not exceed eighty thousand inhabitants, had five thousand people killed and lost eleven thousand prisoners in the battle of Meloria.[7] And it is not necessary to recall the contributions of Athens, Florence, and Venice to the arts, letters, and sciences.

The intellectual influence of this type of state has contributed, together with several other factors, to the creation and preservation

---

[7] In truth, perhaps half the forces sent to Sicily were not composed of Athenian citizens, but, given that these numbered no more than thirty-five or forty thousand, Athens' effort was wondrous. Likewise a part of those who fought in favor of Pisa at Meloria had to be recruited in the Tuscan Maremma, then sparsely populated; thus the effort realized by the hegemonic city, which in a preceding battle had already suffered important losses, remains remarkable.

of that form of political organization that could be called liberal as opposed to its alternative which could be called autocratic. The principal characteristic of the liberal system consists in the fact that the transmission of power is from the bottom to the top—that is, that officials are elected by those who will be subject to them; while in the autocratic system the supreme hierarch nominates his immediate assistants, who in turn nominate subordinate functionaries.[8]

It is known that the old eastern empire, the Mohammedan states, the Roman Empire, Byzantium, and, with some reservations, the monarchies of western Europe from the sixteenth century until the beginning of the nineteenth were organized according to the autocratic systems. On the other hand, besides the city-state of antiquity and the medieval communes, republican governments and parliamentary monarchies can be considered as belonging to the liberal type, although, in truth, in Europe the republics as well as the tempered monarchies might be considered mixed types, because the bureaucracies, which possess a good part of the effective power, are almost always recruited according to the autocratic system.

In general, it can be asserted that autocratic regimes are more permanent than those organized according to the liberal system. The latter are delicate organisms that can function well only when the conditions in the nations adopting them permit it and in periods of economic prosperity and great intellectual achievement. It would be ingenuous to believe that the liberal regimes, in conformity with the political formula that justifies them, rest on the explicit consensus of the numerical majority of the citizens, for, as we have demonstrated elsewhere, in elections the struggle actually develops between diverse organized groups which possess the means to influence the mass of unorganized electors, who choose only between a very few representatives of these groups.[9]

However, in the ensuing struggle to gain the votes of the unorganized majority, each group tries to comply, at least outwardly, with the ideas and sentiments prevailing among the masses. If this at times permits liberal regimes to develop an extraordinary power, on

[8] The meaning, which is certainly a little conventional, that we have given to the adjectives *liberal* and *autocratic* is the same as that already adopted in the *Elementi di scienza politica.*

[9] On this subject, see G. Mosca, *Teorica dei governi* and *Elementi di scienza politica,* already cited.

the other hand it compels the ruling class to submit to the influence of more numerous elements less aware of the true needs of the society. And it is precisely because of this that the major danger threatening liberal institutions consists in the granting of suffrage to the most uneducated classes of the population.[10]

But if the study of the diverse types of organization of the ruling class is important, still more important is the examination of the different methods adopted for its formation, or of the various criteria according to which it admits and retains certain individuals while repulsing many others.

The criterion generally prevailing, and almost indispensable in the formation of a ruling class, consists in the ability to govern or, as Saint-Simon had already perceived, in the possession of those personal qualities which, in a given time and among a given people, are most adaptable to the direction of a society. To this could be added the will for power and an awareness of possessing the necessary qualities, which experience continuous changes since the intellectual, moral, economic, and military conditions of every people are continually in flux, requiring that political and administrative arrangements be modified in parallel fashion.

These modifications at times are slow, and in such a case the new elements infiltrating the ruling class do not rapidly change its spirit and framework. At other times the changes are rapid and tumultuous and then the replacement of old elements by new ones can become, in the course of one or two generations, almost complete. In the former instance, the tendency that we have elsewhere called aristocratic prevails. In the second case, that which we have called democratic prevails.[11]

It is very difficult, in fact almost impossible, to eliminate com-

---

[10] Thus Treitschke in his *Politik* had to admit that logic is the worst enemy of democracy. In fact, a representative regime based on the political formula of popular sovereignty, understood as the sovereignty of the majority, ought to finish with adopting universal suffrage, which eventually will render impossible, or at least very difficult, the correct functioning of this form of government.

[11] See G. Mosca, "Il principio aristocratico e democratico," in *Annuario dell'Università di Torino* for the academic year 1902–1903, and *Elementi di scienza politica,* Part II, Chapter 4.

pletely the action of either of these two tendencies, since an absolute prevalence of the aristocratic one would presuppose that the thought and conditions of life in a human society should never change. Experience teaches that this is absurd. On the other hand, an absolute predominance of the democratic tendency could occur only if children did not inherit the means, connections, and knowledge that allowed their forefathers to obtain the best positions.

It has been argued that private ownership of land, capital, and all the instruments of production has been a chief cause for the inheritance of political influence. It cannot be denied that there is some truth in this assertion but we believe we have already demonstrated that, if the ownership of these instruments is assigned to the state, those who administer the state, always themselves a minority, by accumulating economic and political power would have at their disposal very powerful means to further the career of their children and favorites.

The rapid and almost complete renewal of the ruling class in rather remote periods frequently happened after an invasion by barbarian peoples who still had not found fixed residences. They settled in the conquered country and there took the place of the old rulers. Very often the success of the invaders was owed in large part to the discord and decline of the old ruling class and almost always to the indifference and sometimes also to the connivance of the common people in the invaded country.[12]

Such political cataclysms were not rare in the ancient eastern empires. The Mesopotamian civilization experienced several, and scholars have long been aware of the ruin brought to ancient Egypt by the invasion of the Hyksos. China and India were to experience

12 It is known that for some centuries before the fall of the Roman Empire in the west and until the invasions of the barbarians, Gaul was troubled by the revolt of the Bagaudae and that bands of these elements were recruited among the settlers and the slaves. Also in Africa the revolts of the Circumcellions preceded the invasions of the Vandals. Priscus narrates in the interesting report of his negotiations with Attila that in the court of the king of the Huns he found a Greek who had been made a prisoner by the barbarians and who, when then liberated, was able to attain a good post in the army of the Huns. He declared to the Byzantine ambassador that for a valorous man it was rather preferable to live among the barbarians than be subjected to the continuous torment and extortions of the officials of the empire.

invasions of the same type in various periods, and it is not necessary to recall the fall of the Roman Empire in the west and the invasions of the Arabs and the Turks.

With the advance of civilization the zones inhabited by barbarian and nomadic populations became more and more restricted and those inhabited by dense and stable populations devoted to industry, peaceful commerce, and an intensified agriculture gradually enlarged. Furthermore, the advanced civilization developed means of defense against the barbarians much more efficient than those in use up to the time of Genghis Khan and Tamerlane. Thus cataclysms of the type we have just mentioned have become very difficult, if not to say impossible.

By contrast, in recent and very recent times, rapid and violent renewals of the ruling classes have occurred through the action of new political forces which have arisen within the various countries and through the dispersing of the old ones. In other words, invasions have been replaced by revolutions. On this subject, it will be sufficient to cite the great French Revolution; perhaps also that which took place in Japan from 1853 to 1868; and finally, graver than all, the Russian Revolution.[13] But whatever the cause of the political cataclysms that have changed the composition and order of the ruling class, almost always more or less numerous fragments of the old ruling class have entered into the new one.

From the objective study of history perhaps one can draw the conclusion that the best regimes—that is, those that have been most durable and that have for the longest times known how to avoid those violent crises such as occurred at the fall of the Roman Empire and that from time to time have driven humanity toward barbarism— are the mixed ones. In these regimes, therefore, neither the autocratic nor the liberal system prevails and the aristocratic tendency is tem-

---

[13] It seems, however, that revolutions occurred even in very early times. According to documents translated in the last fifteen years, even ancient Egypt, in the period between the ancient Memphite empire and the new Thebaic empire, from 2360 to 2160 B.C., experienced a period of anarchy, during which the old social hierarchies were upset. It appears that foreign invasions contributed to accentuate the disorder, which, however, had as a principal cause the dissolution of the old governing class. It is interesting to read, after more than forty centuries, the expressions of regret and grief of those who from elevated positions were reduced to misery, while others from the lowest classes of society rose to very high places.

pered by a slow but continuous renewal of the ruling class, which thus allows it to absorb those elements of healthy power that are slowly emerging among the ruled classes. But for such a regime to last, a whole set of circumstances is needed which no legislator's foresight can suddenly create. The multiplicity and equilibrium of ruling forces that only a very advanced civilization can produce are necessary. Other necessities are that religious power be separated from political power, that economic direction is not controlled entirely by the rulers of the state, that arms are not exclusively in the hand of some faction of the society separate and distinct from all the others, and that cultivation and technical preparation are among the requisites permitting entry to the ruling class.

And even this is not enough: also necessary are an education slow in forming and long experience in finding practical ways to check those violent and wicked instincts that often accompany the will for power—instincts that have reappeared so many times during great political crises and after long periods of order and social peace that have led superficial observers to believe such instincts were extinct.

Gaetano Mosca:
The Man and His Times

Gaetano Mosca (1858–1941) was an educator, but not the kind described in George Bernard Shaw's famous line, "He who can, does. He who cannot, teaches." Mosca fruitfully combined experiences as a university professor, government official, elected member of the Italian Chamber of Deputies, Senator, and journalist. An octogenarian at the time of his death, he had varied careers in Italy, his troubled homeland, and the wide range of his experiences is reflected in his writings. His time was one of radical social and political change throughout the world, but especially in Italy; it saw the zenith and decline of liberalism, the extension of democracy, the development of mass socialist movements, the rise of extreme nationalism and imperialism, and successful communist and fascist revolutions. It was also the time of new discussions of elitism, which Mosca is most prominently associated with.

Mosca was a Sicilian by birth and formal education. In the period of Mosca's youth, Sicily was backward socially, politically, and economically. Understandably, some commentators suggest that his writings against mass participatory democracy were influenced by the political culture of his native island during his formative years. The extremely provincial, poverty-stricken Sicilian farm worker or city dweller did not appear to possess the ideal potential for becoming a responsible citizen. The *Risorgimento*, the national liberal revolution in Italy, did not bring social and economic improvement to Sicily. In fact, the changes brought about by the *Risorgimento* aggravated existing conditions. It is not surprising that

Mosca, who was born in Palermo two years before the beginning of the *Risorgimento*, opposed the political ideas and romantic idealism associated with the national movement. To a large degree the *Risorgimento* also meant the coming to power of the bourgeoisie and, in the process, the extension of the governing power to a wider segment of the population. In the view of many, including Mosca, this segment was ill equipped to govern. Hence, the skeptics were not surprised when the emotional high points had passed that most of Italy's profound problems remained unsolved and the promise of solution was not great. Although the *Risorgimento* also put a new emphasis on parliamentary government in Italy, its early achievements were meager, thus Mosca and a large number of persons who thought like him were critical of this political form.

Actually, it was during Mosca's school years in Palermo that the practice of *trasformismo* began in Italy. This practice almost completely negated the possibility of the development of a stable, responsible parliamentary regime. *Trasformismo* emphasized personality, leadership, and opportunism among members of parliament rather than the notions of responsible government and opposition. Parties with alternate solutions to problems did not develop. Instead principles were blended for the purposes of personal gain as key cabinet posts were offered to men with potential followers, no matter what their political coloration might be. In this circumstance, the development of confidence in the parliament, necessary for the success of a parliamentary regime, was not forthcoming. Also, during Mosca's years of study at the University of Palermo the franchise was extended by reducing the voting age from 25 to 21 and lowering the taxpaying requirement from 40 to 19 lire. The result of these changes was an increase in the electorate from approximately 600,000 to over 2,000,000. When Mosca looked about his native Sicily, with its backward conditions, it is not surprising that he had grave doubts about the extension of the right to vote, even though at this time the enfranchisement was limited almost exclusively to the bourgeoisie.

Mosca's first published work was based on the thesis he wrote at the University of Palermo and it was entitled *I fattori della nazionalità* (*The Factors of Nationality*). Applying the realistic approach to social analysis for which he later became famous, he demonstrated in this early work a solid understanding of nationalism and citizen identity. This analysis and his subsequent writings on the subject dealt squarely with questions of national identity, which became critical in the twentieth century.

Soon after obtaining his degree, Mosca left Sicily and travelled to Rome. New experiences on the mainland soon had an impact on his development. In 1871 Rome had become the capital of the newly unified Italy, and when Mosca arrived in 1884 he quickly became a critical observer of national politics and administration in action. He soon finished the first of his major works, *Sulla teorica dei governi e sul governo parlamentare. Studi storici e sociali (On the Theories of Government and Parliamentary Government. Historical and Social Studies)*, published in 1884. The book includes a highly critical analysis of Italian politics and government at that time. It was soon followed by two other works ostensibly in the field of constitutional law. These were *Studi ausiliari del diritto costituzionale (Ancillary Studies of Constitutional Law)*, published in 1886, and *Le costituzioni moderne (Modern constitutions)*, which followed a year later. A foremost Italian political scientist and a Mosca scholar wrote of the former work, using some of Mosca's own words:

> Mosca attributes to constitutional law the responsibility of political science, perceiving it not as "a comment on the Italian or the French constitution" but in a broader and more exact sense, as "a science which examines the laws regulating the social order of the various human societies." [1]

In both of these works Mosca demonstrates his preference for comparative political analysis rather than a formal descriptive approach to constitutional law.

The two books were supposed to enable him to obtain a paid professorship. However, this placement on the academic ladder was denied him. It has been suggested, and acknowledged in his old age by Mosca himself, that the denial of the professorship at that time embittered him in his general outlook, and especially about Italian democracy. He did continue his academic ties as an unpaid lecturer. However, the major alternative work to the professorship proved

[1] Norberto Bobbio, "Introduction" to Gaetano Mosca, *La classe politica*, ed. Norberto Bobbio (Bari: Editori Laterza, 1966), p. x.

very instructive to him in developing his understanding of the operation of parliamentary government. He took a position, which he
kept for ten years, in the Chamber of Deputies editing the official
journal of the parliamentary body. The period in which Mosca
worked in the Chamber was a difficult one for the youthful Italian
Government. The new prime minister, Francesco Crispi, who came
to power in 1887, ushered in a new era of politics. A Sicilian like
Mosca, Crispi was the first person from the great island to become
prime minister. A *Risorgimento* hero, Crispi, before coming to
power, was known as a man of principle who opposed corruption
and political practices such as *trasformismo*. Once in power the new
prime minister seemed to be completely socialized into the existing
system. He did bring about some liberal reforms and, for a time
at least, he had the public posture of a man of action and dedication.
However, he soon began operating as a veritable parliamentary dictator. It was from this last position that Crispi also started Italy on
the road to colonial expansion in Africa. Although his African
adventurism led to Crispi's fall, the seeds of imperial action for Italy
were sown.

It was not only in the Chamber of Deputies that Mosca was
learning new lessons of politics and history. The renowned philosopher Antonio Labriola was teaching at the University of Rome.
Also, in this period, in 1892 to be exact, the Italian Socialist Party
was born. The nascent socialist movement had more than a traditional Marxist coloration. It was marked by a distinct anarchist influence, most closely associated with Mikail Bakunin, a Russian
emigré. The last years of the nineteenth century were characterized
by grave and violent disorders throughout Italy, as workers demonstrated their discontent. Severe governmental repression of the
disorders resulted, and this in turn was answered in 1900 by the
assassination of King Umberto I by anarchists. It was in this setting
that Mosca first judged the operation of parliamentary democracy
at first hand.

After publishing his best known work, *Elementi di scienza
politica* (*The Ruling Class*), Mosca won a professorship at the University of Turin. This book first sets out in detail his ideas on the
ruling class, about which more will be said later. He remained
identified with the University of Turin until 1923. While at Turin

he accepted a second teaching post at Bocconi Commercial University of Milan where he taught constitutional and administrative law and the history of political philosophy. However, he did not limit himself to scholarly and teaching pursuits during the first two decades of the twentieth century. In 1897 he had written a political article of a polemical nature and soon after he began working closely with a leading Sicilian deputy, Marquis Antonio Di Rudini, who also served twice as prime minister. Upon Di Rudini's death Mosca was elected to the Chamber of Deputies in 1909, where he continued to serve until 1919. Furthermore, he served as Under-Secretary for Colonies from 1914 to 1916 and there is little doubt that both his parliamentary and ministerial careers provided him with valuable experience for the development of his political ideas. He continued his political career after 1919 in the Senate, where he had been appointed a life member.

While carrying on his political efforts, he continued to produce scholarly works. His introductory lectures at the University of Turin were published in 1903 under the title *Il principio aristocratico ed il democratico nel passato e nell'avvenire* (*The Aristocratic and the Democratic Principles in the Past and in the Future*). In this theoretical study he discusses a variety of political thinkers and analyzes two basic tendencies in society. The first, the aristocratic tendency, is represented by the old hereditary ruling minority which desires to defend the status quo. The second, the democratic, is represented by the governed masses, who introduce demands for reform which bring about change. In 1908 appeared *Appunti di diritto costituzionale* (*Notes on Constitutional Law*), a well received legal study. In the same period authoritative articles by Mosca were presented in the prestigious *Corriere della Sera* 1901–1925) and *Tribuna* (1911–1921).

The first years of the twentieth century, when Mosca was an active participant in the political system about which he harbored doubts, have been well described by Professor William Salamone in his book *Italian Democracy in the Making: 1900–1914*. The title of this excellent book may be somewhat misleading. Certainly, Mosca did not want to be a party to the extension of democracy. These nascent years of Italian democracy were marked by serious problems and the democratic system with all its limitations had difficulty taking root. Mosca believed that democracy was unworkable. The idea that the masses should be directly involved in the governing process troubled him. In fact, in 1912 when a suffrage bill extending the vote to all males over 30 years old who had served in the armed forces was presented to the Chamber of Deputies, Mosca argued and voted against it. In addition to his fundamental opposition to the broadening of the suffrage, he saw the bill also as a gesture on the part of the wily Prime Minister Giovanni Giolitti, who he thought was endeavoring to strengthen his ruling elite through the facade of democracy. It is not clear whether it was the gesture itself or other factors that disturbed Mosca.

While Mosca was clearly an anti-democrat he was not anti-liberal. In fact, he was a Victorian liberal, or better stated, the Continental equivalent of a Victorian liberal. He appreciated the values of civil liberties and some governmental reform. However, it was questions of leadership that concerned him most, and in this regard he was an elitist. He did not feel that the masses should or could participate in effective governance. For Mosca, this position was not incompatible with liberalism. In fact, he believed true liberalism was antithetical to mass democracy.

His opposition to socialism and later to communism was partially based on the mass bases of these movements. He not only saw them theoretically committed to the masses, but he saw first the Italian Socialist Party, and after its birth the Communist Party, successfully mobilizing large segments of the lower-class population. It should be noted that Mosca was also a harsh critic of Marxist thought.

The coming of fascism to Italy posed a new and more difficult problem for Mosca. He was a skeptic about and in some ways an opponent of the faltering parliamentary regime. The mediocrity of the parliament and its low level of output, especially in responsible selection of leadership, were among the things troubling him most. He had hoped for something better. This hope was intensified by the rise of socialism to a point where he saw the possibility of a socialist take-over. He felt that a new effective elitist government was necessary to forestall such an occurrence. Hence, when fascism came to Italy it seemed possible he would be attracted by the new system, which was strongly anti-communist and anti-socialist and emphasized leadership principles. However, Mosca's views on fascism are not clear cut. Initially, he was at least tolerant, if not totally supportive of the new regime. As time went on, the fascists proved not to be the elitist government that Mosca had hoped for. In fact, the destruction of the liberal climate in Italy was one of the things that disturbed him. It reached a point where he felt he had to speak out. The occasion he selected was a debate in the Senate on the prerogatives of the head of the government, in this case Mussolini. Noting that he had long held an aversion to the parliamentary system he rejected a radical change in it. Also, on other occasions it became evident that his ideas on parliamentary regimes had moderated somewhat, but had not fundamentally changed.[2]

It is somewhat paradoxical, although not surprising, that Mosca was considered by some people, including fascist adherents, to be a precursive thinker to fascism. These people thought his notion of the ruling class was similar to the fascist elite attitude. However Mosca could not agree with this attitude. The popular, vulgar dimension of fascism along with its lack of clarity in historical and social analysis troubled Mosca. Hence, as noted by the late and astute student of Mosca, Renzo Sereno, Mosca opposed fascism on both moral and intellectual grounds.

Many early supporters of fascism in Italy saw it at least in part as a radical movement which appealed to a section of the masses that otherwise would be attracted to left-wing movements. While many aristocratic and middle-class Italian supporters of the fascist regime expected it to moderate its activities when it had won over the masses, Mosca's doubts about repression did not let him accept this. He appreciated the ability of the fascists to forestall a left-wing take-over of government. However, for him a radical mass movement of the right held many of the same dangers as one from the left. Mass, not position on the political spectrum, was the key for him. The fact that he ended his active political career in 1925 as the fascists were solidifying their position was no mere coincidence. Still, for the remainder of his life he did not actively oppose the fascist government.

[2] For a discussion of his later views on parliamentary regimes, see "Cause e rimedi della crisi del regime parlamentare," in *Partiti e sindacati nella crisi del regime parlamentare* (Bari: Gius. Laterza e Figli, 1949), pp. 86–115. This statement was prepared by Mosca in response to an inquiry from the Inter-parliamentary Union.

In 1923 Mosca was called to the University of Rome where he was to hold the most prestigious chair in the field of the history of political theory. His move to Rome followed the preparation of a second and revised edition of *The Ruling Class.* Even before his withdrawal from active political life, he began to devote himself increasingly to his teaching and his scholarly writing. In 1924 he published *Lo stato-città antico e lo stato rappresentativo moderno* (*The Ancient City-State and the Modern Representative State*) as he focused on the study of political theory. In 1925 he published *Encore quelques mots sur le Prince de Machiavelli* (*More Thoughts on Machiavelli's Prince*); this was followed three years later by *L'utopia di Tommaso Moro ed il pensiero comunista moderno* (*The Utopia of Thomas More and Modern Communist Thought*). He continued to teach political theory at the University of Rome until his retirement in 1933, the year that the first edition of *A Short History of Political Philosophy,* then called *Lezioni di storia delle istituzioni e delle dottrine politiche* (*Lessons in the History of Political Institutions and Theory*) appeared. In retirement Mosca revised this work and it came out in another edition in 1937. This is fundamentally the edition that this translation is based on. He died on November 8, 1941, at the age of 83.

Mosca had lived long enough to see the ascension and fall of liberalism and parliamentary democracy in Italy and the rise and the beginning of the decline of fascism in his nation. In the preceding paragraphs, Mosca's careers were traced within the context of some of the major political developments that took place in Italy during his lifetime. The emphasis was on Italy because Mosca must be considered first and foremost as an Italian. While some Italian writers had lengthy experience and significant first-hand knowledge of nations other than their own, and might be considered European in their orientation, this was not the case with Mosca. He was familiar with the literature of Europe and to a degree with that of the United States. In fact, he acknowledged the importance to his thinking of writers like the French historian Taine. Still, this influence was intellectual, not experiential.

It was for the most part on the basis of Italian political experience that Mosca was called conservative, Liberal, anti-democratic, anti-parliamentary, a fascist sympathizer, a realist, and a Machiavellian. Mosca's conservatism was that often associated with those who mistrust the masses. Above all, he was a pessimist who had no faith in radical innovation. Constantly skeptical, he was also an intellectual critic of sharp innovation, especially within the context of the historical review of political change with which he made himself so familiar.

One author of a recent study dealing with the ruling class and crises of parliamentary systems stated:

> Mosca was the prototype of the men of the post-risorgimento, of the generation which matured after 1870, he was a man of the critical age when myths, *idee-forza*, and passions gave way to the construction of the state and civil organization; when politics unveiled its real and prosaic side, not heroic in the romantic sense of gesture and act.[3]

Clearly, Mosca must be considered a realist in his approach to the study of politics. For some persons, such as James Burnham, author of a book called *The Machiavellians*, Mosca's realism and some of his conclusions meant that he was also a Machiavellian.

It is not surprising that with the shift of emphasis among political scientists away from the study of institutional and legal arrangements and toward the realities of the allocation and exercise of power that Mosca's works have served as a source of inquiry for many scholars. As totalitarian and authoritarian regimes and unstable parliamentary systems gave new tests to democratic idealism, increasingly the modern writers who questioned traditional notions of popular sovereignty and majority rule, such as Mosca and his fellow Italians Vilfredo Pareto and Roberto Michels, came in for considerable attention. All three of these writers were concerned with elite theories of power and minority rule. The writings of the three actually complemented one another, although an acrimonious dispute and bitter enmity developed between Mosca and Pareto because the former believed that the latter borrowed his ideas without giving him credit.[4] Clearly, Michels, something of a protégé of Mosca,

[3] Ettore A. Albertoni, *La teoria della classe politica nella crisi del parlamentarismo* (Milan: Istituto Editoriale Cisalpino, 1968), p. 25.

[4] For a part of Mosca's position in the dispute, see "Piccola polemica" in *Partiti e sindacati nella crisi del regime parlamentare*, pp. 116–20. Although partisans for each writer appeared, it is now agreed for the most part that Pareto probably came to the same conclusion as Mosca independent of him.

extended the latter's ideas of a ruling class to modern large-scale organizations.

As noted previously, Mosca's best known work is his *The Ruling Class*. A paragraph from this book clearly sets out its major theme:

> Among the constant facts and tendencies that are to be found in all political organisms, one is so obvious that it is apparent to the most casual eye. In all societies—from societies that are very meagerly developed and have barely attained the dawnings of civilization, down to the most advanced and powerful societies—two classes of people appear—a class that rules and a class that is ruled. The first class always the less numerous, performs all political functions, monopolizes power and enjoys the advantages that power brings, whereas the second, the more numerous class, is directed and controlled by the first, in a manner that is now more or less legal, now more or less arbitrary and violent, and supplies the first, in appearance at least, with the material means of subsistence and with the instrumentalities that are essential to the vitality of the political organism.[5]

Presenting the notion of the ruling class, Mosca acknowledges that in different political cultures and in different historical periods, the ruling class will tend to operate in ways uniquely appropriate to the culture involved. However, no matter where or when, the ruling class endeavors to justify its exercise of power by virtue of what Mosca calls the "political formula." This is an abstraction or myth, such as divine or popular sovereignty and dynastic loyalty. In differing circumstances each ruling class will adopt a "political formula" that best serves its purposes. It is always easier for the majority to accept rule by the minority under the guise of a political formula rather than to accept direct rule by the ruling class. The succinct treatment of the idea of the ruling class found in the last chapter of *A Short History of Political Philosophy* represents Mosca's final version of the ways his thinking evolved on the subject. The ideas on the ruling class and the political formula outlined in the lines above are developed in this chapter with extensive historical argument.[6]

[5] Gaetano Mosca, *The Ruling Class*, trans. Hanna D. Kahn (New York: McGraw-Hill Book Comanpy, 1939), p. 50.

[6] One author, who must be acknowledged as the foremost American scholar on Mosca, has faulted him for not exploiting his historical material suffi-

Even though some critics would dispute the achievements of Mosca's methodology, few persons would deny that within the context of his times he endeavored to be as rigorous in his scholarship as possible. It is noteworthy that one Italian scholar who devoted extensive effort to the study of Mosca, Mario Delle Piane, has written that *The Ruling Class* marks the birth of political science in Italy.[7] Clearly, Mosca was in the forefront of the tradition that gave birth to the development of political science in his nation. The discipline was slow in developing in Italy because of the rigidity and special influence in academic and governmental circles of juridical scholars and historians. The anti-intellectual dimensions of fascism also retarded general free social science development. The fact that Mosca's major efforts were innovative in the social sciences probably was one reason that full recognition of his works in Italy was late in coming and that his reception in other nations, especially in the United States, has in some respects been greater than in the author's nation. Even when he taught constitutional law he seemed to be breaking tradition. There were concerns about him because he was teaching what we could call political science and political sociology. In addition, the fact that he was something of an ideologist where the idea of the ruling class was concerned made him suspect among certain academics. However, it is clear that he carefully endeavored not to confuse what he saw as the scientific study of politics with his expounding of his theory of the ruling class. Furthermore, in applying this theory he carefully limited himself. Unlike Pareto, who dealt with elites and general societal questions, Mosca to the greatest extent applied the notion of the ruling class only to political activities.

Mosca's native country, which served as an important learning laboratory for his creative and analytical thought, while formally committed to the basic tenets of liberal democracy, still finds this democracy under stress. Elsewhere in the Mediterranean basin other more directly elitist solutions to government are being utilized and as one undertakes the study of comparative politics and political

---

ciently. However, when a broad general theory like the ruling class is set forth, this criticism can always be made. See James H. Meisel, *The Myth of the Ruling Class* (Ann Arbor: The University of Michigan Press, 1962), pp. 62–63.

[7] "Mosca, Gaetano," *The International Encyclopedia of the Social Sciences*, Vol. 10 (New York: The Macmillan Company and The Free Press, 1968), pp. 504–7.

Index